AMNESTY IN
INTERNATIONAL LAW

THE LEGALITY UNDER
INTERNATIONAL LAW OF NATIONAL
AMNESTY LAWS

—

Ben Chigara

UNIVERSITY OF WARWICK

An imprint of **Pearson Education**

Harlow, England · London · New York · Reading, Massachusetts · San Francisco
Toronto · Don Mills, Ontario · Sydney · Tokyo · Singapore · Hong Kong · Seoul
Taipei · Cape Town · Madrid · Mexico City · Amsterdam · Munich · Paris · Milan

Pearson Education Limited

Edinburgh Gate
Harlow
Essex CM20 2JE

and Associated Companies throughout the world

Visit us on the World Wide Web at:
www.pearsoneduc.com

First published 2002

© Pearson Education Limited 2002

ISBN 0582 437938

British Library Cataloguing-in-Publication Data
A catalogue record for this book is available from the British Library

Library of Congress Cataloging-in-Publication Data
A catalog record for this book is available from the Library of Congress

10 9 8 7 6 5 4 3 2 1
06   05   04   03   02

Typeset in 10/13pt Sabon by 35
Printed and bound in Great Britain by Biddles Ltd.,
Guildford and King's Lynn

To the memory of one who bore the sweetest name:

MOTHER

—

The hope of a secure and livable world lies with disciplined

nonconformists, who are dedicated to justice, peace, and

brotherhood. . . . In any cause that concerns the

progress of mankind, put your faith in

the nonconformist!

Martin Luther King, Jr (1981) *Strength to Love.*

CONTENTS

Treaties, Conventions and Declarations   xi
Cases and Incidents   xiii
Abbreviations   xvi
Acknowledgements   xvii

1 PROBLEMATISING NATIONAL AMNESTY LAWS:
  STATE PRACTICE   1
  Introduction   1
  On justice   2
  On crimes against humanity   6
  Amnesia: assumptions and challenges   8
      (a) Imposed national amnesty laws   9
      (b) Elective national amnesty laws   12
      (c) Theoretical, policy and practical problems with national
          amnesty laws   13
  Conclusion   21

2 NATIONAL AMNESTY LAWS: LIMITS OF STATE
  DISCRETION UNDER INTERNATIONAL LAW   23
  Introduction   23
  Perspectives on municipal and international legal systems   26
  Declaration of national amnesty laws as exercise of
     State sovereignty   28
  Conclusion   39

3 THE RIGHTS, JUSTICE DYNAMIC AND PHYSIOLOGICAL
  NEEDS OF THE STATE   41
  Introduction   41
  Rights, victims and the rule of law   41
      (a) The rule of law   42
      (b) Victims and the post-violation era   45
  National imperatives: to anaesthetise or to quicken the law   48
      (a) Determining needs of a State: lessons from Maslow's
          hierarchy of needs   48
      (b) Determining needs of a State: lessons from Pavlov's
          theory of classical conditioning   53
  Conclusion   56

4 SCHIZOPHRENIC STATE PRACTICE: TO PROHIBIT OR TO
AUTHORISE NATIONAL AMNESTY LAWS? 57
Introduction 57
State assertions of emerging norms of customary law and
their motivations 59
Identification and application of the law 73
Making and unmaking of law in the international legal system 75
   (a) Settled practice of States regarding crimes that offend all
of humanity 77
   (b) Values recognised by practice of State deference to
declarations of national amnesty laws that purport to
expunge criminal and/or civil liability of agents of a prior
regime alleged to have violated basic human rights of
individuals 80
   (c) Values stressed by international treaties on crimes against
humanity 85
   (d) Values stressed by customary international law 89
Conclusion 90

5 AMNESTY, STATE DISCRETION AND INTERNATIONAL
CONSTRAINT: WHAT MODEL? 92
Introduction 92
State discretion versus *opinio communitatis* 92
Attribution theory and international law as the 'bystander' where
expression of State discretion challenges *opinio communitatis* 101
Graeco–Roman tradition 106
The positive human rights law tradition 107
   (a) Requirement of reasonableness 110
   (b) Requirement of natural justice 112
   (c) Codification in official records 117
   (d) Legality of national amnesty laws under international law 119
Truth and reconciliation commissions and international law 121
Conclusion 122

6 POSITIVE HUMAN RIGHTS LAW TRADITION: EXCLUSION
OF THE NATIONAL AMNESTY LAWS TRADITION? 125
Introduction 125
Persistent and increasing universal force of the United Nations
versus inconsistent, intermittent force of a handful of States'
declarations of national amnesty laws 125
The positive human rights law tradition eclipses and compels
to submission competing and parasitic traditions 127

Taming impunity for violation of basic human rights of
   individuals: human rights treaties emerge that have
   supervisory organs: 129
     (a) Monitoring of States Parties' compliance with their
         obligations under the International Convention on the
         Elimination of All Forms of Racial Discrimination (1965)
         by the Committee on the Elimination of Racial
         Discrimination   130
     (b) Monitoring of States Parties' compliance with their
         obligations under the International Covenant on Civil and
         Political Rights (1966) by the Human Rights Committee   132
     (c) Monitoring of States Parties' compliance with their
         obligations under the International Covenant on
         Economic, Social and Cultural Rights (1966)   134
     (d) Monitoring of States Parties' compliance with their
         obligations under the Convention against Torture and
         Other Cruel, Inhuman or Degrading Treatment or
         Punishment (1984) by the Committee against Torture   137
     (e) Monitoring of States Parties' compliance with their
         obligations under the Convention on the Elimination of
         All Forms of Discrimination against Women (1979) by
         the Committee on the Elimination of Discrimination
         against Women   140
     (f) Monitoring of States Parties' compliance with their
         obligations under the Convention on the Rights of the
         Child (1989) by the Committee on the Rights of the Child   141
     (g) Some issues on the monitoring by treaty bodies of States
         Parties' compliance with treaty obligations   143
What about immunity for acts done in the name of the State?   145
     (a) Immunity of a former head of State   146
     (b) Acting under superior orders   152
     (c) The proposed International Criminal Court and amnesty   155
Conclusion   161

7 CONCLUSIONS   163
   Submissions   166

Bibliography   171
Index   180

TREATIES, CONVENTIONS AND DECLARATIONS

African Charter on Human and Peoples' Rights, 26 June 1981 Banjul, OAU Doc. CAB/LEG/67/3/Rev 5; 21 ILM 59   **67, 70, 119**

American Convention on Human Rights, 22 November 1969 San Jose, PAUTS 36; 9 ILM 673   **33, 70**

Charter of the Organisation of African Unity, 25 May 1963, Addis Ababa, 479 UNTS 39; 2 ILM 766   **67**

Charter of the Organisation of American States and 1967 Protocol, 30 April 1948, Bogota, 119 UNTS 4; PAUTS 1   **67**

Convention against Torture and Other Cruel, Inhuman or Degrading Treatment or Punishment (1984), (1984) 23 ILM 1027   **7, 14, 37, 50, 85, 87, 116, 136–40**

Convention on the Liability of Operators of Nuclear Ships, 25 May 1962 Brussels, 1 Ruster, p.405   **35**

Convention on the Non-Applicability of Statutory Limitations to War Crimes and Crimes Against Humanity, G.A. Res. 2391 (XXIII), Annex, 23 UNGAOR Supplement (No. 18) at 40, UN Doc. A/7218 (1968)   **7, 121**

Convention on the Prevention and Punishment of the Crime of Genocide (1948) 78 UNTS 277   **50, 85–7, 89, 159**

Convention on the Privileges and Immunities of the United Nations, 13 February 1946, London, UNTS 15; UKTS 10 (1950), Cmd 1803   **30–31**

Convention on the Rights and Duties of States, 26 December 1933, Montevideo, 165 LNTS 19; PAUTS 37   **67**

Declaration on Principles of International Law concerning Friendly Relations and Co-operation among States in Accordance with the Charter of the United Nations (1970) Annex to United Nations General Assembly Resolution 2625 (XXV)   **67**

Diplomatic Conference on Maritime Law, Standing Committee, Doc. CN-6/SC17   **35**

Draft Code of Crimes against the Peace and Security of Mankind, Report of the International Law Commission of the work of its Forty-eighth Session, 51st Session Supplement No. 10, UN Doc. A/51/10 (1966)   **38**

European Convention on Human Rights 87 UNTS 103; ETS 5; UKTS 38 (1965), Cmnd 2643   **70**

International Convention on the Elimination of All Forms of Racial Discrimination (1965) UKTS Misc. No. 77 (1969), Cmnd 4108   **118, 126, 129–32, 136**

International Convention on the Suppression and Punishment of the Crime of Apartheid, GA Res. 3068 (XXVIII) (1973)   **67, 74, 101**

International Covenant on Civil and Political Rights (1966), UKTS 6 (1977); 999 UNTS 171   **31–32, 51, 69, 108, 115–16, 118, 128, 132–4**

International Criminal Tribunal for Rwanda, Rules of Procedure and Evidence, UN
    Doc. ITR/3/REV.1 (1995) entered into force 29 June 1995   **77, 85, 123**
London Charter of 1946, UKTS 4 (1945); UNTS 251   **78, 85–6, 121, 153**
Nuremberg Rules, in Agreement for the Prosecution and Punishment of the Major
    War Criminals of the European Axis, 82 UNTS 279   **121**
Rome Statute of the International Criminal Court, UN Doc. A/CONF.183/9 (1998)
        85, 123, 152–61, 170
International Covenant on Economic, Social and Cultural Rights (1966) **129, 134–7**
International Convention against the Taking of Hostages (1979), UKTS 81; 18 ILM
    1456   **14, 85, 88**
Vienna Convention on the Law of Treaties, 23 May 1969, UN Doc. A/Conf. 39/27;
    UKTS 58 (1980), Cmnd 7964   **36, 103–5**
United Nations Charter, 26 June 1945, San Francisco, UKTS 67 (1946), Cmd 7015;
    1 UNTS xvi   **29, 30–31, 52, 68–9, 102, 118, 125–6, 129**
United Nations General Assembly Declaration on the Right and Responsibility of
    Individuals, Groups and Organs of Society to Promote and Protect Universally Rec-
    ognised Human Rights and Fundamental Freedoms (1999), A/Res/53/144, 8 March
    1999   **126**
Universal Declaration of Human Rights (1948) UN Doc. A/811   **56, 67, 69, 98,
        105, 108–9, 118–19, 126–9, 165, 169**
Convention against the Taking of Hostages (1979) 18 ILM 1456   **14, 85**

CASES AND INCIDENTS

Administrator of German Property v Knoop [1933] Ch 439   **27**

Advisory Opinion on the Legality of the Threat or Use of Nuclear Weapons (1996) 35(4) ILM 809   **38**

Alabama Claims Arbitration (1872) Moore 1 Int Arbitration 495   **103**

Alexander Padilla and Mr Ricardo III Sunga (legal counsel) v The Philippines (2000) (Communication No. 869/1999), UN Doc. CCPR/C/70/D/869/1999   **108**

Ameer Keshavjee v Canada (2000) (Communication No. 949/2000), UN Doc. CCPR/C/70/D/949/2000   **108**

Amoco International Finance Corp. v Iran (1987) 15 Iran–USCTR 189   **25**

Anglo Norwegian Fisheries case (United Kingdom v Norway) ICJ Rep (1951) p.116   **76, 150–1**

Arvo Karttunen v Finland (Communication No. 387/1989), UN Doc. CCPR/C/46/D/387/1989; IHRR vol. 1 No. 1 (1994) p.78   **69**

Assenov Case (Assenov and Others v Bulgaria) No. 90/1997/874/1086   **130**

Associated Provincial Picture House Ltd v Wednesbury Corporation [1948] 1 KB 223   **110–12**

Asylum Case (Columbia v Peru) ICJ Rep (1950), p.266   **56**

Attorney-General of the Government of Israel v Eichmann (1961) 36 ILR 277   **160**

AZAPO Case, CCT 17/96   **2, 61–6, 74–5, 81–5, 97–8, 104, 108, 111, 113**

Barbie Case, France Court of Cassation (Criminal Chamber) 20 December 1985, 78 ILR 125   **7, 66**

Barbuit's Case (1735) 25 ER 77   **27, 66**

Barry Hart v Australia (2000) (Communication No. 947/2000), UN Doc. CCPR/C/70/D/947/2000   **108**

Belgium v Spain ICJ Rep (1970) p.3   **149**

Benedictine Nuns Case, 8 June 2001   **159–61**

Blackburn v Attorney-General [1971] 2 All ER 430   **27**

Bouterse Case, Amsterdam Court of Appeal, 20 November 2001   **7**

Carlton Linton v Jamaica (Communication No. 255/1987), UN Doc. CCPR/C/46/D/255/1987; IHRR vol. 1 No. 1 (1994) p.73, paras 9 and 10   **69**

Case concerning the Arrest Warrant of 11 April 2000 (Democratic Republic of Congo v Belgium)   **160**

Case concerning East Timor (Portugal v Australia) (1995) 34(6) ILM 1583   **29**

Court of the First Circuit v Richard Gonsales, State of Hawai'i FC-CR. No. 98–2047, 14 July 1999   **49**

Dimitry L. Gridin v Russian Federation (2000) (Communication No. 770/1997), UN Doc. CCPR/C/ 69/D/770/1997   **108**

Durayappah v Fernando [1967] 2 AC 337   **113**

El autor v Alemania (2000) (Communication No. 808/1998), UN Doc. CCPR/C/70/D/
  808/1998   108
Emperor of Australia v Day, 2 Giff 628   27
Heathfield v Chilton (1767) 98 ER 50   27
I Congreso del Partido [1981] 3 WLR 328   27
Kambanda, Jean (ICTR-97–23-S) www.ictr.org/ENGLISH/ cases/ Kambanda/index.htm
                                                                               66
Larry Salvador Tovar Acuna v Venezuela (1999) (Communication No. 739/1997),
  UN Doc. CCPR/C/65/D/739/1997   108
Lenford Hamilton v Jamaica (Communication No. 333/1988), UN Doc. CCPR/C/50/
  D/333/1988; IHRR vol. 1 No. 3 (1994) p.60   69
Llandovery Castle Case (1921), Supreme Court of Leipzig   153
Lotus Case (France v Turkey) Permanent Court of International Justice Reports, Series
  A, No. 10, p.254   73
Malone v Commissioner of Police for the Metropolis (No. 2) [1979] 2 All ER 620
                                                                               27
Winfat Enterprises (HK) Co. Ltd v Attorney-General for Hong Kong [1985] AC 733
                                                                               27
Massacre Las Hojas v El Salvador, Case 10.287, Report No. 26/92, IACHR OEA/
  Ser.L/V/II.83 Doc. 14 at 83 (1993)   63, 114
Military and Paramilitary Activities in and against Nicaragua (Nicaragua v US) Mer-
  its, ICJ Rep (1986) p.14 (Judgment of June 27)   37, 127
Netherlands v US (1928) 2 RIAA 829   28
North Sea Continental Shelf Cases (Federal Republic of Germany v Denmark; Federal
  Republic of Germany v The Netherlands) ICJ Rep (1969) p.3   52, 72, 76
Pearberg v Varty [1972] 2 All ER 62   113
Peleus Trial, War Crimes Reports (1945) 1, 12. (British Military Court Hamburg)
                                                                              153
Peter Chiiko Bwalya v Zambia (Communication No. 314/88), UN Doc. CCPR/C/48/
  D/314/1988; IHRR vol. 1, No. 2 (1994) p.84   69
Prosecutor v Furundzija Case No. IT-95–17/1-T (10 December 1998) (1999) 38 ILM
  317   38–9
Prosecutor v Tadic IHRR vol. 4 (1997) p.645   108
Prosecutor v Jean-Paul Akayesu, Case No. ICTR-96–4-T Decision of 2 September
  1998   108
R v Commission for Racial Equality, ex parte Hillingdon London Borough Council
  [1982] AC 779   113
R v Secretary of State for the Home Department, ex parte Brind and Others [1991] 1
  AC 696   74
R v Bow Street Metropolitan Stipendiary Magistrate and Others, ex parte Pinochet
  Ugarte (No. 3) [1999] 2 WLR 827   6, 16–17, 27, 37–8, 60, 66, 74, 85,
                                                               89, 116, 146–52
Reservations Case, ICJ Rep (1951) p.15   7, 149
Ridge v Baldwin [1964] AC 40   112
Rodger Chongwe v Zambia (2000) (Communication No. 821/1998), UN Doc. CCPR/
  C/70/D/821/1998   108

Sei Fuji v State of California (1952) 19 ILR 312   69
Short v Poole Corporation [1926] Ch 66   **111**
The Prosecutor of the Tribunal v Slobodan Milosevic and Others www. un.org/icty/ indictment/english/mil-ii990524e .htm   **10, 66**
Velasquez Rodriguez Case IACHR (1998) Series C, No. 4   **33, 38**
Winfat Enterprises (HK) Co. Ltd v Attorney-General for Hong Kong [1985] AC 733   27
Trendtex Trading Corporation v Central Bank of Nigeria [1977] 1 All ER 881   27
Island of Palmers Case (Netherlands v USA) (1928) 2 RIAA 829   28
Case Concerning East Timer (Portugal v Australia) 34 ILM 1583   29
Barcelona Traction Case ICJ Reports (1970) 3   37, 149
Texaco v Libya (1977) 53 ILR 389   103
Glasgow Corporation v Muir [1943] AC 448   111
London Passenger Transport Board v Upson [1949] AC 155   112
Prosecutor v Dusko Tadic (Jurisdiction) (1996) 35 ILM 32   7

ABBREVIATIONS

ACHPR	African Charter on Human and Peoples' Rights
AJIL	American Journal of International Law
BYIL	British Yearbook of International Law
CAT	Committee against Torture
CEDAW	Committee on the Elimination of Discrimination against Women
CERD	Committee on the Elimination of All Forms of Racial Discrimination
CESCR	Committee on Economic, Social and Cultural Rights
CRC	Committee on the Rights of the Child
DRC	Democratic Republic of Congo
ECOSOC	Economic and Social Council
EJIL	European Journal of International Law
EU	European Union
GATT	General Agreement on Tariffs and Trade
HRC	Human Rights Committee (United Nations)
ICC	International Criminal Court
ICCPR	International Covenant on Civil and Political Rights
ICESCR	International Covenant on Economic, Social and Cultural Rights
ICJ	International Court of Justice
ICTR	International Criminal Tribunal for Rwanda
ICTY	International Criminal Tribunal for the former Yugoslavia
ILC	International Law Commission
IMT	International Military Tribunal
ITLOS	International Tribunal for the Law of the Sea
NGOs	Non-governmental organisations
PCIJ	Permanent Court of International Justice
UDHR	Universal Declaration of Human Rights
UN	United Nations
UNC	United Nations Charter
UNGA	United Nations General Assembly
VANPAJR	Voluntarily adopted national amnesty law that constitutes a necessary pillar of the State's constitution, and that is not an affront to contemporary standards and notions of justice in the light of developments since adoption by the United Nations General Assembly of the Universal Declaration of Human Rights and which is reasonable and consistent with *norms jus cogens*.
VCLT	Vienna Convention on the Law of Treaties
WTO	World Trade Organisation
ZANU (PF)	Zimbabwe African National Union Patriotic Front

ACKNOWLEDGEMENTS

This project began when I was invited in 1999 to contribute to an edited collection of essays on the constitutional implications of the *Pinochet Case*, edited by Professor Diana Woodhouse and published by Richard Hart. This book examines broader issues on the subject that I was not able to consider for the essay collection. In writing these few pages I have benefited enormously from the masterly encouragement of Professor John Dugard of the University of Leiden, Professor Neil Duxbury of the University of Manchester and Dr Edward Kwakwa, Assistant Legal Counsel, World Intellectual Property Organisation, who each commented on selected draft chapters of the book. I am grateful also to Beatrice Dal Cin of the University of Bristol, to Cathy Jenkins of the School of Oriental and African Studies and to Professor John Merrills of the University of Sheffield whose timely interventions while I was working on this book proved most useful. Providence was, as ever, most magnanimous. Of course any mistakes are mine alone.

1

PROBLEMATISING NATIONAL AMNESTY LAWS: STATE PRACTICE

INTRODUCTION

The argument is often made that justice must sometimes defer to measures targeted at securing political stability, especially where investigation and prosecution of crimes against humanity '*would*' undermine the rehabilitation process of a State from totalitarian rule to another system of government, usually democracy. Implicit in this argument are two points which protagonists appear to shy away from. The first is that justice is not, and cannot be, an agent or catalyst of the process of committing a State to a more desirable system of government. Further, that justice and measures targeted at committing a State to democratic practice are mutually exclusive. The second is that equality before the law is not an absolute idea. Rather, it is relative, and amnesia is presented as the virtuous guarantor of the safe passage from totalitarian to democratic rule. Discourse which labels as '*transitional justice or transformative justice*'[1] national amnesty laws that purport to extinguish legal liability of agents of a prior regime alleged to have violated basic human

---

[1] See McAdams, A. J. (1997) *Transitional Justice and the Rule of Law in New Democracies*, University of Notre Dame Press, London, p.1; Kritz, N. J. (ed.) (1995) *Transitional Justice: How Emerging Democracies Reckon with Former Regimes*, United States Institute of Peace Press, vol. 1, p.1; Roht-Arriaza, N. (ed.) (1995) *Impunity and Human Rights in International Law and Practice*, Oxford University Press, New York, p.1; Welscher, L. A. (1991) *Miracle, A Universe: Settling Accounts with Torturers*, Penguin Books, London, Chap. 1; Stotzky, I. P. (ed.) (1993) *Transition to Democracy in Latin America: The Role of the Judiciary*, Westview Press, Boulder Co., Chap. 1; Brysk, A. (1994) *The Politics of Human Rights in Argentina: Protest, Change, and Democratization*, Stanford University Press, Stanford CA, Chap. 1; Akhavan, P. (1996) 'The Yugoslav Tribunal at Crossroads: The Dayton Peace Agreement and Beyond', *Human Rights Quarterly*, vol. 18 No. 1, p.259.

rights of individuals invokes a sense of juridical legitimacy about such laws. However, neither the question of national amnesty laws for such offences as normative standard, nor that of amnesty's legitimacy – assuming that it had a normative pedigree – are givens in international law. This chapter evaluates the validity of the argument that justice must sometimes defer to political measures targeted at committing to democratic practice States that once were living theatres of breach of basic human rights of individuals. The tension at the core of this argument has been described invariably as the tension between the need to remember and the threat posed to memory by historical relativism,[2] and as a manifestation of the interactive evolutionary relationship that prefigures the relationship between international law and peace agreements.[3] By examining on the one hand, resilience of philosophical assumptions that underpin the idea of amnesty and on the other, the *'claimed utility'* of national amnesty laws, amnesia to crimes against humanity is shown to be both inconsistent and incompatible with international law. Further, processes that sponsor amnesia and by which individual policy preferences are aggregated into binding collective decisions of the executive are shown to be normatively unjustifiable. On the contrary, they are opposable to attempts to establish democratic practice in formerly totalitarian States. Because national amnesty laws discussed in this book presuppose breach of basic human rights of individuals or commission by agents of a prior regime of what international law regards as high crimes,[4] and because arguments that favour amnesia for crimes against humanity oppose established notions of justice as fairness, it is necessary to begin with a brief consideration of what is meant first, by justice and secondly, by crimes against humanity.

ON JUSTICE

Manifest in the idea of amnesty is the utilitarian argument that not justifying victims of crimes against humanity is itself acceptable where that action results in the achievement of a greater social good.[5] That social good is often perceived as the purchase, through the currency of national amnesty laws, of the threat of disruption to the new social order posed by those that perpetrated

---

[2] See Braude, C. and Spitz, D. (1997) 'Memory and the Spectre of International Justice: A Comment on *AZAPO. AZAPO v President of the Republic of South Africa*', *South African Journal on Human Rights*, vol. 13 No. 2, p.269 at p.277.

[3] See Bell, C. (2000) *Peace Agreements and Human Rights*, Oxford University Press, Oxford, pp.65–66.

[4] Discussing high crimes, see Warbrick, C. and McGoldrick, D. (1999) 'The Future of Former Head of State Immunity after *Ex parte Pinochet*', *International and Comparative Law Quarterly*, vol. 48 No. 4, p.937 at p.938.

[5] See Mill, J. S. (4th ed. 1869) *On Liberty*, Longmans, Green, Reader, and Dyer, London, Chap. IV.

the crimes against humanity should attempts be made to prosecute them. Therefore, Rawls' theory of justice as fairness, which places the notion of justice between the principle of retribution[6] and the principle of average utility,[7] fits the task of evaluating the justiceability of amnesty laws that purport to expunge criminal and/or civil liability of agents of a prior regime alleged to have violated basic human rights of individuals. By Rawls' own admission, the theory of justice as fairness is an extension of Locke, Rousseau and Kant's ideas of justice as social contract. Contracts by their very nature depend on:

(1) the allocation of bargaining power between parties,
(2) the allocation of contractual risks between parties,[8] and
(3) the legal system's response to outcomes based on the above-mentioned social, private arrangements.

Rawls' theory of justice as fairness is premised on a hypothetical genesis where members of a community come together to create rules by which future conduct of agents of the community must comply. At that moment all members of the community are both equal and disinterested in the nature of the rules created. He writes that the principles of justice are chosen behind a veil of ignorance[9] and confer basic rights and duties.[10] By these principles:

> 'men decide in advance how they are to regulate their claims against one another and what is to be the foundation charter of their society. Just as each person must decide by rational reflection what constitutes his good, that is, the system of ends which it is rational for him to pursue, so a group of persons must decide once and for all what is to count among them as just and unjust. The choice which rational men would make in this hypothetical situation of equal liberty, assuming for the present that this choice problem has a solution, determines the principles of justice.'[11]

Justice is evidenced by practice of principles, which

> 'free and rational persons concerned to further their own interests would accept in an initial position of equality as defining the fundamental terms of their association. These principles are to regulate all further agreements; they specify the kinds of social cooperation that can be entered into and the forms of government that can be established.'[12]

---

[6] Rawls, J. (1986) *A Theory of Justice*, Oxford University Press, Oxford, pp.3–5.

[7] Ibid. p.150.

[8] See e.g. Wheeler, S. and Shaw, J. (1994) *Contract Law: Cases, Materials and Commentary*, Oxford University Press, Oxford, pp.453–470.

[9] Rawls, J. (1994) 'The Main Idea of the Theory of Justice', in Singer, P. (ed.) *Ethics*, Oxford University Press, Oxford, p.363.

[10] Ibid. p.362.

[11] Ibid.

[12] Ibid.

Therefore, Rawls' theory of justice as fairness combines legal equality of all members of the community with a disinterested predetermination under the veil of ignorance of how breaches of its rules will be dealt with. In this sense, the law exists and operates to justify victims of breaches of their predetermined legal rights. This is consistent with Mill's assessment of the utility of law. Mill writes that, 'In the conduct of human beings towards one another, it is necessary that general rules should for the most part be observed in order that people may know what they have to expect...'[13] However, national amnesty laws for their part disregard the rights of victims. They treat victims as if they did not have predetermined rights at the moment of abuse, and if they did, as if they had not been breached at all. The law does not regard perpetrators of crimes against humanity as having trampled upon predetermined legal rights. Whether one is a victim of crimes against humanity or a beneficiary of a national amnesty law, previously determined legal rights and duties of citizens have no significance. What matters is whether there is sufficient threat of disruption of the incoming government's agenda by those that committed the alleged crimes against humanity. If that threat is deemed to exist, the incoming government either accepts the outgoing government's demand for an amnesty or offers them one. Fear then masters law. For this reason national amnesty laws that purport to expunge criminal and/or civil liability of agents of a prior regime alleged to have violated basic human rights of individuals appear to contradict the theory of justice as fairness because they violate the basis and ethos of law as *self-constituting*.[14] They oppose also the function of law as a community's preferred agent for distinguishing acceptable conduct from unacceptable conduct. Without that possibility, even the continued survival of the community is threatened. They appear to cast 'fear' as the arbiter in the determination whether or not crimes against humanity should be investigated and prosecuted. If investigation and prosecution of criminals threatens order, then that threat should displace previously determined legal standards of a community. The danger is created then that victims' legal rights and the community's values are set to zero where the prior regime procures for itself an amnesty law that claims to extinguish all criminal and/or civil liability attributed to its agents by threatening to disrupt the new social order if its agents are ever prosecuted for breaching basic

---

[13] Mill, J. S., note 5 above, at p.143. See also Griset, P. L. (1991) *Determinate Sentencing – The Promise and the Reality of Retributive Justice*, State University of New York Press, Albany; Fell, G. S. (1991) 'Street-crime Victim Compensation, Retributive Justice, and Social-contract Theory', in Sank, D. and Caplan, D. I. (eds) *To Be a Victim – Encounters with Crime and Injustice*, Plenum Press, New York/London, p.87; and Feather, N. T (1998) 'Reactions to Penalties for Offences Committed by the Police and Public Citizens: Testing a Social-cognitive Process Model of Retributive Justice', *Journal of Personality and Social Psychology*, vol. 75 No. 2, p.528.

[14] See Allot, P. (1999) 'The Concept of International Law', *European Journal of International Law*, vol. 10, p.31.

human rights of individuals. In this sense, such national amnesty laws set back national and international society's social gains by attempting to reconstitute social values and starting all over again. Allot comments:[15]

> 'The state of international law at any time reflects the degree of development of international society. Recent developments in international society have made necessary and inevitable the coming-to-consciousness of international law as the fully effective law of a fully functioning international society.'

National amnesty laws that purport to erase criminal and/or civil liability of agents of a prior regime alleged to have violated basic human rights of individuals attempt to edit life's irreversible and uneditable record. Their very declaration is itself a recognition that crimes against humanity have occurred but that no one should be investigated or prosecuted. Their very declaration simultaneously asserts the occurrence of crimes against humanity and rejection of the relevance of existing law to those breaches of a community's predetermined legal standards. This compromise is implied all the time in discourse, which calls these national amnesty laws *'transitional justice or transformative justice'*.[16] In short whether national amnesty laws are clothed with justificatory cloaks or with euphemistic labels the fact remains that they are inconsistent with the notion of justice as fairness. Rawls' theory of justice as fairness is evident in the practice of most States. National constitutions, which may be written[17] or unwritten,[18] evidence a country's preferred choice of the first principles of a conception of justice which is to regulate all subsequent criticism and reform of institutions.

> 'Then, having chosen a conception of justice, we can suppose that they are to choose a constitution and a legislature to enact laws, and so on, all in accordance with the principles of justice initially agreed upon. Our social situation is just if it is such that by this sequence of hypothetical agreements we would have contracted into the general system of rules which defines it.'[19]

A national constitution has not been heard of which declares that citizens have basic rights, which, if violated, will be compensated for by the State forgiving perpetrators of those violations, even without prior investigation of their involvement in the alleged breaches, and without prosecution. Declaration of national amnesty laws that purport to expunge criminal and/or civil liability of agents of a prior regime alleged to have violated basic human rights of individuals appears to be unjust. Moreover:

---

[15] Ibid.
[16] See above at p.1.
[17] A common feature among States that emerged from the post-war decolonisation process.
[18] Such as the British constitution, old, efficient and self-evident, yet unwritten.
[19] Rawls, J., note 9 above.

'the idea that human beings have rights as humans is a staple of contemporary world politics. International conventions, both global and regional, state it, at length and in relation to a large number of rights. People speaking for States proclaim it. Groups other than States assert it in its collective form . . . Non-governmental organizations make its observance their *raison d'être*. Individuals *in extremis* appeal to it. Reporters presume it. And scholars try to make sense of it . . .'[20]

Current State practice shows that the way in which a government treats its own citizens is now a legitimate matter of international scrutiny by the United Nations and human rights organisations such as Interights, Amnesty International and Rights Watch.[21] Article 5 of the International Criminal Tribunal for the territory of the former Yugoslavia lists murder, extermination, enslavement, deportation, imprisonment, torture, rape, persecutions on political, racial and religious grounds, and other inhuman acts as war crimes that must be punished.

ON CRIMES AGAINST HUMANITY[22]

Crimes against humanity have been described variously as acts that trample underfoot the laws of God and humanity,[23] crimes *jus cogens*,[24] and grave violations of human rights.[25] It is settled that international law recognises crimes against humanity, and that crimes against humanity do not require a

---

[20] Vincent, R. J. (1986) *Human Rights and International Relations*, Cambridge University Press, Cambridge, p.7.

[21] Examples of this practice include direct intervention of SADC forces in Lesotho (1998), NATO in Kosovo (1999), ECOWAS in Sierra Leone (1997), the United Nations in Iraqi (1990), the United Nations sanctions against Indonesia of 1999, and United Nations sanctions against apartheid South Africa and racist Rhodesia in the 1970s.

[22] See generally Robertson, G. (1999) *Crimes Against Humanity: The Struggle for Global Justice*, Allen Lane, London; van Schaack, B. (1999) 'The Definition of Crimes Against Humanity: Resolving the Incoherence', *Columbia Journal of Transnational Law*, vol. 37 No. 3, p.787; Hovannisian, R. G. (ed.) (1999) *Remembrance and Denial: The Case of the Armenian Genocide*, Wayne State University Press, Detroit MI; Freeman, M. (1999) 'Genocide and Gross Human Rights Violations in Comparative Perspective', *Ethnic and Racial Studies*, vol. 22 No. 6, p.1072; Fenrick, W. J. (1999) 'Should Crimes Against Humanity Replace War Crimes?' *Columbia Journal of Transnational Law*, vol. 37 No. 3, p.767; Bassiouni, M. (1999) *Crimes Against Humanity*, Martinus Nijhoff, Dordrecht/London.

[23] The first recorded such trial occurred in the fifteenth century, at Bresach. See Birkett, J. (1947) 'International Legal Theories Evolved at Nuremberg', *International Affairs*, vol. 23, p.317.

[24] That is, crimes against which there can be no derogation. *R v Bow Street Metropolitan Stipendiary Magistrate and Others, ex parte Pinochet Ugarte (No. 3)* [1999] 2 WLR 827 at p.841, HL, *per* Lord Browne-Wilkinson.

[25] See Freeman, M. (1999) 'Genocide and Gross Human Rights Violations in Comparative Perspective', *Ethnic and Racial Studies*, vol. 22 No. 6, p.1072, and Robertson, G. (1999) *Crimes Against Humanity: The Struggle for Global Justice*, Allen Lane, London.

connection to international armed conflict.[26] The *Barbie Case*[27] has helpfully defined crimes against humanity as:

> 'inhuman acts and persecution committed in a systematic manner in the name of a State practicing a policy of ideological supremacy, not only against persons by reason of their membership in a racial or religious community, but also against the opponents of that policy, whatever the form of their opposition'.

The French court distinguished crimes against humanity from war crimes in that while prosecution of war crimes is constrained by specific time limits imposed by the statute setting up the tribunal for that purpose,[28] war crimes are directly connected to the existence of a situation of hostilities. However, even if they could also be classified as war crimes, crimes against humanity are not constrained by or subject to statutory limitation.[29] Article 1 of the Convention on the Non-Applicability of Statutory Limitations to War Crimes and Crimes against Humanity (1968) prohibited the prescription of crimes against humanity whether committed in time of war or in peace. Article 1 of the International Convention on the Suppression and Punishment of the Crime of Apartheid (1973) declares that apartheid is a crime against humanity that constitutes a serious threat to international peace and security. The Convention against Torture and Other Cruel, Inhuman or Degrading Treatment or Punishment (1984), which makes torture a crime against humanity, clearly states in Article 2(2) that no special context needs to be established before torture can be alleged. Customary international law recognises that a crime against humanity may be committed in time of peace.[30] In a succinct examination of the constitutive elements of a crime against humanity for the Amsterdam Court of Appeal in the *Bouterse Case*[31] Dugard wrote that to qualify as crimes against humanity the acts in question:

---

[26] See *Prosecutor v Dusko Tadic (Jurisdiction)* (1996) 35 ILM 32 at p.72, ICTY. See also Dugard, J. (1997) 'Retrospective Justice: International Law and the South African Model', in McAdams, A. J. (ed.) *Transitional Justice and the Rule of Law in New Democracies*, University of Notre Dame Press, Notre Dame and London, p.269, at p.274.

[27] France Court of Cassation (Criminal Chamber) 20 December 1985, 78 ILR p.126.

[28] Ibid. p.127.

[29] Ibid. pp.127–128. For commentary on whether this decision eradicates the substantive distinction between crimes against humanity and war crimes and leaves that determination to the context in which the act complained of occurred, see Fenrick, W. J. (1999), 'Should Crimes Against Humanity Replace War Crimes?' *Columbia Journal of Transnational Law*, vol. 37 No. 3, p.767, and van Schaack, B. (1999) 'The Definition of Crimes Against Humanity: Resolving the Incoherence', *Columbia Journal of Transnational Law*, vol. 37 No. 3, p.787.

[30] Discussing the obsolescence of the nexus requirement that crimes against humanity must be linked to a situation of armed conflict, see the ICTY Appeals Chamber in *Prosecutor v Dvsko Tadic (Jurisdiction)* (1996) 35 ILM 32 at p.72, para.140.

[31] Decision of 20 November 2000 regarding the case of the former military ruler Lt. Col. D. D. Bouterse of the Republic of Surinam. Professor Dugard appointed as expert to the court.

(1) Must be committed against a civilian population. This requirement is commonplace in instruments defining the crime against humanity, the notable exception being the 1996 ILC Draft Code.[32]

(2) Must be collective in nature. The emphasis is not on the individual victim but rather on the collective, the individual being victimised not because of his individual attributes but because of his membership of a targeted civilian population.

(3) Not any act of murder or torture against a civilian population will qualify as a crime against humanity. Additionally there must be evidence that the acts were committed as part of State (or organised non State) action or policy in a systematic, widespread or large-scale manner.

(4) The jurisdictional element that distinguishes crimes against humanity from other international crimes and the national crimes of (say) murder, torture, etc. is the requirement that the act be systematic, widespread or large scale. However, it is not necessary that the acts be both widespread (large scale) and systematic. International instruments speak of widespread or systematic acts. The plan may be inferred from a series of events, such as the general historical circumstances and the overall political background against which the criminal acts are set.

(5) There is no requirement that the acts be carried out in a discriminatory or persecutory manner.

(6) A person charged with a crime against humanity must clearly have the necessary *mens rea* to commit the crime.

Enormous international energy has been and continues to be allocated to condemnation of crimes against humanity through various channels. That alone may be sufficient to ask whether amnesia for crimes against humanity is an option. However, there are of course more compelling grounds for posing the same question. One is the significance of ordering societies through legal frameworks premised on the notion of justice if rules are selectively applied.

AMNESIA: ASSUMPTIONS AND CHALLENGES

The Etymological Dictionary of English places the origin of the words '*amnesty*' and '*amnesia*' in the Greek word '*amnestia*' which means forgetfulness.[33] State practice on granting of national amnesty to people that otherwise would be charged with crimes against humanity[34] points to various and even

---

[32] UNGAOR 51st Session, Supplement No. 10 (A/51/10), p.10.

[33] Skeat, W. W. (1909) *An Etymological Dictionary of the English Language*, Clarendon Press, Oxford, p.127.

[34] See McAdams, A. J. (1997) *Transitional Justice and the Rule of Law in New Democracies*, University of Notre Dame Press, London.

unreconcilable motivations. Consequently, the philosophical derivatives of amnesty also tend to vary. Nonetheless, two categories of these derivatives are immediately observable. One points to *imposed national amnesty laws* while the other points to an aggregate of influences that result in *elective national amnesty laws*.

(a) Imposed national amnesty laws

Imposed national amnesty laws are granted to members and officials of the outgoing totalitarian government by itself, with the consent of the incoming government. They are contractual in that often the outgoing government makes them a fundamental condition of its surrender of public office. They are some-times peddled as 'negotiated amnesties' though the incoming government has neither the bargaining power to prevent declaration of such amnesty laws, nor sufficient control of the determining political, social milieu to prevent them. A good example of this is the agreement reached in the twilight hours of the apartheid regime of South Africa between the National Party and the African National Congress on how to deal with criminals that perpetrated the crimes of apartheid. Dugard[35] writes that:

> The option of prosecution of the leaders of the apartheid State before domestic courts was impossible as there were no victors in the process that brought to an end apartheid and the leaders of the apartheid State were themselves a party to the negotiated settlement. In essence the choice was between unconditional am-nesty, favoured by the National Party, or conditional amnesty. The latter option was chosen.

Whether such contracts are void on grounds of duress is another matter. However, it must be stressed that but for the national amnesty laws that result from such agreements, the autocratic reign of terror accompanied by gross violation of basic human rights of individuals would continue for an indeterminable future.[36] Therefore, such amnesties become the crucible in which the moral, ethical and legal imperatives of justice and the political necessities of extricating the State from further human rights abuse occur. The law that secured for Senator Pinochet Ugarte and his government and its officials amnesty from prosecution for events that occurred in Chile between

---

[35] Dugard, J. (1997) 'Is the Truth and Reconciliation Process Compatible with International Law? An Unanswered Question', *South African Journal on Human Rights*, vol. 13 No. 2, p.258.

[36] A point often missed in discourse on the Chilean amnesty. See Gareton, M. A. (1999) 'Chile 1997–1998: The Revenge of Incomplete Democratisation', *International Affairs*, vol. 75, p.261. See also Chigara, B. (2000) 'Pinochet and the Administration of International Criminal Justice', in Woodhouse, D. (ed.) *The Pinochet Case: A Legal and Constitutional Analysis*, Hart Publishing, Oxford, p.115 at p.123.

11 September 1973 and 10 March 1978 – the worst period of human rights violations under the military government – is yet another example. Trading off their legal entitlement to pursue in the courts of law perpetrators of human rights violations for peace and the chance to re-establish themselves as a democracy is said to be the price that Chileans paid to end military governance. Senator Pinochet Ugarte is reported to have stated: 'Touch one hair on the head of one of my soldiers, and you lose your new democracy.'[37] By maximising the threat of disruption, Senator Pinochet Ugarte was able to extract from the incoming civilian administration amnesty for crimes that international law condemns in the strongest possible terms. Negotiated settlements that secure this kind of amnesty for persons alleged to have violated basic human rights of others expose a tenuous dichotomy between human rights and peace so commonly alluded to in human rights and other United Nations treaties. Bell writes that linking of human rights protections with peace-building is problematic and controversial not least because it is often challenged as partisan and/or idealistic.[38] Because the laws at issue when such amnesty laws are contemplated often have a dual existence as national laws on the one hand, and as international laws on the other, it is important that breaches of international law be accounted for by international processes, whatever approaches are taken domestically to address violation of national laws. Schabas[39] writes that because human rights obligations are contracted on an international level, they pierce the hitherto impenetrable wall of State sovereignty: 'Where these obligations are breached, the individual may be punished for such international crimes as a matter of international law, even if his or her own State, or the State where the crime was committed, refuses to do so.' This approach is evident in the case of Slobodan Milosevic whose conduct while head of State has resulted in charges of genocide and breach of humanitarian law under both national law and international humanitarian law.[40] On 23 June 2001 the Yugoslav government issued a decree allowing the extradition of suspects (including Slobodan Milosevic) to the International Criminal Tribunal for the former Yugoslavia.[41] This approach ensures that whether or not national practice corrodes legitimacy of national laws, international law's legitimacy is not correspondingly compromised by mimick-

---

[37] Cassel, D. (1998) 'Transitional Justice and the Rule of Law', *American Journal of International Law*, vol. 92, p.601 at p.602.

[38] See Bell, C. (2000) *Peace Agreements and Human Rights*, Oxford University Press, Oxford, p.5.

[39] Schabas, W. A. (2000) *Genocide in International Law*, Cambridge University Press, Cambridge, p.2.

[40] *The Prosecutor of the Tribunal v Slobodan Milosevic and Others* www.un.org/icty/indictment/english/mil-ii990524e .htm. See *The Times*, 23 May 2001.

[41] See 'Way Cleared for Milosevic Trial', *Sunday Times*, 24 June 2001.

ing domestic practice of not enforcing national laws. Evidence shows that the end of State terror and atrocity sometimes sparks off euphoria that anaesthetises the international sphere into a willing spectator of the approaches adopted at national level. The demise of the apartheid regime in South Africa and the national strategies adopted to deal with crimes of State terror and atrocity during apartheid is a case in point. At other times the end of State terror and atrocity is greeted with international preparedness to prosecute breaches of international human rights laws as was the case in Rwanda, Sierra Leone and the former Yugoslavia. Dugard[42] writes that in a state of euphoria over the abandonment of apartheid, the international community was in no mood to set up an international tribunal for apartheid's criminals. But euphoria alone is not able permanently to tranquillise requirements of justice as fairness in a Rawls sense.[43] Such negligence on the part of the international community undermines credibility of international legal norms, as no one knows when they will apply and when they will not. This negligence is apparent in the South African amnesty law of 1995 in that it makes no attempt to bring within the ambit of the amnesty inquiry acts that constituted a crime under international law but were not criminal under the law of apartheid. Dugard observes that 'Death and suffering caused by forcible population removals, inhuman influx control laws and arbitrary detention-without-trial laws permitting merciless interrogation in solitary confinement that qualified as crimes against humanity, are excluded from the amnesty process, presumably because they were authorised by South African Statute.'[44] This negligence of the United Nations in not enforcing its own laws in the face of nation States' claims of the right to declare pardon for breaches of international law breeds confidence in would-be criminals that they can get away with it. But the steady galvanising of the universal culture of human rights is challenging the validity under international law today of such national amnesty laws as the Chilean amnesty law of 1978 and other similar amnesty laws. The collapse of national amnesty laws that sought to remove criminal and/or civil liability of agents of a prior regime alleged to have violated basic human rights of individuals confirms the Rawls pragmatic of the need to uphold society's previously established legal standards by enforcing corresponding sanctions whenever breaches of those standards occur. The collapse of such national amnesty laws is something that will be stopped only by their rejection in the first place – whether they are imposed, elected or otherwise. This is the fact that those that argue that peace and justice are separable prefer to shy away

---

[42] Dugard, J. (1997) 'Is the Truth and Reconciliation Process Compatible with International Law? An Unanswered Question', *South African Journal on Human Rights*, vol. 13 No. 2, p.258.

[43] See above at pp.2–5.

[44] Dugard, J., note 42 above, at p.260.

from.[45] They argue that by rigidly insisting on requirements of justice the human rights school has prolonged conflicts such as the war in the former Yugoslavia. They criticise privileging of justice for victims of crimes against humanity in the search for peace agreements as a mechanism for rejecting deals capable of shortening conflicts and saving lives. An anonymous writer to the *Human Rights Quarterly* put it this way: 'The quest for justice for yesterday's victims of atrocities should not be pursued in such a manner that it makes today's living the dead of tomorrow. That, for the human rights community, is one of the lessons from the former Yugoslavia.'[46] This writer shares Bell's view that it is not enough to examine the connection between human rights abuses and the speed with which they are resolved, but to go beyond that and analyse the question whether protecting human rights through the implementation of human rights conventions and customs plays a positive role in conflict management, resolution, or transformation.[47] Even more, because international criminal law requires evidence of *mens rea* for the charge of crime against humanity, confronting those engaged in the forbidden acts necessarily facilitates proof of the crimes when the time comes for trial. Silence of the human rights community at the time of the atrocities advocated by some may have the opposite effect of emboldening the criminals into thinking that any State had capacity to act as they were acting.

(b) Elective national amnesty laws

Elective national amnesty laws have more to do with what are often referred to as practical considerations necessary for the State to make reasonable transition from autocratic to democratic rule.[48] The outgoing autocratic government does not make granting of amnesty a condition of its surrender of public office. However, the incoming government decides that granting amnesty to personnel of the previous government that would otherwise be charged with crimes against humanity is beneficial to the State. This superimposes an executive decision over a judicial consideration of the legal rights of the victims of totalitarian rule. Further, the legal duties of the recipients of the amnesty to the State and to other citizens of the State are not enforced. Even more, the families and relatives of the victims of the previous administration are left in no doubt of the legal value of their loved ones' lives who become sacrifices of a political dream – the dream of stability and democracy. Thus, State orches-

---

[45] See Anonymous (1996) 'Human Rights in Peace Negotiations', *Human Rights Quarterly*, vol. 18 No. 2, p.249 at p.250.

[46] Ibid. p.258.

[47] Bell, C. (2000) *Peace Agreements and Human Rights*, Oxford University Press, Oxford, pp.5–6.

[48] Discussing the Mozambique and South African amnesties, see Cassese (1998) 'Reflections on International Criminal Justice', *Modern Law Review*, vol. 61 No. 1, p.1 at pp.3–6.

trated transactions which purport to exchange the legal rights of the victims and the legal duties of those that should be prosecuted for crimes against humanity for the unfathomable hope only that stability and democracy will be realised are problematic for three reasons.

(c) Theoretical, policy and practical problems with national amnesty laws

First, national amnesty laws are problematic in that they refer to property rights of victims whose title never passes on to the State for it to be able to trade them off for any other good. Macpherson writes that:

> 'John Locke repeatedly and explicitly defined men's properties as their lives, liberties, and estates. For Hobbes, the things in which a man had property included "his own life and limbs; and in the next degree, (in most men), those that concern conjugal affection; and after them riches and means of living". One's own person, one's capacities, one's rights and liberties were regarded as individual property. They were even more important than individual property in material things and revenues, partly because they were seen as the source and justification of individual material property.'[49]

If basic human rights are the property of individuals,[50] and in this case the property of victims, it is difficult to see how title to those basic rights of victims transfers from the victims themselves to the government so that it legitimately can exchange them for another good. Justification of rights of victims of some of the worst excesses of human rights violations becomes simply consideration for transfer of civil power from one government to the next. But law ought to act on behalf of victims to justify them. Not to do so would be to complete their extermination and annihilation. Writes Jankelevitch:

> 'Within the framework of the prevalent moral amnesty long granted to murderers, all those who were deported, executed or massacred, have none but us to think of them. If we stopped thinking of them, we would complete their extermination: they would be definitively annihilated.'[51]

---

[49] Macpherson, C. B. (1997) 'Human Rights as Property Rights', *Dissent*, 24 No. 1, p.72.

[50] Discussing the Principle of Generic Consistency, see Gewirth, A. (1982) *Human Rights: Essays on Justification and Applications*, University of Chicago Press, Chicago/London, pp.1–15. In this connection see also Vincent, R. J. (1986) *Human Rights and International Relations*, Cambridge University Press, Cambridge, Chap. 1: The Idea of Human Rights. Milne writes that: 'If there are human rights, they must be universal moral rights. They must be universal because they are rights which people have simply as human beings irrespective of nationality, religion, citizenship, marital status, occupation, income or any other social or cultural characteristic, and also irrespective of sex. . . . Can there be such rights? Yes, if there is a universal morality which includes them. Is there such a morality? According to a famous theory there is, and it is usually called in English *natural law*.' Milne, A. J. M. (1984) 'The Idea of Human Rights: A Critical Inquiry', in Dowrick, F. E. (ed.) *Human Rights: Problems, Perspectives and Texts*, Gower, Aldershot, Chap. 1.

[51] Cited in Cassese, A. (1998) 'Reflections on International Criminal Justice', *Modern Law Review*, vol. 61 No. 1, p.1 at p.2.

In his preface to Dyzenhaus' *Judging the Judges, Judging Ourselves* Asmal talks of law as a humanising agent, and as a sanctuary for the perplexed.

> 'law is that to which we turn, these days, for collective self-expression. . . . In South Africa, this disappointment – the distance between law's humanistic promise and its workaday betrayals – has been stark over the last four decades. The question is whether we can change this, today, and how.'[52]

The correct view is that neither the regime that inflicted terror and atrocities on its subjects nor the incoming one seeking to commit the State to democratic practice have ownership of victims' personal rights. Therefore, those responsible for breaching victims' basic rights, which are recognised in treaties and conventions, customary international law and *jus cogens*, ought to be prosecuted for those breaches. It appears also that the new government has no right to impede the deported, the tortured, those taken hostage, and those whose loved ones were murdered from taking independent action against perpetrators of crimes against humanity. In fact, the incoming government has a duty under international law to prosecute those alleged to have committed grave violations of human rights. Both the Convention against Torture and Other Cruel, Inhuman or Degrading Treatment or Punishment (1984) which came into force on 26 June 1987[53] and the International Convention against the Taking of Hostages (1979) which came into force in 1983[54] require States to adopt measures for their enforcement within their territories. Article 2 of the Convention against Torture obliges States to take effective legislative, administrative, judicial or other measures to prevent acts of torture in any territory under their jurisdiction. No exceptional circumstances whatsoever, whether a state of war or a threat of war, internal political instability or any other public emergency, are a sufficient justification of torture. A claim that one was acting under a superior's orders or a public authority will not suffice as a justification of torture. Even more, by Article 5(1) each State Party shall take such measures as may be necessary to establish its jurisdiction over the offences referred to in Article 4 in the following cases: (a) when the offences are committed in any territory under its jurisdiction or on board a ship or aircraft registered in that State; (b) when the alleged offender is a national of that State; and (c) when the victim is a national of that State if that State considers it appropriate.

Secondly, State orchestrated transactions that purport to exchange the legal rights of victims of human rights violations and the legal duties of those that should be prosecuted for those crimes, for the hope only that stability and democracy will be realised at some unidentifiable point in the future, are

---

[52] Dyzenhaus, D. (1998) *Judging the Judges, Judging Ourselves: Truth, Reconciliation and the Apartheid Legal Order*, Hart Publishing, Oxford, p.vii.
[53] GA Res. 39/46, Annex, 39 UNGAOR Supplement No. 51, at p.197, UN Doc. A/39/51 (1984).
[54] UKTS 81 (1983), Cmnd; (1979) 18 ILM 1456.

problematic for policy reasons. Consistent application of rules of law enhances the legitimacy of both the rules themselves and the legal system in which they operate. Inconsistent application of a rule of law weakens its legitimacy, and that of the legal system in which it is inconsistently applied. Inconsistency in the application of rules of law blurs the distinction between valid and invalid rules. Applying a rule incoherently can have one or all of three possible effects. Franck writes that:

> 'incoherence nullifies the flawed act of validating or withholding validation. Second, it undermines the standards, rules and processes for bestowing status or validity. Third, it derogates from the legitimacy of the institution that is charged with validating. Thus, in the UN context, when the GA fails to follow the Organization's own rules, standards or procedures for accrediting delegates, it damages the claim of the whole UN system to be taken seriously as bestower of status.'[55]

There is, therefore, a sense in which the sterile debate about whether or not international law is law is actually fanned by United Nations practice when the General Assembly or the Security Council, or both, pick and choose cases where international standards will apply. Dworkin writes that 'fair play' is the hallmark of legitimacy in any legal order.

> 'Most would be dismayed by laws that treat similar accidents or occasions . . . differently on arbitrary grounds. [While] . . . each point of view must be allowed a voice in the process of deliberation, the collective decision must nevertheless aim to settle on some coherent principle whose influence then extends to the natural limits of its authority. If there must be compromise because people are divided about justice, then the compromise must be external, not internal; it must be compromise about which scheme of justice to adopt rather than a compromised scheme of justice.'[56]

As an index of legitimacy, consistency requires that a rule, whatever its content, be applied uniformly in every 'similar' or 'relevant' instance.[57] Thus, international standards that proscribe against crimes against humanity ought to be upheld whenever there is conduct that falls within their sphere. I am not advocating legal formalism here,[58] nor am I advocating mechanical jurisprudence, which Hart correctly regards as impossibility. He writes:

---

[55] Franck, T. (1990) *The Power of Legitimacy Among Nations*, Oxford University Press, New York/Oxford, p.41.

[56] Dworkin, R. (3rd ed. 1990) *Law's Empire*, Fontana Press, London, pp.193–194.

[57] Ibid.

[58] See Simmonds, N. E. (1996) *Central Issues in Jurisprudence: Justice, Law and Rights*, Sweet and Maxwell, London, pp.87–89; Hart, H. L. A. (2nd ed. 1994) *The Concept of Law*, Clarendon Press, Oxford, pp.126–135. I would argue that life itself is not formal. Some people die before they are even born. So death does not necessarily follow birth. Although we try to formalise our weather, sometimes 'it winters' at the peak of summer and 'summers' at the peak of winter. Even the *Oxford English Dictionary* places 'success' before 'work'. Formalism is not entirely helpful.

'If the world in which we live were characterized only by a finite number of features, and these together with all modes in which they could combine were known to us, then provision could be made in advance for every possibility. We could make rules, the application of which to particular cases never called for a further choice. Everything could be known, something could be done and specified in advance by rule. This would be a world fit for "mechanical" jurisprudence.'[59]

Rather, I am arguing for a deference of executive action to enforcement of fundamental rules of international law where particular human conduct falls within their sphere of operation. The prohibition of torture by anyone at any time applies to uphold, enhance and declare the sanctity of human dignity. The State cannot forgive breaches of international human rights law. It is powerless so to do because the rights in question are the property of the victims of those particular breaches, and victims never pass title of those rights to the State. 'The modern concept of property is pretty well confined to the right of an individual or corporation – a natural or artificial person – to exclude others from some use or enjoyment of some thing.'[60]

Thirdly, State orchestrated transactions which purport to exchange legal rights of victims of crimes against humanity on the one hand, and the legal duties of those that should be prosecuted for crimes against humanity on the other, for the unfathomable hope only that stability and democracy will be realised, are problematic because they conflict with substantive international law. This is illustrated by the case of *R v Bow Street Metropolitan Stipendiary Magistrate and Others, ex parte Pinochet Ugarte (No. 3)*[61] which focused international attention especially on the deliberations of the House of Lords, which was not accustomed to working under intense international interest. As the Law Lords considered whether or not Senator Pinochet Ugarte should be extradited to face charges of crimes against humanity as Spain had requested, in Britain, as in Chile, Spain and other parts of the world, Senator Pinochet Ugarte was hailed by some as a victim and by others as a culprit whose escape from well-established norms of international law was coming to an end. Even when Jack Straw, British Home Secretary, finally halted extradition proceedings against Senator Pinochet Ugarte in 2000, and allowed the Senator to return to Chile for health reasons, worldwide celebrations of that decision were matched by condemnations of it.

The international warrant of arrest that triggered proceedings against Senator Pinochet Ugarte in London had been issued by the Spanish court at Madrid

---

[59] Hart, H. L. A. (2nd ed. 1994) *The Concept of Law*, Clarendon Press, Oxford, p.128.
[60] Macpherson, C. B. (1997) 'Human Rights as Property Rights', *Dissent*, vol. 24 No. 1, p.72 at p.73.
[61] [1999] 2 WLR 827, HL.

alleging that during his rule of Chile, between 1973 and 1990, Senator Pinochet Ugarte had ordered his officials to commit acts of *torture* and of *hostage taking*.[62] Thus, Senator Pinochet was alleged to have breached norms of international law founded on customary international law, conventions and treaties.[63] The prohibition of torture 'has evolved into a peremptory norm of *jus cogens*, that is, a norm that enjoys a higher rank in the international hierarchy than treaty law and even "ordinary customary" rules'.[64] Charges of torture are commonplace in the leading cases on crimes against humanity.[65] Therefore, when executive decisions compromise enforcement of norms of *jus cogens*, they undermine the very core of international standards. In the view of Lords Millet and Phillips torture and hostage taking are '*international crimes* for which there could be no immunity even before the [Torture] Convention came into effect and consequently there is no immunity under customary international law'.[66] 'No immunity' in this sense underlines the seriousness of the offence that even the mere thought of granting national amnesty to those alleged to have committed crimes against humanity runs counter to the spirit and purpose of these special norms. The provisions of the Torture and Hostage Taking Conventions discussed above strengthen this view.

Fourthly, State orchestrated transactions which purport to exchange the legal rights of victims of crimes against humanity on the one hand, and the legal duties of those that should be prosecuted for those crimes on the other, for the hope only that stability and democracy will be realised, are problematic for practical reasons. Can a society, writes Hayner, build a democratic future on a foundation of blind, denied, or forgotten history?[67] What if the democracy hoped for in the sacrifice of the victims' rights is not achieved? Developments unfolding in Zimbabwe at the time of writing, and whose end appears unpredictable though sufficiently worrying, illustrate vividly the danger posed.[68] If sacrifice of victims' equal treatment before the law is regarded as consideration for the better common good of achieving democracy, what should happen if the stability and democracy hoped for prove elusive? Does the amnesty become void, and its beneficiaries subject to investigation and prosecution for

---

[62] *Ex parte Pinochet Ugarte (No. 3)* [1999] 2 WLR 827 at p.834.

[63] See Chigara, B. (2000) 'Pinochet and the Administration of International Criminal Justice', in Woodhouse, D. (ed.) *The Pinochet Case: A Legal and Constitutional Analysis*, Hart Publishing, Oxford, p.115 at p.116.

[64] *Ex parte Pinochet Ugarte (No. 3)* [1999] 2 WLR 827 at p.841, *per* Lord Browne-Wilkinson.

[65] See proceedings of the Nuremberg trials of 1945; the International Criminal Tribunal for the Territory of the former Yugoslavia (ICTY); and the International Criminal Tribunal for Rwanda (ICTR).

[66] *Ex parte Pinochet Ugarte (No. 3)* [1999] 2 WLR 827 at p.829.

[67] Hayner, P. B. (2001) *Unspeakable Truths: Confronting State Terror and Atrocity*, Routledge, New York, p.5.

[68] See *The Times*, Commentary, 12 April 2000, p.29.

crimes against humanity? This makes the amnesty approach to resolution of crimes against humanity fickle. Amnesty laws are not the only means by which reconciliation can be achieved by a community emerging from State terror and atrocity. Provided that they do not cover atrocious crimes that international law obliges States to punish, they perhaps can be used to facilitate such reconciliation.[69]

Geras[70] argues that individuals have basic rights against personal violation. The threshold against violation of these basic rights must be kept very high if society's welfare considerations are to be maintained. Political considerations alone are not sufficient justification for violation of these basic personal human rights. However, the granting of amnesty to agents of a prior regime alleged to have violated basic human rights of individuals sets to zero the rights of victims. It is as if they never had any human dignity positively recognised by law.

Investigation and prosecution of crimes against humanity benefits those alleged to have committed those crimes by destigmatising them as criminals when they are acquitted of the charges, or when they personally come to terms with their own self-delusion after conviction and sentencing for their flagrant disrespect of society's most prized values. The hope that those convicted might reflect on their waywardness while serving their sentences appears to be a better risk to take, even if all they ever do is only serve their time, than that of letting them go scot free with the hope that that in itself will expedite transition to democratic rule. The latter approach unfairly empowers potential beneficiaries of national amnesty laws for violation of basic human rights of individuals, so that by maximising the threat of disruption, they can go unpunished. Forever, society remains hostage to masters of violence.

Privileging over prosecution of crimes prohibited often by both national and international law in order to pursue a political dream whose realisation can not be guaranteed has been attempted in several countries.[71] Several reasons have been proffered in support of this treatment of persons that have committed crimes against humanity. The first is that fragile democracies may not be able to survive the destabilising effects of politically charged trials because, often, countries emerging from dictatorship are polarised and unstable.[72] Therefore, prosecuting crimes against humanity in such cases is counter-productive.

---

[69] See Orentlicher, D. F. (1991) 'Settling Accounts: The Duty to Prosecute Human Rights Violations of a Prior Regime', *Yale Law Journal*, vol. 100, p.2537 at p.2546.

[70] *Amnesty: Rights and Wrongs*. Paper presented at Conference on Amnesty, Truth and Reconciliation, University of Hull, 10 April 2000.

[71] Examples include Zimbabwe, Haiti, South Africa, Mozambique, Uganda, Argentina, Uruguay, Bolivia, the Philippines, Chile, Chad, El Salvador, Germany and more recently, Sierra Leone. See Hayner, P. B. (1994) 'Fifteen Truth Commissions – 1974 to 1994: A Comparative Study', *Human Rights Quarterly*, vol. 16 No. 4, p.597.

[72] Orentlicher, D. F., note 69 above, at p.2546.

Hayner aptly captures the helplessness of States in addressing this problem through the words of a United States State Department Official who stated:

> 'There is a need to empty wounds of all the old infection before healing can start. But in some countries, like Angola and Mozambique, I'm not sure you'd have anything left if you cleaned out all the infection. I used to feel very strongly that truth needs to come out. But there are others here that don't feel that way; they feel that it is most important to focus on the elimination of future abuses . . .'[73]

Emerging democratic practice has more to lose in a situation where the community is divided than where it is united under the banner of reconciliation and amnesty. Secondly, the military may not take kindly to prosecution of members of the former military government. Therefore, the civilian government should proceed cautiously without tempting the military to demonstrate where their sympathy lies. It has been argued already that this is problematic because there is no explanation how the property rights of victims pass to the State so that it can then trade them as consideration for the promise of murderers and torturers not to disrupt efforts to commit the State to democratic practice. Even more, these claims threaten to divert jurisprudence from a study of law to a study of sacrificial religious philosophy where one goal is juxtaposed against another and the pair is perceived as a binary opposition rather than as a complement. Derrida[74] traces the inculcation of the sacrificial logocentric bias of Western philosophy to Platonism. In *Phaedrus* Plato recounts the myth of *Theuth*, in which writing as a form of a gift that can aid one's memory is presented to Ra,[75] the father-god, who refuses it because he perceives it to be a *dangerous drug* that impedes the memory and therefore usurps the active functioning of the brain. Says the King:

> 'If men learn this, it will implant forgetfulness in their souls; they will cease to exercise memory because they rely on that which is written, calling things to remembrance no longer from within themselves, but by means of external marks.'

Plato refers to writing as *pharmakon*, by which he means a remedy-poison.[76] Derrida argues that because writing is perceived as a supplement to speech, to presence of mind, to the origin as logos and logos as origin, and because it is expelled for threatening to supplant it altogether, the rejection by philosophic

---

[73] Cited in Hayner, P. B., note 71 above, at p.610.

[74] Derrida, J. (1981) *Dissemination* (translated by Barbara Johnson), University of Chicago Press, Chicago, pp.76–168.

[75] Ra is an Egyptian god. If Plato is Derrida's myth of origin, then 'the West's' philosophical foundations can be said to recede into Africa.

[76] Hamilton, E. and Huntington, C. (eds) (1964) *Plato, The Collected Dialogues*, Pantheon, New York.

tradition of a radical ambiguity or originary bivalence is exposed.[77] This
exposure appears to suggest that the violence of exclusion is imbedded in our
philosophical traditions which for the stabilisation of concepts and ideas
appear to depend on a process of radical expulsion, exclusion and rejection of
the opposite idea: *the sacrifice*. Through this violence or sacrifice, order is
established because the difference between the good idea that is kept and the
bad idea that is sacrificed is established. Good and bad are just as distinct and
as separate from each other as they sound in our ears. We must not suggest
that even in the best of us lies some evil, and in the worst of us lies some
good. No. The difference is obvious and beyond comparison. One problem
with this approach is that the very *sacrifice* that is excluded appears to be the
matrix for difference, the matrix for pluralism and the matrix for unsifted
knowledge.

> 'The *pharmakon* is the origin, the foundation of oppositions that come into
> being by its expulsion. Far from being dominated by any oppositions, writing is
> the condition for the very possibility of opposition; it cannot be contained by
> any oppositions, but remains ever in excess of them. Writing is insubordinate in
> principle and, more importantly, of principle as such. The emergence of the
> logos as the condition of truth, of the presence of the idea itself, is thus traced to
> the expulsion of an otherness in which it originates. . . . This obstacle to truth,
> the rival to truth, is likewise its originary model. This opposition of same to
> same, where rival model and obstacle are one, displays the dynamics of violent
> mimesis of the victimary hypothesis.'[78]

This approach alienates violence from the community by protecting the community from its own violence. However, it also appears to mystify the origin
of violence by assigning it to the victim. The result is that the same violence,
which must be eliminated, is protected. Therefore, the community is ever in
search of new victims in which it blindly seeks its 'store of deep background'.[79]
The ugliness of this violence lies in that often the privileged idea is applied to
define or interpret its opposite, and we accept the outcome of that process as
'rational'. For the purposes of this study, the question whether a better understanding of customary international law can be arrived at from a reconciliation of that which the process of formulating rules of customary international
law has privileged as a rule of customary international law, and that which
it has excluded as its other or opposite takes priority. Derrida argues that
the other is not merely the opposite of the privileged idea. To hold that view

---

[77] McKenna, A. J. (1992) *Violence and Difference*, University of Illinois Publishing Co., Illinois,
p.28.
[78] Ibid. p.32. See also Derrida, J. (1981) *Positions* (translated by Alan Bass), The Athlone Press,
London, pp.24–25.
[79] Derrida, J., note 74 above, at p.128.

would be to perpetuate the violence that gives rise to the sort of interpretation and valuations that are coterminous with it.

> 'All translations into languages that are the heirs and depositories of Western metaphysics thus produce on the *pharmakon* an effect of analysis *that violently destroys it, reduces it to one of its simple elements by interpreting it, paradoxically enough, in the light of the ulterior developments it itself has made possible.* Such an interpretative translation is thus as violent as it is impotent: it destroys the *pharmakon* but at the same time forbids itself access to it, leaving it untouched in its reserve.'[80]

When applied by organs of the State, including judicial institutions, this approach to interpretation and application of ideas is not entirely helpful because of the paradoxes that it raises. This could be resolved by employing reverse reasoning techniques to test the strength of ideas that are otherwise regarded as 'givens'.[81] The idea that prosecution of crimes against humanity and consolidation of stability for the purposes of furthering democratic practices are mutually exclusive in countries that are on the mend from totalitarian rule to democratic rule is not given. The idea that prosecution of crimes against humanity and efforts to consolidate stability of a State that is in transition from totalitarian rule to democracy are mutually exclusive is a myth that deserves no acceptance especially because through codification of customary international law, and through treaties aimed at developing international law, the international community has opted comprehensively to proscribe crimes against humanity.

CONCLUSION

National amnesty laws that purport to expunge criminal and/or civil liability of agents of a prior regime alleged to have violated basic human rights of individuals are based on three unreconcilable facts. The first is the *non-event* of the transfer of the property rights of victims of human rights violation from the victims themselves to the State. Victims' property rights must be shown to have transferred from the victims themselves on to the State before the State legitimately can claim to be trading off those property rights for any other good in the interest of the State. How this can happen is perhaps still beyond the comprehension of the present writer. Yet not to insist on this would imply that victims are mere property of the State. Such a doctrine is unsupportable. Victims possess basic human rights, which are their property *qua* individuals. It is a fraudulent government that claims to have authority to pardon those

---

[80] See McKenna, A. J., note 77 above, at p.33. Emphasis added. See also Derrida, J. (1981) *Positions* (translated by Alan Bass), The Athlone Press, London, p.20.
[81] McKenna, A. J., note 77 above, at p.19.

that breached victims' basic rights without demonstrating first when and how those rights had actually been conveyed to it. The second is that those that breached victims' basic rights immediately incurred international responsibility for those breaches. International law grants universal jurisdiction for prosecution of crimes against humanity.[82] In particular, it obliges States to adopt internal measures for the prosecution of these crimes. Therefore, amnesia does not appear to have been contemplated in the formulation of the norm against crimes against humanity. The third is based on the *fear* of the new government that prosecution of crimes against humanity committed by members and officials of the outgoing regime, or to put it another way, justifying the victims of crimes against humanity by prosecuting those responsible for breaching victims' basic human rights, will be met with violence that disrupts the process of rehabilitating the State from totalitarian rule to democratic rule. It is the further threat of criminal behaviour of the outgoing government and its agents that forces the incoming government to suspend the function of judicial institutions. The hope that under this cloud of terror hung over the State by the outgoing government, both while it was violating individuals' basic rights and after it has handed over power to the new government, democratic practice will be established appears misplaced.

It has been argued that title to property rights of victims never transfers to the State. Therefore, the State is incapable of forgiving those that breached the rights of victims on behalf of the victims, even in exchange for the promise of the violators that they will not disrupt the new government's agenda. However, assuming that the incoming government could trade off those rights, it is under a specific duty under international law to prosecute crimes against humanity. If they were accepted as part of statecraft in modern international law, national amnesty laws that purport to expunge criminal and civil liability of agents of a prior regime potentially would threaten to convert jurisprudence from a study of positive laws to a study of sacrificial philosophy. Therefore, it appears that for now national amnesty laws that purport to expunge criminal and/or civil liability of agents of a previous regime alleged to have violated basic human rights of individuals are not acceptable under international law. Their service of institutionalised violence opposes democratic practice even though it is often argued that they help to establish democracy. The suggestion that rehabilitation of a State from totalitarian rule to democratic practice is mutually exclusive to justice is an apology for setting to zero the inalienable rights of victims of crimes against humanity. It protects and perpetuates violence and fraud in the State system.

---

[82] Discussing law as a universalising system of rules, and law as a presence of the social past, and law as an organising of the social present and law as a conditioning of the social future, see Allot, P. (1999) 'The Concept of Law', *European Journal of International Law*, vol. 10, p.31 at p.32.

2

NATIONAL AMNESTY LAWS: LIMITS OF STATE DISCRETION UNDER INTERNATIONAL LAW

INTRODUCTION

Continuing resort by States to declare national amnesty laws that meet with tacit approval or outright rejection of other States compels inquiry into an old question, that is, what does international law allow States to do, and what does it not allow them to do? Framing the question this way is vulnerable to the charge of presuming the relationship or connection between international law and national law because implicit in the question is the view that it is international law that prescribes the constituency of national law and not vice versa. Because national law evolved prior to the practice of States which began gradually to grow from the second half of the Middle Ages[1] of creating rules of conduct in areas of mutual interest it appears more logical to assume that it is national law that prescribed jurisdiction of international law. Theorists have remained locked in debate on the connection between national and international law, and the interaction of their jurisdictions. On its surface this debate appears to be a contest between monism and dualism.[2] More

---

[1] See Harris, D. J. (5th ed. 1998) *Cases and Materials on International Law*, Sweet and Maxwell, London, p.1; Brownlie, I. (5th ed. 1998) *Principles of Public International Law*, Oxford University Press, Oxford, pp.31–56; Cassese, A. (1994) *International Law in a Divided World*, Clarendon Press, Oxford, pp.34–38; Jennings, R. and Watts, A. (eds) (9th ed. 1992) *Oppenheim's International Law*, Longman, London, p.4; Brierly, J. L. (6th ed. 1963) *The Law of Nations*, Oxford University Press, Oxford, p.41.

[2] See Jennings, R. and Watts, A. (eds) (9th ed. 1992) *Oppenheim's International Law*, Longman, London, pp.53–81; Fitzmaurice, G. (1957–II) 'The Principles of International Law Considered from the Standpoint of the Rule of Law', *Recueil des cours*, vol. 92, p.1; Fitzmaurice, G. (1956) 'The Foundations of Authority of International Law and the Problem of Enforcement', *Modern Law Review*, vol. 19, p.1; Dixon, M. (3rd ed. 1998) *Textbook on International Law*, Blackstone Press, London, pp.77–78.

profoundly, the debate reflects also a battle for the generic origin of the rule of law.[3] Resort to the question of purpose and function of international law affects the particulars and peculiarities of the debate so that focus falls on the social utility of the law, which is arguably of more consequence than the question of the theoretical connection between national and international legal systems. The law is a mode of the self-constituting of a society. It is that which constitutes and manifests society's common interest and organises the making and application of social standards to which all members of the society must submit. 'International society is the collective self-constituting of all human beings, the society of all societies. International law is the law of international society.'[4] The judicial prosecution at Bresach in the fifteenth century of a war criminal for trampling underfoot the laws of God and man, and of war criminals at the end of the Second World War, and of crimes against humanity at the International Criminal Tribunal for the former Yugoslavia (ICTY) and the International Criminal Tribunal for Rwanda (ICTR), and of General Pinochet in the United Kingdom in 1998; and the establishment in 1946 of the International Court of Justice (ICJ) and progressive creation thereafter of permanent international tribunals, including the International Tribunal for the Law of the Sea (ITLOS), and the adoption in 1998 of the Statute of Rome which refers to the creation of a permanent International Criminal Court (ICC) typically point to international society's efforts to apply a particular law – international law, to submit national strategies of dealing with issues that affect all of humanity to the international domain. The impressive labyrinth of inter-governmental and non-governmental organisations that serve the global community in various ways points to international society's favour in certain instances to apply international strategies of dealing with issues that affect all of humanity to national ones. Pronouncements of national Home Affairs Government Departments on issues such as asylum and immigration always refer to international obligations that States must honour when formulating or applying their asylum or immigration laws. The conduct of commerce and trade suggests supremacy of international norms, even though they apply unfairly sometimes to developing countries whose concerns are not adequately reflected in the bulk of international trade laws. For instance the GATT/WTO regime has been raised on the doctrine of sanctity of contracts. Arbitration tribunals have no regard whatsoever to principles of equity, or to duress or unconscionability, insisting on the sacrosanctity

---

[3] See Koskenniemi, M. (1989) *From Apology to Utopia: The Structure of International Legal Argument*, Finnish Lawyers' Publishing Company, Helsinki, pp.194–206.
[4] Allot, P. (1999) 'The Concept of International Law', *European Journal of International Law*, vol. 10, p.31 at p.32.

of contracts.[5] Thus, where nationalisation of foreign multinational enterprises is an issue, focus falls on prompt, adequate and efficient compensation[6] regardless of the context of the circumstance. Sornarajah[7] regrets that counter-measures, the weapon of the strong and not of the weak, has been rubber-stamped into the Dispute Settlement System of the Marakesh Agreement 1994 which set up the World Trade Organisation. But what sanctions can Mozambique, Jamaica or Venezuela impose with any effect on the United States? Nonetheless, international economic law points to a subordination of national practice to international standards. A host of international treaties going several hundred years back point also to the existence of a diverse range of international standards that impinge national capacity unilaterally to act on issues of international concern. Moreover, after several decades of work on Draft Articles on State Responsibility, the International Law Commission,[8] whose purpose is to promote the progressive development and codification of international law in its document of 11 August 2000, stated in Article 3 that the characterisation of an act of a State as internationally wrongful is governed by international law. Further, such characterisation is not affected by the characterisation of the same as lawful by internal law.[9] The irrelevance of the domestic provisions in situations where internationally prohibited offences have been committed is developed in Article 32[10] which provides that the responsible State may not rely on the provisions of its internal law as justification for failure to comply with its obligations under international law. Again

---

[5] See Sornarajah, M. (2000) *The Settlement of Foreign Investment Disputes*, Kluwer, Netherlands. But in *Amoco International Finance Corp. v Iran* (1987) 15 Iran–USCTR 189 para. 220, the arbitration tribunal suggested that 'the choice between all the available methods must rather be made in view of the purpose to be attained, in order to avoid arbitrary results and to arrive at an equitable compensation in conformity with the applicable legal standards . . .'. This case and its type can be distinguished from other property type cases in that it involved determination of the value of the nationalised enterprise according to speculative market value of company shares. Where the value of the nationalised enterprise is not derived from such speculative factors as value of company shares on the stock market, tribunals have homed in on the prompt adequate and sufficient compensation (PAEC) principle often referred to as the Hull principle after United States Secretary of State Hull who in 1940 stated in connection with the Mexican government's decision to expropriate foreign oil interests that: 'the right to expropriate property is coupled with and conditioned on the obligation to make adequate, effective and prompt compensation. The legality of an expropriation is in fact dependent upon the observance of this requirement.' See Harris, D. J. (5th ed. 1998) *Cases and Materials on International Law*, Sweet and Maxwell, London, p.568. See also (1987) *Third Restatement of United States Foreign Relations Law*, vol. 2, para.712.
[6] See e.g. the decision of the Iran–United States Claims Tribunal in *Amoco International Finance Corp. v Iran* 15 Iran–USCTR 189 where the tribunal focused on the Khemco Agreement.
[7] Sornarajah, M. (2001) *Developing Country Perspective of International Economic Law in the Context of Dispute Settlement*. Paper presented at Manchester University School of Law Conference on Perspectives in International Economic Law, 4 May 2001.
[8] Established by the UNGA in compliance with Article 13 of the UNC.
[9] A/CN.4/L.600, p.2.
[10] Ibid. p.11.

this throws a shadow of illegality on national amnesty laws that purport to expunge criminal and/or civil liability of agents of a prior regime alleged to have violated basic human rights of individuals because, as will become clear shortly, both customary international law and treaty law impose a duty on States either to prosecute or extradite to another State, which is willing to prosecute, persons alleged to have committed certain offences. Further, the defence of necessity may not be invoked where:

(1) the international obligation arises from a peremptory norm of general international law;
(2) the international obligation in question excludes the possibility of invoking necessity; or
(3) the State has contributed to the situation of necessity.[11]

National amnesty laws that purport to expunge criminal and/or civil liability of agents of a prior regime alleged to have violated basic human rights of individuals certainly evidence breach of peremptory norms of general international law for which necessity as a defence is not available. Thus, such national amnesty laws provide an opportunity for a study on the modern limits on State discretion of international constraint. The question raised by the national amnesty laws tradition is this: to what extent is declaration of national amnesty – itself an assertion of national sovereignty – subject to review of international law? This chapter evaluates the connection between national and international law in the context of State practice regarding national amnesty laws that purport to expunge criminal and/or civil liability of agents of a prior regime alleged to have violated basic human rights of individuals. It shows that increasingly, and with strong reference to positive international human rights law, both State practice of denouncing these national amnesty laws and judicial decisions of national courts and international tribunals favour review by international law of them. This strengthens the view that, presently, declaration of national amnesty laws for crimes of a past regime, whatever its motivation,[12] may be illegal under international law.

PERSPECTIVES ON MUNICIPAL AND INTERNATIONAL LEGAL SYSTEMS

Akehurst[13] refers to two doctrines, by which international law may be integrated into British law, pointing to dualist claims about the relationship between national law and international law. By the doctrine of incorporation,

---

[11] Article 26. Ibid. p.9.
[12] See Chap. 1 above.
[13] Malanczuk, P. (ed.) (7th ed. 1997) *Akehurst's Modern Introduction to International Law*, Routledge, London, pp.69–70.

customary international law automatically forms part of English and Scots law. Judicial support for this proposition is abundant. The Court of Appeal stated in *Trendtex Trading Corporation v Central Bank of Nigeria*[14] that: 'the rules of international law, as existing from time to time, do form part of our English law'. By the doctrine of transformation, which increasingly appears to be taking over from the doctrine of incorporation, rules of customary international law form part of English law only in so far as they have been accepted by English Acts of Parliament and judicial decisions. In cases affecting private rights,[15] English courts have tended not to give effect to international treaties in the absence of an enabling Act of Parliament.[16] Dualism therefore regards national law and international law as two separate systems in which the external obligations of a State under international law have only a political relation to its use of internal law making powers within the national system.

> . . . Thus, a State which through its municipal law is violating international law will be in breach of external obligations and may be made the object of sanctions. The offending municipal law, will, however, be law until, or rather unless, the State is forced, through sanctions or other pressures, to change it.[17]

Lauterpacht[18] and others[19] hotly contest this. Current developments in international law of reviewing declarations of amnesties by States and of supervising governments' application of sovereign authority[20] favour Kelsen's[21] monist description of both the basis of the rule of law and the relationship between

---

[14] [1977] 1 All ER 881. In 1735 the Lord Chancellor stated in *Barbuit's Case* that 'the law of nations in its fullest extent is and forms part of the law of England': (1735) 25 ER 77. See also *Heathfield v Chilton* (1767) 97 ER 50; *Emperor of Australia v Day* 2 Giff 628 at p.678. More recent cases include: *I Congreso del Partido* [1981] 3 WLR 328; *R v Bow Street Metropolitan Stipendiary Magistrate and Others, ex parte Pinochet Ugarte (No. 3)* [1999] 2 WLR 827.

[15] See e.g. *Administrator of German Property v Knoop* [1933] Ch 439; *Blackburn v Attorney-General* [1971] 2 All ER 430; *Malone v Commissioner of Police for the Metropolis (No. 2)* [1979] 2 All ER 620 at pp. 637–638; *Winfat Enterprises (HK) Co. Ltd v Attorney-General for Hong Kong* [1985] AC 733.

[16] Jennings, R. and Watts, A. (eds) (9th ed. 1992) *Oppenheim's International Law*, Longman, London, p.59, n.24.

[17] McCoubrey, H. and White, N. D. (3rd ed. 1999) *Textbook on Jurisprudence*, Blackstone Press, London, p.154.

[18] He writes: 'Within the community of nations, the essential feature of the rule of law is constantly put in jeopardy by the conception of the sovereignty of States which deduces the binding force of international law from the will of each individual member of the international community.' Lauterpacht, H. (1966) *The Function of Law in the International Community*, Archon Books, Hamden/Connecticut, p.3.

[19] Especially Kelsen. See generally Kelsen, H. (1967) *The Pure Theory of Law*, University of California Press, Berkeley.

[20] Above.

[21] See Kelsen, H. (1934) 'The Pure Theory of Law: Its Method and Fundamental Concepts, Part I', *Law Quarterly Review*, vol. 50, p.475; Kelsen, H. (1935) 'Pure Theory of Law (Part II)', *Law Quarterly Review*, vol. 51, p.518.

national law and international law. Kelsen's model of a legal system is based on a hierarchy of norms in which each norm is validated by a prior norm until the point of origin of legal authority is reached – the *grundnorm*. A purported norm of the legal system that does not link up in this hierarchical chain leading back to the *grundnorm* can not be a norm of the legal system. Therefore, the *grundnorm* is the starting-point of any chain of legal norms. It is 'the apex of a normative pyramid which through a long line of connections, authorises the decisions and actions taken in the system at ground level, i.e., in the determination of particular issues and cases'.[22] Accordingly, there is only one legal order comprising both international and domestic law. Any municipal law that violates international obligations is to a greater or lesser extent invalid.[23]

DECLARATION OF NATIONAL AMNESTY AS EXERCISE OF STATE SOVEREIGNTY

Traditional international law was raised on the bedrock of national sovereignty of States.[24] The United Nations adopted in 1945 the principle that State members of the organisation are sovereign equals.[25] Further, sovereignty was privileged above other principles by the requirement that: 'All members shall refrain in their international relations from the threat or use of force against the territorial integrity or political independence of any State, or in any other manner inconsistent with the Purposes of the United Nations.'[26] Juridically, sovereignty is a tripartite idea comprising the external, internal and territorial dimensions. Judge Huber stated in the *Island of Palmers Case*[27] that: 'Sovereignty in the relations between States signifies independence, independence in regard to a portion of the globe is the right to exercise therein, to the exclusion of any other State, the functions of a State.' The external dimension is implied all the time when States refer to their authority to determine their relations with other subjects of international law without prior authorisation or control of another State.[28]

---

[22] McCoubrey, H. and White N. D., note 17 above, at p.149.

[23] Ibid. p.154. Arguing that the human rights order manifests nothing more than heroic monism, see Mak, T. D. (1995) 'The Case against an International War Crimes Tribunal for the Former Yugoslavia', *International Peacekeeping*, vol. 2 No. 4, p.536 at pp.544–550.

[24] On the evolution of the juridical concept of sovereignty in international law, see Chigara, B. (2001) *Legitimacy Deficit in Custom: A Deconstructionist Critique*, Ashgate, Aldershot, Chap. 2.

[25] See Article 2.1 of the United Nations Charter, 26 June 1945, San Francisco, UKTS 67 (1946), Cmd 7015; 1 UNTS xvi.

[26] Article 2.4 of the United Nations Charter, ibid.

[27] *Netherlands v US* (1928) 2 RIAA 829. See also Harris, D. J. (5th ed. 1998) *Cases and Materials on International Law*, Sweet and Maxwell, London, pp.190–200.

[28] See Mugerwa, N. (1968) 'Subjects of International Law', in Sorensen, M. (ed.) *Manual of Public International Law*, p.253.

External sovereignty reflects also a more deeply rooted ideological construct, namely, internal sovereignty. Internal sovereignty refers to the State's exclusive right or competence to determine the character of its own institutions, to ensure and provide for their operation, to enact laws of its own choice, and to ensure their respect.[29] The territorial sovereignty of a State refers to the State's exclusive authority over all persons and objects existing on, under or above its territory.[30] Central to territory is the presence of a community whose members do not extend their allegiance beyond that of their sovereign. Thus, during the Second World War, the hosting by the United Kingdom of 'governments in exile'[31] created the legal fiction that the countries these governments claimed to represent still existed as sovereign States, when they had neither a territory under their control, nor a population strictly aligned to them. This fiction relied for its realistic appeal on the hope that those governments would recover control of their former territories at some point in the future. In the event, that hope was realised. The *East Timor Case*[32] indicates that had events of the Second World War conspired to produce a different final result, that fiction would have been discarded, and the governments in effective control recognised.

Although the external aspect of sovereignty appears to be the only one implied whenever sovereignty is invoked in international law, sovereignty is the sum total of all three aspects. Sovereignty so described forms one of the fundamental principles of international law.[33] One consequence of perceiving sovereignty in this manner is that in theory, every sovereign power is a legal despot in the sense that it is free from legal constraint. Therefore, it can appropriate, without their consent, the property rights of victims of breaches of human rights to trade them off for the promise of the perpetrators of those breaches not to threaten the new political order.[34] While Hobbes and Bodin

---

[29] Ibid.

[30] On the inviolability of territorial sovereignty, see Article 2.7 of the United Nations Charter, 26 June 1945, San Francisco, UKTS 67 (1946), Cmd 7015; 1 UNTS xvi; Cassese, A. (1986) *International Law in a Divided World*, Clarendon Press, Oxford, p.78.

[31] Poland, Norway, the Netherlands, Belgium, Luxembourg, Yugoslavia, and Greece.

[32] *Case concerning East Timor (Portugal v Australia)* (1995) 34(6) ILM 1583. In August 1975, Indonesia forcibly entered East Timor, throwing out the Portuguese authorities that the United Nations had long recognised as the Administrator of the non-self governing territory (NSGT). Over the next 20 years, UNGA Resolutions and Security Council Resolutions condemned Indonesia's action and instructed Indonesia to withdraw from East Timor in order for the Timor people to exercise their right to self-determination. Until October 1999 Indonesia remained in *de facto* control of East Timor. In that period several States including Australia did business with Indonesia rather than the supposed Administrator of the NSGT, Portugal, whenever East Timor's rights were concerned.

[33] For a thorough discussion on the fundamental principles governing international relations, see Cassese, A., note 30 above, at pp.126–165.

[34] For discussion of human rights as property rights of individuals whose title never passes to the State, denying the fiction that the State can pardon on behalf of victims those that breached their human rights, see Chap. 1 above.

may have found compelling the notion of an all-powerful State–sovereign in the sixteenth century,[35] it is difficult to find justification for similar compulsion in the twenty-first century. On the contrary, solidification of developments that occurred particularly in the twentieth century[36] demonstrate to a great extent an insatiable political, social and economic yearning among States for a conception of sovereignty that distributes rather than centralises authority.[37] Functionally, the role of these regional and international bodies has become so fundamental that few international transactions pass without having at some stage been referred to an international organisation.[38]

The decline in the practice of States of monolithic sovereignty intensified after the Second World War when States forged ahead with the creation of international organisations that they bequeathed with power to supervise States' own exercise of sovereign authority within their territories. The United Nations, which is the most 'universal organisation' around, is a vivid illustration of that practice. Article 104 of the United Nations Charter[39] obliges each member State to accord the organisation within its own territory such legal capacity as may be necessary for the exercise of its functions. The 1946 Convention on the Privileges and Immunities of the United Nations stated that

---

[35] Fear of the fragmentation of the newly formed States because of religious and other civil crises was always threatening. See Lapidoth, R. (1992) 'Sovereignty in Transition', *Journal of International Affairs*, vol. 45, p.325 at pp.326–327.

[36] Kwakwa writes that: 'There has been a rapid growth in the number of multilateral treaties which seek to regulate a much more extensive range of issues among States in areas of human rights, politics, economics and other social issues. The European nations are ceding some of their sovereignty to a common European Union; the African States are signing up for the African Charter on Human and Peoples' Rights which subjects their human rights practices to review by an African Commission on Human Rights; and under the Vienna Convention on Diplomatic Relations, States incur responsibility for action within their own territory arising from non-adherence to the principle of diplomatic immunity.' Kwakwa, E. (1995) 'Internal Conflicts in Africa: Is There a Right of Humanitarian Action?' *African Yearbook of International Law*, p.9 at p.21.

For a lucid discussion of exclusive competence of regional organisations and how that impacts on monolithic notions of sovereignty, see especially Neuwahl, N. A. (1991) 'Joint Participation in International Treaties and the Exercise of Power by the EEC and its Member States: Mixed Agreements', *Common Market Law Review*, vol. 28, p.717 at pp.719–736. Moreover, the Marakesh Agreement setting up the WTO accepts membership of supranational organisations such as the EU.

[37] While in the remote past the king or prince was considered as the sovereign, the American Declaration of Independence of 1776 favoured popular sovereignty. The French Constitution of 1791 declared that sovereignty belonged to the nation. The English legal system talks of 'The Queen in Parliament', or parliamentary sovereignty. On economic, social, and political justifications for divided sovereignty, see Kwakwa, E., note 36 above, at pp.18–22.

[38] See e.g. Vignes, D. (1st ed. 1983) 'The Impact of International Organisations on the Development and Application of Public International Law', in Macdonald, R. St J. and Johnston, D. M. (eds) *The Structure and Process of International Law*, Sweet and Maxwell, New York, p.809.

[39] United Nations Charter, 26 June 1945, San Francisco, UKTS 67 (1946), Cmd 7015; 1 UNTS xvi.

Article 104 confers on the United Nations juridical personality which enables it among other things to contract with States, acquire and dispose of immovable and movable property, and to institute legal proceedings.[40] The United Nations Security Council has authority to compel States, including non-members of the United Nations, to enforce United Nations economic embargoes or other measures against a State or a group of States.[41] The Human Rights Committee of the United Nations created by the International Covenant on Civil and Political Rights[42] is an ongoing institution that gives institutional support to the Covenant's norms. It is concerned with enforcement by States Parties of the Covenant and its Optional Protocols. Article 40 of the Covenant which sets out the function of the Committee requires States Parties to submit reports on the measures that they have adopted to give effect to the rights recognised under the convention, and to report on the progress made in the enjoyment of those rights.[43] The Committee reviews these reports and then transmits its comments to the States Parties. The Optional Protocol of the Covenant, itself a separate agreement, authorises the Committee to receive communications from individuals claiming to be victims of violations by States Parties of the Covenant, to study them, and to forward its views about those communications to the relevant individuals and States.[44] In addition, it submits through the Economic and Social Council an annual report to the United Nations General Assembly. Its functions in each of these modes are different.[45] Ghandhi writes that:

'It is clearly not a legislative body. Its promulgation of "general comments", which have developed into a particularly important freestanding method of interpreting the Covenant (and the Optional Protocol) may, however, be described aptly as a quasi-legislative function. It is clearly not a court of law, tribunal or a formal judicial body. Nevertheless, when acting under its authority in the

---

[40] See Article 1. Section 1 of the Convention on the Privileges and Immunities of the United Nations, 13 February 1946, London, UKTS 10 (1950), Cmd 1803; UNTS 15.

[41] Article 2.6 of the United Nations Charter. During the Rhodesian crisis even Switzerland that had vigorously opposed the suggestion that it was bound to apply sanctions under Article 2.6 of the United Nations Charter did take measures to prevent the use of Swiss territory for the avoidance of United Nations sanctions against Rhodesia. See Greenwood, C. (1992) 'New World Order or Old? The Invasion of Kuwait and the Rule of Law', *Modern Law Review*, vol. 55 No. 2, p.153 at p.160.

[42] UN Doc. CCPR/C/2/Rev.4 (1994).

[43] On how members that serve on the committee are elected, and procedural matters of the work of this Committee, see Steiner, H. J. and Alston, P. (1996) *International Human Rights in Context*, Clarendon Press, Oxford, pp.500–554.

[44] See Ghandhi, P. R. (1998). *The Human Rights Committee and the Right of Individual Communication, Law and Practice*, Ashgate, Aldershot, p.40.

[45] For commentary see McGoldrick, D. (1991) *The Human Rights Committee, Its Role in the Development of the International Covenant on Civil and Political Rights*, Clarendon Press, Oxford, pp.52–55.

individual communication procedure the Committee has conducted its business and formulated its "views" under article 5.4 of the Optional Protocol in a way which approximates as nearly as possible to the way which a court of law operates. Its "views" read like judgments of a court. Nevertheless, the decisions of the Committee are not formally binding legally such as those of a court of law. Under the inter-State procedure, the function of the Committee is to act in a fact-finding and conciliatory role and it may hear oral argument in these proceedings. When exercising its role under the article 40 reporting system, its duty is to "consider" and "study" such reports by engaging in a constructive dialogue with States Parties.'[46]

Because members of the Committee are independent experts acting in their personal capacities[47] and not government representatives acting under instruction of their respective governments, the Committee enjoys a higher than average public perception of independence, credibility, and lack of bias.[48] The work of the Committee has provided impetus for much positive change in the welfare of citizens of countries where general or particular Covenant rights have not been readily recognised. Exposing to the international community governmental deficiencies in delivery of Covenant rights almost always results in the particular government even reluctantly adopting the Committee's recommendations for improvement. Thus, the supervisory function of the Human Rights Committee in the enforcement of Covenant rights affects States Parties' application of their sovereign authority. The Covenant determines the boundaries of State rights and citizens' civil rights. The Committee seeks to ensure that these boundaries are enforced. In 1992, the Committee made it clear that amnesties covering acts of torture are generally incompatible with the duty of States to investigate such acts.[49] The Committee is but one of several institutions[50] created in the aftermath of the Second World War, whose effect has been to diminish the monolithic sovereignty's domestic jurisdiction argument and its defence of violation of human rights. The United Nations Commission on Human Rights, which is responsible for at least 13 thematic mandates, including torture and cruel, inhuman or degrading treatment; enforced or voluntary disappearances; summary or arbitrary executions; and

---

[46] Ghandhi, P. R., note 44 above, at pp.40–41. See also O'Flaherty, M. (1996) *Human Rights and the UN: Practice before the Treaty Bodies*, Sweet and Maxwell, London, pp.17–52.

[47] International Covenant on Civil and Political Rights, Article 28.3.

[48] This perception is compromised by factors such as part-time membership on the Committee by persons that continue to hold government posts. See Steiner, H. J. and Alston, P. (1996) *International Human Rights in Context*, Clarendon Press, Oxford, p.502.

[49] General Comment No. 20 (44) (on Article 7) UN Doc. CCPR/C21/Rev.1/Add. 3, para.15 (1992).

[50] These include the United Nations Commission on Human Rights, the United Nations Committee against Torture, the United Nations Commission on Status of Women, and the Committee on Rights of Child.

arbitrary detention,[51] together with other international institutions, serve to entrench the view that a State's treatment of its own citizens, and its internal governance on many significant matters, is subject to the norms of international human rights law.[52] Therefore, national laws, including national amnesty laws, are very much open to scrutiny of international law inasmuch as they affect the international crusade for a universal culture of human rights unleashed by the Universal Declaration of Human Rights.

Many international organisations have power to establish their own rules of operational procedure. Article 60 of the American Convention on Human Rights[53] authorised the Inter-American Court of Human Rights to draw up its statute, and to adopt its own Rules of Procedure. Article 44 of the Convention authorises any person or group of persons, or any non-governmental entity legally recognised in one or more member States of the United Nations, to lodge petitions with the Commission of complaints of violation of that Convention by a State Party. The American Court of Human Rights held in the *Velasquez Rodriguez Case*[54] that the requirement on States to 'ensure the rights set forth in the convention' in Article 1.1 of the American Convention on Human Rights obliged States, including Honduras, to investigate and punish any violation of the rights recognised. Both the Inter-American Court and Commission of Human Rights[55] have held that the amnesties granted by Argentina and Uruguay are incompatible with the American Convention on Human Rights. Similar developments in Europe and Africa that derive from the European Convention on Human Rights and the African Charter on Human and Peoples' Rights respectively negate claims of the practice in modern international law of monolithic sovereignty espoused by Hobbes and Boden in the sixteenth century.[56]

These examples show that international organs have been formed that supervise exercise by States of sovereign authority.[57] Particularly in the fields

---

[51] Steiner, H. J. and Alston, P. (1996) *International Human Rights in Context*, Clarendon Press, Oxford, pp.362–363.

[52] See also Marks, S. (2000) *The Riddle of All Constitutions: International Law, Democracy, and the Critique of Ideology*, Oxford University Press, Oxford. Marks considers whether there has emerged through custom, the norm of democratic governance in international law.

[53] American Convention on Human Rights, 22 November 1969, San Jose, PAUTS 36; (1969) 9 ILM 673.

[54] IACHR (1998) Series C, No. 4, para.165.

[55] Inter-American Commission on Human Rights, Report No. 29/92 (Uruguay) 82nd Session OEA/LV/11.82. Doc. 25 (2 October 1992); ibid. Report No. 24/92 (Argentina). Doc. 24.

[56] See p.29 above.

[57] On theories on internationational organisations and how their proliferation in international life has amended conception of sovereignty and non-interference, see among others, Amerasinghe, C. F. (1994) 'Interpretation of Texts in Open International Organisations', *British Yearbook of International Law*, vol. 45, p.175; Anand, R. P. (1986–II) 'Sovereign Equality of States in International Law', *Recueil des cours*, vol. 197, p.13; Chen, B. (Greed ed. 1951) *The International Law*

of human rights, environmental protection and world trade, the international institutions and organs created have tremendous scope and potential to affect actions of independent sovereign States. The theoretical problem raised by this development often is about how, and not why, these bodies acquire legal capacity.[58] This suggests that there is a clear recognition by the international community that these bodies have a fundamental role to play in international life. Therefore, the sovereign will of the State is not uncapped, but very much under supervision of international law and special interest international institutions and organisations.[59]

---

of Recognition, Stevens and Sons, London; Conlon, P. (1995) 'Lessons from Iraq Sanctions Committee as a Source of Sanctions Implementation Authority and Practice', *Virginia Journal of International Law*, vol. 35 No. 3, p.633; Craven, M. C. R. (1995) 'What's in a Name? The Former Yugoslav Republic of Macedonia and Issues of Statehood', *Australian Yearbook of International Law*, vol. 16, p.199; Crawford, J. (1979) *The Creation of States in International Law*, Clarendon Press, Oxford; Crawford, J. (1976–77) 'The Criteria for Statehood in International Law', *British Yearbook of International Law*, p.93; Fitzmaurice, G. (1956) 'The Foundations of the Authority of International Law and the Problem of Enforcement', *Modern Law Review*, vol. 19, p.1; Greenwood, C. (1992) 'New World Order or Old? The Invasion of Kuwait and the Rule of Law', *Modern Law Review*, vol. 55 No. 2, p.153; Halderman, H. (1962) 'Legal Basis For United Nations Armed Forces', *American Journal of International Law*, vol. 56, p.488; Koskienemi, M. (1995) 'International Law in a Post-Realist Era', *Australian Yearbook of International Law*, vol. 16, p.1; Koskenniemi, M. (1989), *From Apology to Utopia: The Structure of International Legal Argument*, Finnish Lawyers Publishing Company, Helsinki; Lauterpacht, H. (1976–IV) 'The Development of the Law of International Organisations by the Decisions of International Tribunals', *Recueil des cours*, vol. 152 p.377; Lauterpacht, H. (1948) *Recognition in International Law*, Cambridge University Press, Cambridge; Martinez, M. (1996) *National Sovereignty and International Organisations*, Kluwer Law International, The Hague; Bos, M. (1980) 'Theory and Practice of Treaty Interpretation', *Netherlands International Law Review*, vol. 27, p.3; Muller, A. (1995) *International Organisations and their Host States: Aspects of their Legal Relationships*, Kluwer Law International, The Hague; Parry, C. (1949) 'The Treaty Making Power of the United Nations', *British Yearbook of International Law*, vol. 20, p.108; Schneider, J. (1963) *Treaty Making Power of International Organisations*, Rue Du Cardinal Lemoine, Paris; White, N. (1996) *The Law of International Organisations*, Manchester University Press, New York/ Manchester; Higgins, R. (1963) *The Development of International Law Through the Political Organs of the United Nations*, Clarendon Press, Oxford; Zacher, M. W. (1970) *Dag Hammaskjold's United Nations*, Columbia University Press, New York/London; McDougal and Associates (1987) *Studies in World Public Order*, New Haven Press, New Haven; Kairys, D. (1982) *The Politics of Law: A Progressive Critique*, Pantheon Books, New York; Davies, M. (1996) *Delimiting the Law*, Pluto Press, London; Weatherill, S. (1995) *Law and Integration in the European Union*, Clarendon Press, Oxford; Kritsiotis, D. (1993) 'The Legality of the 1993 US Missile Strike on Iraq and the Right of Self-Defence in International Law', *International and Comparative Law Quarterly*, vol. 45, p.162.

[58] See Chinkin, C. (1993) *Third Parties in International Law*, Clarendon Press, Oxford, Chap. 4; Detter, T. (1962) 'The Organs of International Organisations Exercising their Treaty-Making Power', *British Yearbook of International Law*, vol. 38, p.421; Seyested, F. (1964) 'Is The International Personality of Intergovernmental Organisations Valid vis-a-vis Non-Members?' *Indian Journal of International Law*, vol. 4, p.233; Weissberg, G. (1961) *The International Status of the United Nations*, Oceana, Dobbs Ferry.

[59] In 1955, the International Law Commission (ILC) observed that the United Nations and all its international organisations of comparable capacity could own ships, and that the United Nations

The idea of an uncapped will of the State is difficult to justify in normative terms also. Normatively, there is a clear distinction between State and society because the State is not the originator of all rights that exist in society. Groups existed, and had rights, even before the evolution of the State. Pluralist writers[60] point to the very real constraints which associations and groupings can place upon the freedom of the State. Writing in the nineteenth century, Tocqueville observed that in the United States citizenship was not 'granted' by the State but was the attribute of autonomous individuals seen as having rights prior or superior to the State and recognised as such by the Constitution and the courts.[61] In these terms, decentralisation of power is desirable, while the concentration of authority in an omnipotent, centralised State tends to threaten liberty and to stifle creativity. This decentralisation of authority to international institutions has a direct effect on what States can and can not do in the exercise of their sovereignty. Thus, national amnesty laws are a legitimate target of inquiry regarding the constraint and discretion that international law allows States. Moreover, and much to the disappointment of dualist writers, States have developed through international law norms whose enforcement does not depend on the consent of States.[62] Norms that belong to the category of peremptory general international law, otherwise known as *jus cogens*,[63]

---

could register its own ships with the particular State whose flag the ship could then fly. This was meant to satisfy the requirements under Article 4 of the Provisional articles on the regime of the high seas, by which ships carry the nationality of the State in which they are registered. They shall sail under its flag and, save in the exceptional circumstances expressly provided for in international treaties or in these articles, shall be subject to its exclusive jurisdiction in the high seas. See UN Doc. A/CN. 4/103. At the adoption of the Convention on the Liability of Operators of Nuclear Ships (Brussels, May 1962) the Conference adopted a resolution which observed that the majority of States present at the Conference favoured the principle of allowing inter-governmental organisations to accede to the Convention, and to operate nuclear ships subject to that Convention. See Convention on the Liability of Operators of Nuclear Ships, Brussels, 25 May 1962, 1Ruster, p.405. See also Diplomatic Conference on Maritime Law, Standing Committee, Doc. CN-6/SC17.

[60] For a lucid discussion on the use of and internal effects on a State system of power, see Craig, P. (1990) *Public Law and Democracy in the United Kingdom and the United States of America*, Oxford University Press, Oxford, Chap. 6. The views of the pluralists are of course not uncontroversial. The undoubted merit of their argument lies, however, in the very fact that they focus on the reasons why sovereignty should or should not be said to reside in a particular institution; and because they focus on the consequences which should or should not flow from this ascription of power. While attention to other issues sparked off by pluralists can do much to enrich the debate, space precludes such an effort here.

[61] See O'Donnell, G. (2000) 'The Judiciary and the Rule of Law', *Journal of Democracy*, vol. 11, No. X, pp.25–31 at p.29. See also, Tocqueville, A. (Commager, H. S. (ed.) 1946) *Democracy in America*, Oxford University Press, Oxford, p.51.

[62] See Jennings, R. and Watts, A. (eds) (9th ed. 1992) *Oppenheim's International Law*, Longman, London, p.54.

[63] See Malanczuk, P. (ed.) (7th ed. 1997) *Akehurst's Modern Introduction to International Law*, Routledge, London, p.57.

overarch national constitutions. Crimes against humanity possess universal jurisdiction, which means that every country in the world has the right to arrest and charge in its own national courts persons alleged to have committed breaches. In some cases, there is a duty on every nation to either prosecute or extradite fugitives to another country that is ready to prosecute those crimes.[64] Therefore, in the ordering of constitutions,[65] international law appears to overarch national constitutions, denying States the defence of national sovereignty for breaches of international law.

Norms of *peremptory* general international law sometimes referred to as norms *jus cogens* are of such importance to the international legal system[66] that even in the exercise of their sovereign right to enter treaties one with another, States may not breach norms of this category. The Vienna Convention on the Law of Treaties[67] states in Article 53 that:

> A treaty is void, if, at the time of its conclusion, it conflicts with a peremptory norm of general international law. For the purposes of the present Convention, a peremptory norm of general international law is a norm accepted and recognised by the international community of States as a whole as a norm from which no derogation is permitted and which can be modified only by a subsequent norm of general international law having the same character.

Article 64 states that: 'If a new peremptory norm of general international law emerges, any existing treaty which is in conflict with that norm becomes void and terminates.' Therefore, States can not contract out of compulsory norms of international law. This provision applies to local custom as much as it applies to treaties, custom not being mentioned in the treaty merely because the treaty itself was intended to codify the law of treaties only.[68] Peremptory norms of international law are not many in number because of the high standard that has been set in the definitional article. A rule cannot become a peremptory norm unless it is 'accepted and recognised by the international community as a whole'. An overwhelming majority of States is required, cutting across cultural, economic, ideological and religious differences. In the

---

[64] See Article 4 of the Convention on the Prevention and Punishment of the Crime of Genocide (1948) 78 UNTS 277.

[65] See Marks, S. (2000) *The Riddle of All Constitutions: International Law, Democracy, and the Critique of Ideology*, Oxford University Press, Oxford, pp.101–120.

[66] See International Law Commission's elucidation of the ICJ's decision in the *Barcelona Traction Case*, ICJ Rep (1970) p.3, in *Yearbook of the International Law Commission*, No. II Part II, 1976, p.109 at p.119. See also Zacklin, R. 'Beyond Kosovo: the United Nations and Humanitarian Intervention', The Josephine Onoh Memorial Lecture 2000, Studies in Law Series, University of Hull, p.12.

[67] 23 May 1969, UN Doc. A/Conf. 39/27; UKTS 58 (1980), Cmnd 7964.

[68] Malanczuk, P. (ed.) (7th ed. 1997) *Akehurst's Modern Introduction to International Law*, Routledge, London, p.57.

Barcelona Traction Case[69] the International Court of Justice (the Court) stated that norms *jus cogens* can derive from contemporary international law's outlawing of 'acts of aggression, and of genocide, as also from the principles and rules concerning basic rights of the human person including protection from slavery and racial discrimination', giving weight to academic opinion on that question. Nonetheless, the Court did not go so far as identifying these norms as *jus cogens*. However, some commentators have indicated that this shows that the prohibitions on the use of force, racial discrimination, genocide, torture, slavery and gross violation of human rights have achieved the status of *jus cogens*.[70] Akehurst[71] writes that apart from the 'basic rights of the human person' that the Court alludes to in the *Barcelona Traction Case*, the only other norm that receives anything approaching universal acceptance of States is the rule against aggression. This view is supported by the Court's decision in the *Nicaragua Case (Merits)*,[72] and by Christenson who sees the indispensable function of *jus cogens* as that of meeting the compelling need for ensuring public order in the international community.[73]

Relative to the 'basic rights of the human person', the House of Lords in *Ex parte Pinochet (No. 3)* stated that the international crime of torture justifies States in taking universal jurisdiction over torture wherever committed.[74] *Per* Lord Browne-Wilkinson:

'I have no doubt that long before the Torture Convention of 1984 State torture was an international crime in the highest sense. . . . the objective was to ensure a general jurisdiction so that the torturer was not safe wherever he went. . . . The purpose of the Convention was to introduce the principle *aut dedere aut punire* – either you extradite or you punish.'[75]

---

[69] ICJ Rep (1970) p.3.

[70] See Whiteman, M. (1977) 'Jus Cogens in International Law', *Georgia Journal of International and Comparative Law*, p.607. In his commentary on Article 38(1)(d) of the Statute of the International Court of Justice, Brownlie writes that: 'Whatever the need for caution, the opinions of publicists are used widely. The law officers' opinions tendered confidentially to the executive in Great Britain contain references to the views of Vattel, Calvo, Hall, and others, and the opinions themselves represent the views of experts, including Harcourt, Phillimore, and Finlay. Arbitral tribunals and national courts make extensive use of the writings of jurists.' Brownlie, I. (5th ed. 1998) *Principles of Public International Law*, Oxford University Press, Oxford, pp.24–25.

[71] Note 68 above, at p.58.

[72] *Case concerning Military and Paramilitary Activities in and against Nicaragua (Nicaragua v US) Merits*, ICJ Rep (1986) p.14, para.190, judgment of 27 June.

[73] Christenson, G. A. (1987) 'The World Court and Jus Cogens', *American Journal of International Law*, vol. 81 p.93.

[74] *R v Bow Street Metropolitan Stipendiary Magistrate and Others, ex parte Pinochet Ugarte (No. 3)* [1999] 2 WLR 827 at p.841 *per* Lord Browne-Wilkinson.

[75] Ibid. For further commentary see Chigara, B. (2000) 'Pinochet and the Administration of International Criminal Justice', in Woodhouse, D. (ed.) *The Pinochet Case: A Legal and Constitutional Analysis*, Hart Publishing, Oxford, pp.115–128.

Torture and offences *jus cogens* justify universal jurisdiction in spite of where they are committed because they offend against all of humanity. According to the International Law Commission:

> 'the responsibility engaged by the breach of these obligations is engaged not only in regard to the State which was the direct victim of the breach, it is also engaged in regard to all the other members of the international community, so that, in the event of a breach of these obligations, every State must be considered justified in invoking – probably through judicial channels – the responsibility of the State committing the internationally wrongful act.'[76]

In its Draft Code of Crimes against the Peace and Security of Mankind of 1996, the International Law Commission sought to oblige States to try or extradite persons alleged to have committed crimes against humanity.[77] Thus, for their enforcement human rights possess both a personal and a communal status. According to Macpherson, one's own person, one's capacities, one's rights and liberties are one's own individual property. They are even more important than individual property in material things and revenues, partly because they are the source and justification of individual material property.[78] Because human rights are the inalienable property of individuals *qua* individuals, and, in this case, the property of victims of a previous regime, title to that property or to those basic rights of victims cannot be transferred to the incumbent government. Therefore, no government can legitimately deal with victims' property rights as sacrifice for the purchase of national stability and a chance to establish democracy basically because no government could demonstrate ever that it had acquired victims' inalienable rights. Moreover, the International Law Commission, the House of Lords in *Ex parte Pinochet (No. 3)*, the Inter-American Court of Human Rights in the *Velasquez Rodriguez Case*,[79] the Trial Chamber of the ICTY in *Prosecutor v Furundzija*,[80] and the International Court of Justice in the *Barcelona Traction Case* and more recently in its *Advisory Opinion on the Legality of the Threat or Use of Nuclear Weapons*,[81] all characterised inalienable human rights of individuals as having a communal dimension in their protection, which empowers the international community to bring to book those that trample on others' inalienable human rights. This dimension of basic human rights of individuals rejects therefore

---

[76] *Yearbook of the International Law Commission*, No. II Part II, 1976, p.109 at p.119.

[77] Article 6, Draft Code of Crimes against the Peace and Security of Mankind, *Report of the International Law Commission of the Work of its Forty-eighth Session*, 51st Session, Supplement No. 10, UN Doc. A/51/10 (1966).

[78] Discussed in Chap. 1 above. Macpherson, C. B. (1997) 'Human Rights as Property Rights', *Dissent*, vol. 24 No. 1, p.72.

[79] IACHR (1998) Series C, No. 4, para.165.

[80] Case No. IT-95–17/1-T (10 December 1998); (1999) 38 ILM 317 at paras151–157.

[81] (1996) 35(4) ILM 809.

that a government can rely on the exercise of its sovereign powers to pardon those responsible for the breaches of victims' rights where those breaches have offended all of humanity. The Trial Chamber of the ICTY in *Prosecutor v Furundzija*[82] held that amnesties for torture are null and void and will not receive foreign recognition.[83]

CONCLUSION

This chapter considered the connection between national and international law in the context of State practice on national amnesty laws that purport to expunge criminal and/or civil liability of agents of a prior regime alleged to have violated basic human rights of individuals. It has shown that the increasing practice of States of creating norms that discourage and even prohibit States from granting previous governments amnesty for violation of human rights manifests two significant issues. First, by creating international institutions that supervise recognition of covenant, treaty and general international law human rights, States have demonstrated a commitment to ensuring recognition of basic human rights at all times. Monolithic sovereignty can no longer serve as a bar to international law's insistence that States ought to recognise and justify violations of basic individual human rights of their citizens. Secondly, for their enforcement human rights are ascribed with both a personal and a communal status. The *personal prefix* recognises that human rights are the property of individuals *qua* individuals. Where these rights have been breached, it is the personal property of victims of those breaches that is violated. Title to that personal property or to those basic rights of victims does not transfer to the incumbent government. Therefore, no government can claim legitimately to have authority to deal with victims' personal titles as sacrifice for the country's restoration to normality because no government can ever acquire or inherit victims' personal titles in their basic human rights. The *communal prefix* to the enforcement of human rights is evident in the judicial decisions of national and international organs created to supervise States' recognition of human rights, and of *ad hoc* tribunals established to justify violation of victims' basic rights. They all appear to assert that human rights of individuals possess for their enforcement a communal dimension. This communal dimension derives from two sources. The first is the duty to try or extradite to another country able to do so, persons alleged to have violated human rights of individuals. The second is the universal jurisdiction that crimes against humanity have been endowed with, which compels the international

---

[82] Case No. IT-95–17/1-T (10 December 1998); (1999) 38 ILM at paras 151–157.
[83] For an alternative view see Mak, T. D. (1995) 'The Case against an International War Crimes Tribunal for the Former Yugoslavia', *International Peacekeeping*, vol. 2 No. 4, pp.536–563.

community to pursue violators wherever they may be merely because they have trampled underfoot the basic individual human rights of others. No previous government can exercise its sovereign competence to pardon either itself or a previous government for breaches of victims' rights where those breaches have affected the communal or international notions of basic human rights because no individual government has title to deal with that property. Therefore, national amnesty laws that seek to extinguish international human rights offences of a past regime, whatever their motivation,[84] appear to be illegal under current international law. The enforcement by States of that illegality may have surged in recent times, foregrounding rules of general international law that already existed.

---

[84] See Chap. 1 above.

3

THE RIGHTS, JUSTICE DYNAMIC AND PHYSIOLOGICAL NEEDS OF THE STATE

INTRODUCTION

The previous chapter critiqued national amnesty laws from a legalistic view that portrayed human rights as property with legal title that bestows competencies on the holder and imposes on others negative duties not to breach such title(s). It appeared also to condone use by the international community of its aggregate power to seek out and punish those that offended its morals. This chapter attempts to balance the power dynamic in discourse on national amnesty laws that purport to expunge criminal and/or civil liability of agents of a prior regime alleged to have violated basic human rights of individuals by considering whether the needs of State doctrine[1] provides any real justification for privileging amnesia over justice.

RIGHTS, VICTIMS AND THE RULE OF LAW

When a government for whatever reason adopts a policy that results in the systematic abuse of basic rights of individuals, a dynamic is unleashed that further divides the population into sub-communities. As a consequence, the sub-communities created transcend previous economic and other social divisions that may have subsisted. They include the following: victims, perpetrators, agitators, and a polarised judiciary.[2] Positivism's insistence that valid

---

[1] On needs of State doctrine, see Chap. 1 above. See also Rawls, J. (1999) *A Theory of Justice*, Oxford University Press, Oxford.

[2] Mejia writes that with a polarised judiciary, 'people no longer know where to seek justice.... Guatemala is fast becoming the example of a country with no rule of law. Impunity is a phenomenon that is the cornerstone of the judiciary's impotence. It is important for those seeking justice

rules of the legal system should be enforced places on the judiciary the burden
whether it should enforce rules that offend against fundamental principles of
justice[3] and the rule of law[4] merely because they satisfy all the set rules on law
creation. A major challenge thereafter is how to attend to or how to diminish
these divisions so that the pain and suffering caused, together with the resulting
psychological and emotional traumas, can start to heal.[5] However, before these
sub-communities can revert to being as single a community as is realistically
possible, they each look to law for protection, justification, and vindication.
Law's humanistic appeal casts it as the favourite and principal architect of this
agenda. Their expectation of what the law should do for them becomes a test
of law's efficacy. Law's response to each of their 'rational' expectations becomes
the test for law's approval or disapproval. But is the law so easily suited both
to soothe and to justify; to reconcile and to harness a broken community's
reserves in order to deal with the present as well as to confront the future?

(a) The rule of law

Use of the phrase 'rule of law' is much in evidence. Jurists, journalists, aca-
demics and politicians use it often without clarifying what they mean. Discourse
on the subject points to two models of the idea. The one associated with
Aristotle regards the 'rule of law' as 'the rule of reason'. Contemporary proponents of this model include Ronald Dworkin,[6] whose holistic interpretive

---

to perceive international concern regarding the absence of the rule of law'. Mejia, R. M. (1999)
'The Struggle against Impunity in Guatemala', *Social Justice*, vol. 26 No. 4, pp.55–83 at p.55. See
also ECOSOC Resolution E/CN.4/RES/2000/42 of 20 April 2000 on Independence and Imparti-
ality of the Judiciary, Jurors and Assessors and the Independence of Lawyers, at www.unhchr.ch/
Huridocda/Huridoca.nsf/TestFrame/6bb989fe108bac42802568d400538f5a/Opendocument.

[3] Discussing the question whether one should regard as continuing to be legally valid something
that offended against fundamental principles of justice and the rule of law when it was legally valid
in terms of the positive law of the legal system which had perished, and using as an example 1945
Germany after National Socialism had been defeated, and 1989 Germany after the collapse of the
German Democratic Republic, see Alexy, R. (1999) 'A Defence of Radbruch's Formula', in
Dyzenhaus, D. (ed.) *Recrafting the Rule of Law: The Limits of Legal Order*, Hart Publishing,
Oxford, pp.15–39. Rephrasing the question, Alexy asks: 'can something be illegal today which in
the past was legal?' In the context of South Africa, the question that will not go away is whether
the (1995) national amnesty law is the correct response to crimes of apartheid which the United
Nations in several of its Human Rights Conventions and GA Resolutions and Declarations
labelled as 'crimes against humanity'. Outlining the legal issues and social implications, see
Dyzenhaus, D. (1998) *Judging the Judges, Judging Ourselves*, Hart Publishing, Oxford, pp.150–
178 and Rivers, J. (1999) 'The Interpretation and Invalidity of Unjust Laws', in Dyzenhaus, D.
(ed.) *Recrafting the Rule of Law: The Limits of Legal Order*, Hart Publishing, Oxford, pp.40–65
respectively.

[4] Discussed below.

[5] See Harries, K. (1997) 'Social Stress and Trauma: Synthesis and Spatial Analysis', *Social Science
and Medicine*, vol. 45 No. 8, pp.1251–1264.

[6] See Dworkin, R. (1990) *Law's Empire*, Fontana Press, Glasgow.

theory has been criticised as being both naive and parochial.[7] Dworkin's holistic interpretive theory of law asserts that there must be at least *prima facie* moral grounds for claims of the existence of legal rights and duties. For this reason, legal rights are a species of moral rights.[8] Dworkin refutes one of positivism's central claims that the existence and content of the law can be identified by reference to social sources of the law[9] without reference to morality except where the law thus identified has itself incorporated moral criteria for the identification of the law.[10] Thus, to resolve a hard case, a judge must 'choose between eligible interpretations by asking which shows the community's structure of institutions and decisions – its public standards as a whole – in a better light from the standpoint of political morality'. In doing so the judge directly engages his own moral and political convictions in the determination of a case, arriving at a decision that reflects 'not only his opinions about justice and fairness, but his higher order convictions about how these ideals should be compromised when they compete',[11] a process summed up in the exploits of Judge Hercules.[12] Dworkin's holistic interpretive theory of law is often criticised as being an unconvincing departure from positivism.[13] Even more, it is parochial because 'it supposes that any particular order includes a judiciary empowered to test legislation in accordance with a foundational constitutional document such as the Bill of Rights'.[14]

The other model, associated with Montesquieu, regards 'the rule of law' as 'those institutional restraints that prevent governmental agents from oppressing the rest of society'.[15] It is the latter that impressed Tocqueville[16] whose 1835 treatise *Democracy in America* continues to inspire discussion of the idea. He writes:

---

[7] See Dyzenhaus, D. (1999) *Recrafting the Rule of Law: The Limits of Legal Order*, Hart Publishing, Oxford, pp.1–12 at pp.1–2. See also Shklar, J. N. (1987) 'Political Theory and the Rule of Law', in Hutchinson, A. C. and Monahan, P. (eds) *The Rule of Law: Ideal or Ideology*, Carswell, Toronto, p.1.

[8] See Dworkin, R., note 6 above, at pp.258–260.

[9] These include legislation, judicial decisions, social customs.

[10] Hart, H. L. A. (2nd ed. 1994) *The Concept of Law*, Clarendon Press, Oxford, p.269.

[11] Dworkin, R., note 6 above, at p.256.

[12] Ibid. p.239.

[13] Simmonds writes that rules of law are 'publicly ascertainable in that their content can be established simply by reference to empirical facts, without without making any moral judgments'. Simmonds, N. E. (1986) *Central Issues in Jurisprudence: Justice, Law and Rights*, Sweet and Maxwell, London, p.84. Thus, Dworkin's claim undermines the separation of law and morality which is essential to law's basic function. For a fuller response to Dworkin's attack on positivism, see Hart, H. L. A. (2nd ed. 1994) *The Concept of Law*, Clarendon Press, Oxford, *Postscript*, at pp.268–276.

[14] Dyzenhaus, D. (1999) *Recrafting the Rule of Law: The Limits of Legal Order*, Hart Publishing, Oxford, pp.1–2.

[15] Ibid.

[16] Tocqueville, A. (Commager, H. S. (ed.) 1946) *Democracy in America* (translated by H. Reeve) Oxford University Press, Oxford, p.51.

'In America the principle of the sovereignty of the people is not either barren or concealed, as it is with some other nations; it is recognised by the customs and proclaimed by the laws; it spreads freely and arrives without impediment at its most remote consequences. If there be a country in the world where the doctrine of the sovereignty of the people can be fairly appreciated, where it can be studied in its application to the affairs of society, and where its dangers and its advantages may be foreseen, that country is assuredly America.'

Of the United States Supreme Court he remarked that: '. . . a more imposing judicial power was never constituted by any people'.[17] Judges have enormous power, and people are proudly conscious of their rights and are ready to demand their enforcement at public gatherings and in law courts. The courts have enormous power even in 'the absence of what we [Europeans] term the Government, or the Administration. Written laws exist in America, and one sees that they are daily executed [despite the fact that] . . . the State has no administrative functionaries of its own stationed in the different points of its territory'.[18] Tocqueville attributed this social arrangement to three factors, all of which combined to result in the rule of law that can be described as those institutional restraints that prevent governmental agents from oppressing the rest of society. To paraphrase O'Donnell, the first refers to what he calls 'the behaviour and beliefs of individuals'. Generally, people did not question the reason for complying with judicial decisions. Perhaps the courts that guaranteed their civil liberties had to be supported if individuals' rights were to be sustained.

The second factor that facilitated the rule of law, and which pointed to the source of individual rights, was the institutional design of American society. The federal structure and the practice of holding frequent elections for all public offices were pivotal in restraining the executive.

'federalism created several legal jurisdictions and many potential conflicts among them. This required an institution placed above the contending parties – even above the federal government – with the authority to establish what was the law of the land. . . . this institution – the judiciary – had to have its authority vested in it by the supreme law of the land, the Constitution.'[19]

The effect on the restraint on executive power of federalism was strengthened by the fact that public office bearers everywhere were elected or appointed for a fixed period only, after which they retired to private life. According to Tocqueville, communities 'in which secondary functionaries are elected are inevitably obliged to make great use of judicial penalties as a means of

---

[17] Tocqueville as cited in O'Donnell, G. (2000) 'The Judiciary and the Rule of Law', *Journal of Democracy*, vol. 11 No. 1, pp.25–31 at p.25.
[18] Ibid. pp.25–26.
[19] Ibid. p.26.

administration'.[20] Further, the authority to declare statutes unconstitutional was vested in all courts. Thus, 'the American Magistrate . . . gives rise to immense political influence. . . . Few laws can escape the searching analysis of the judicial power for any length of time.'[21]

The third factor that facilitated the rule of law as constraint on the executive's misapplication of public authority derives from macro-social factors.[22] The first settlers in America had arrived in pursuit of freedom and personal autonomy.[23] That spirit remained in their society and was imbedded in their culture. It underpinned the Constitution when it was written. This, according to Tocqueville, fostered first the view that every individual is a career of rights that public officers must respect and foster, and secondly, that 'Providence has given to every human being the degree of reason necessary to direct himself in the affairs which interest him exclusively'.[24] Thus, the rule of law model based on institutional restraints that prevent governmental agents from oppressing the rest of society is premised on the existence of a legitimate, independent and active judiciary on the one hand, and a vigorous civil society that possesses rights which it is ready to go to great lengths to enforce through the courts on the other. Absence or rejection of these attributes in any setting results in an atmosphere inimical to the social equality of conditions conducive to enforcement or justification of basic human rights of individuals.

(b) Victims and the post-violation era

Reference to a community of victims presupposes an acceptable empirical test of victimhood, if there is one. Such a test would be useful especially where one of the sub-communities created by a previous government's abuse of basic human rights of individuals claimed to have overriding priority in the restorative[25] processes that follow directly from the disempowerment of the victimiser. But is there such a test? According to Friedrichs'[26] theory of radical victimology there is. This theory which advocates for a legal recognition of victims' rights

---

[20] Ibid. p.27.

[21] Ibid. pp.26–27.

[22] Ibid.

[23] Ibid. p.85.

[24] See O'Donnell, G. (2000) 'The Judiciary and the Rule of Law', *Journal of Democracy*, vol. 11 No. 1, p.25 at p.28.

[25] This word creates an often non-existent glorious past in the history of a nation. It is used here to mean nothing more than that which is desirable but which the past may never have had.

[26] Friedrichs, D. (1983) 'Victimology: A Consideration of the Radical Critique', *Crime and Delinquency* vol. 29 pp.283–294. For Young, radical victimology is also about the need within communities to determine and address the risk and effect of crime on individual members of that community: Young, J. (1986) 'The Failure of Criminology: The Need for a Radical Realism', in Matthews, R. and Young, J. (eds) *Confronting Crime*, Sage, London, p.23.

and a direct role for the victim within the criminal justice system was sponsored initially by public outrage at the poor treatment of victims of crime, and was immediately thereafter co-opted into political agendas of Western democracies. Giving the victim a role within the criminal justice system has the advantages of not increasing the power of the State in criminal proceedings[27] and of not winding back the clock to the time when the victim of crime was perceived as nothing more than an object of pity and compensation alone.[28]

McShane and Williams[29] define a victim as 'someone whose victimisation continues within the criminal justice processing system'. However, system victimisation or second victimisation usually presupposes a previous victimisation. The pre-legal system era is often credited with evidence of generous sensitivities to the victim. In that era:

> 'Victims and their relatives controlled the extent of retribution and, consequently, the extent of their satisfaction with the punishment meted out to the offender. The threat of blood feuds was high enough, however, to require societal intervention. Law . . . began the process of restricting the role of the victim. With the advent of such notions as the "King's Peace," the victim began to fade from his or her key role in the criminal process and, in a move calculated to reinforce central authority, the State took over the role of the victim. True, individual victims showed up to testify at trials, or gave information to the criminal justice system in a variety of ways, but they were no longer the accusers and prosecutors who brought the offender to justice. . . . banished from a major role in the criminal process, victims lost the important right to determine the essence of a transgression and the State began to use law to define offenses independent of the victim's sense of harm. . . . this point marked the beginning of neglect of the victim. . . . the modification of the victim's role from a person who has been harmed in some way to one who provides emotional credibility to the prosecution.'[30]

This appropriation of crimes by State systems, and the neglect of victims' sense of harm and essence of transgression, appear to have contributed immensely to the perception of victims also as those individuals that suffer at the hands of the State.[31] However, through human rights treaties and through customary international law,[32] international law has engineered a system of rules which if efficiently applied may result in greater application of the principle *aut*

---

[27] See McShane, M. D. and Williams, F. P. (1992) 'Radical Victimology: A Critique of the Concept of Victim in Traditional Victimology', *Crime and Delinquency*, vol. 38 No. 2, pp.258–271 at p.259.

[28] See Geis, G. (1990) 'Crime Victims: Practice and Prospects', in Lurigo, A. *et al.* (eds) *Victims of Crime*, Sage, Newbury Park, CA, at pp.251–268.

[29] McShane, M. D. and Williams, F. P., note 27 above, at p.261.

[30] Ibid. p.260.

[31] See Schwendinger, H. and Schwendinger, J. (1970) 'Defenders of Order or Guardians of Human Rights?' *Issues in Criminology*, vol. 7, pp.72–81.

[32] See Chap. 2 above.

dedere aut punire, that is, either you extradite or you punish perpetrators of torture, introduced by the torture convention.[33] The principle opposes it appears unilateral use of State discretion to appropriate basic human rights of victims of human rights violations by agents of a prior regime. This prohibition on all States suggests that it is illegal under international law for States to adopt domestic or municipal criminal procedures that condone or exonerate from prosecution agents of a prior regime alleged to have violated basic human rights of individuals.[34] The Human Rights Committee of the United Nations established to supervise State compliance with the Covenant on Civil and Political Rights, and which periodically gives general comments on obligations of States arising from particular articles of the Covenant,[35] in 1992 stated that national amnesty laws that purport to expunge criminal and/or civil liability of agents of the State alleged to have violated basic human rights of individuals through use of torture are 'generally incompatible with the duty of States to investigate such acts; to guarantee freedom from such acts within their jurisdiction; and to ensure that they do not occur in the future'.[36] Policy reasons for this include justification of victims' rights and upholding of the rule of law. By quickening the law that prohibits such actions so that those offences are prosecuted, law's integrity and efficacy as a tool of social control is maintained.[37] Anaesthetising the law so that those offences are not prosecuted casts doubt, first on the power of the particular rules of the legal system, and secondly, on law's utility in general.[38]

Advancing the case for judicial resolution of crimes against humanity Jankelevitch[39] writes that:

'all those who were deported, executed or massacred, have none but us to think of them. If we stopped thinking of them, we would complete their extermination; they would be definitively annihilated. . . . Those who have vanished forever now exist on through us in the devoted faithfulness of our memory; were we to forget them . . . they would simply cease to be. Should we even begin to forget the ghetto fighters, they would be murdered a second time.'

---

[33] See Chigara, B. (2000) 'Pinochet and the Administration of International Criminal Justice', in Woodhouse, D. (ed.) *The Pinochet Case: A Legal and Constitutional Analysis*, Hart Publishing, Oxford, p.115 at p.118.

[34] See also Report of the Committee against Torture, UNGAOR, 45th Session Supplement No. 44, Annex V, pp.109–113; UN Doc. A/45/44 (1990).

[35] Scharf, M. P. (1996) 'Swapping Amnesty for Peace: Was There a Duty to Prosecute International Crimes in Haiti?' *Texas International Law Journal*, vol. 31 No. 1, pp.1–41 at p.26.

[36] United Nations Human Rights Committee, ICCPR, Addendum, UN Doc. CCPR/C21/Rev.1/Add.3 at 4 (1992).

[37] On legitimacy, see Chap. 1.

[38] See Chigara, B. (2001) *Legitimacy Deficit in Custom: A Deconstructionist Critique*, Ashgate, Aldershot, Chap. 1: Juridification of Custom.

[39] Cited in Cassese, A. (1998) 'Reflections on International Criminal Justice', *Modern Law Review*, vol. 61 No. 1, pp.1–10 at p.1.

When rights of victims are enforced justice is achieved. Declarations of rights, which are not accompanied by enforcement of those rights, amount to political rhetoric. If people were to choose between rights which if breached would attract no penalty or sanction to the one breaching those rights, and rights which if breached exacted legal penalties on the one breaching them, perhaps not even one person would prefer the former rights. People believe in legally enforceable rights. When legally enforceable rights are not enforced victims of breach become also victims of State ineptitude.

NATIONAL IMPERATIVES: TO ANAESTHETISE OR TO QUICKEN THE LAW?

Some legal philosophers observe both a descriptive and a normative parallel between the State as a legal subject of the international legal system on the one hand, and on the other the individual as a subject of municipal law. With reference to the doctrines of State sovereignty and of individual liberty, Koskenniemi writes that both doctrines 'describe social life in terms of the activities of individual agents ("legal subjects", citizens, States) and set down the basic conditions within which the relations between these agents should be conducted'.[40] This parallelism enables us to bring to bear on our analysis of the conduct of States as social agents in the international legal system, social theories on conduct of individuals as social agents within their communities. Maslow's[41] theory of motivation and Pavlov's[42] theory of classical conditioning are helpful in the determination of State needs following removal from public office of a regime that violated basic human rights of individuals.

(a) Determining needs of a State: lessons from Maslow's hierarchy of needs

The needs of State doctrine has emerged in the literature as the strongest defence for national amnesty laws that purport to expunge criminal and/or civil liability of agents of a prior regime alleged to have violated basic human rights of individuals.[43] Its main tenet is that while there is a need to empty wounds of all the old infection before healing can start, in some cases there would be nothing left if the infection were cleaned out.[44] Therefore, such cases

---

[40] Koskenniemi, M. (1989) *From Apology to Utopia: The Structure of International Legal Argument*, Finnish Lawyers' Publishing Company, Helsinki, p.192.
[41] See Atkinson, R. *et al.* (10th ed. 1990) *Introduction to Psychology*, Harcourt Brace Jovanovich, London, pp.524–526.
[42] Ibid. pp.248–256.
[43] See e.g. Scharf, M. P. (1996) 'Swapping Amnesty for Peace: Was There a Duty to Prosecute International Crimes in Haiti?' *Texas International Law Journal*, vol. 31 No. 1, pp.1–41.
[44] Hayner, P. B. (1994) 'Fifteen Truth Commissions – 1974 to 1994: A Comparative Study', *Human Rights Quarterly*, vol. 16, p.597 at p.610.

should be allowed to give priority to reconstruction of the State and to maximising social and economic capital on those projects that strengthen and
push the nation forward rather than on those that retain social division and
insist on a form of legal vengeance. However, determination of what the
prime need(s) is (are) of any one State at any one moment is similar to the
question: what is the prime need of any one individual at a particular time?
The fact is that the answer to that question always is a matter of interpretation. From time to time, the rich tapestry of life throws at us situations whose
demand for answers is so quizzical that only the brave dare rush to make
suggestions. Take the case of Elias Gonsales who survived the storm that
killed his mother and other immigrants escaping from Cuba to the United
States in 2000. The United States courts[45] had to decide, under much media
and public interest, whether the boy should be allowed to stay with his relatives in Miami, or be returned to his father in Cuba. Or that of Mozambique
immediately after the floods of February 2000 that overwhelmed and devast-
ated the country's infrastructure.[46] Determination of what the prime need of
the subject is in each of these cases is not easily done. Yet fate has condemned
humanity forever to have to give sufficient answers to that question whenever
it arises. Where the question involves a State, the stakes are always much
higher than where an individual has to make that determination for himself.
Thus, the question whether exemptions should ever be made that authorise
deviation from the legal duty of States to prosecute persons alleged to have
breached basic human rights of individuals[47] raises major concerns for all of
humanity. That politically this is still a thorny issue among States can be seen
in the manner that it exercises governments' activities. On 26 April 2001, in a
debate of the House of Commons Standing Committee established by the
British Parliament to scrutinise the International Criminal Court (ICC) Bill
[Lords], the question whether the international community should intervene in
domestic plans of a State emerging from State tyranny dominated proceedings
on 26 April 2001. It was suggested that:

> 'It is not up to us in this country to determine how the peoples of a country that
> has experienced serious conflict should resolve such matters. It was not up to us
> to interfere in South Africa with the way in which Archbishop Desmond Tutu
> and the authorities ran the Truth and Reconciliation Commission. . . . it was not
> the job of a freelance Spanish magistrate or the Home Secretary to interfere in
> the reconciliation process in Chile and the case of former President Pinochet.

---

[45] See *Court of the First Circuit v Richard Gonsales*, State of Hawai'i FC-CR. No. 98–2047,
14 July 1999.
[46] See BBC NEWS, 'Mozambique Picks up the Pieces', http://news6.thdo.bbc.co.uk/hi/english/
world/africa/newsid_734000/734865.stm.
[47] See Chap. 1 above. See also Scharf, M. P., note 43 above, at p.40.

Arguably, the reconciliation process was impeded rather than advanced by what happened on this side of the Atlantic. There is an important lesson for us to learn. We must allow nations that have been through a difficult civil war or internal conflict scope to reconcile their different factions. I think that we all accept that it will not be possible to impose solutions from outside. My Hon. Friend the Member for Chesham and Amersham referred to Dayton, where an attempt was made at reconciliation. In another case, the British Government urged the Government of Sierra Leone to take into their ranks people guilty of heinous crimes whom they had sought to oppose.'[48]

To determine the effect on a community (both national and international) of granting exemption from prosecution of offences proscribed by law, it may be useful to refer to psychological learning theories.

Maslow's theory of motivation is premised on the idea that human behaviour is based on a hierarchy of needs. These needs are ordered, ascending from the basic biological needs to the more complex psychological motivations that become important only after the basic needs have been satisfied. The needs at one level must be at least partially satisfied before those at the next level become important determiners of action. The first basic need according to Maslow is the physiological need to satisfy hunger, thirst and so forth. This is followed immediately by safety needs, by which he means the need to feel secure, safe and out of danger.[49] Therefore, until physiological and safety needs have been at least significantly satisfied, their satisfaction will dominate a person's actions and higher motives are of little significance.

'Only when basic needs can be satisfied easily will the individual have the time and energy to devote to aesthetic and intellectual interests. Artistic and scientific endeavours do not flourish in societies in which people must struggle for food, shelter and safety. The highest motive – *self-actualisation* – can only be fulfilled after all other needs are fulfilled.'[50]

Maslow acknowledges that not all people achieve self-actualisation. However, many people experience transient moments of self-actualisation which Maslow calls peak experiences. A peak experience is characterised by 'happiness and fulfillment – a temporary, non-striving, non-self-centred state of perfection and goal attainment'.[51] If we substituted for Maslow's pen, the pen of any one of the committees that drafted either the Universal Declaration of Human Rights (1948), or the Convention on the Prevention and Punishment of the Crime of Genocide (1948),[52] or the Convention against Torture and

---

[48] See www.publications.parliament.uk/pa/cm200001/cmstand/d/st010426/ pm/10426s01.htm.
[49] See Table 1 below.
[50] Atkinson, R. *et al.*, note 41 above, at p.525.
[51] Ibid. p.526.
[52] UKTS 58 (1970); 78 UNTS 277. Came into force on 12 January 1961.

Other Cruel, Inhuman or Degrading Treatment or Punishment (1984),[53] or the International Covenant on Civil and Political Rights (1966),[54] or of the International Law Commission,[55] then we might end up with a hierarchy of State needs that in many ways epitomised the one discussed below.

The physiological needs of the State include all three aspects of sovereignty,[56] which ensure existence of the State itself.[57] These physiological needs of the State to have a defined territory, a permanent population that owes allegiance to no other sovereign than itself, an effective government and the capacity to enter into relations with other States[58] need to be satisfied for a State to exist.[59] Further, the EU requires evidence that new entities aspiring for statehood in

Table 1.   Maslow's hierarchy of needs

---

7. Self-actualisation needs: to find self-fulfilment and realise one's potential
⇑
6. Aesthetic needs: symmetry, order, and beauty
⇑
5. Cognitive needs: to know, understand, and explore
⇑
4. Esteem needs: to achieve, be competent, and gain approval and recognition
⇑
3. Belongingness and love needs: to affiliate with others, be accepted, and belong
⇑
2. Safety needs: to feel secure and safe, out of danger
⇑
1. Physiological needs: hunger, thirst, and so forth

---

[53] (1984) 23 ILM 1027. Came into force on 26 June 1987.

[54] UKTS 6 (1977); 999 UNTS 171. Came into force on 23 March 1976.

[55] A creation of Article 13 of the Charter of the United Nations which charges the General Assembly of the organisation to initiate studies and make recommendations for the purpose *inter alia* of encouraging the progressive development of international law and its codification. The International Law Commission was established by the General Assembly in 1947 and charged with the task of codifying and developing international law. For its achievements see Harris, D. J. (5th ed. 1998) *Cases and Materials on International Law*, Sweet and Maxwell, London, pp.65–67.

[56] Namely internal, external and territorial. For discussion of see Chap. 2 above.

[57] See Henkin, L. (2nd ed. 1979) *How Nations Behave*, Columbia University Press, New York.

[58] See Murphy, S. D. (1999) 'Democratic Legitimacy and the Recognition of States and Governments', vol. 48 No. 3, pp.545–581 at p.546. See also Brownlie, I. (1982) 'Recognition in Theory and Practice', *British Yearbook of International Law*, vol. 53, pp.197–211.

[59] See Crawford, J. (1976–77) 'The Criteria for Statehood in International Law', *British Yearbook of International Law*, vol. 48, p.93; Crawford, J. (1979) *The Creation of States in International Law*, Clarendon Press, Oxford. On EU practice on State recognition, and in particular its policy regarding recognition of States that broke away from the former Yugoslavia, see Warbrick, C. (1992) 'Recognition of States', *International and Comparative Law Quarterly*, vol. 41 No. 2, p.473.

Eastern Europe and the Soviet Union demonstrate that they have constituted themselves on a democratic basis and accepted the appropriate international obligations and have committed themselves in good faith to a peaceful process and to negotiations. The appropriate international obligations include:

(1) Respect for the provisions of the United Nations Charter and the commitments subscribed to in the Final Act of Helsinki and in the Charter of Paris, especially with regard to the rule of law, democracy and human rights.

(2) Guarantees for the rights of the ethnic and national groups and minorities in accordance with the commitments subscribed to in the framework of the Conference on Security and Co-operation in Europe (CSCE).

(3) Respect for the inviolability of all frontiers which can only be changed by peaceful means and by common agreement.

(4) Acceptance of all relevant commitments with regard to disarmament and nuclear non-proliferation as well as to security and regional stability.

(5) Commitment to settle by agreement, including where appropriate by recourse to arbitration, all questions concerning State succession and all regional disputes.[60]

This extension by a supranational organisation[61] of international requirements for recognition of an entity aspiring towards statehood not only restates some of the fundamental principles of international law outlined in the United Nations Charter,[62] but also maps out what are perhaps the critical concerns of international life. Nonetheless, it is not clear that customary international law imposes a general duty on States to practice democratic governance.[63] However, it underlines the need of States to be accepted by other States as States *per se*.

These physiological needs would be followed in the hierarchy by security needs of the State. Current practice of States shows that both external and

---

[60] See EC Foreign Ministers Declaration on the Guidelines on Recognition of new States in Eastern Europe and the Soviet Union of 16 December 1991, (1993) *European Journal of International Law*, vol. 4 No. 1, p.72. See also www.ejil.org.

[61] Categorising international organisations into universal, supranational, inter-governmental and non-governmental and discussing the qualities of each, see Martinez, M. (1996) *National Sovereignty and International Organisations*, Kluwer Law International, The Hague; Maunu, A. (1995) 'The Implied External Competence of the European Community after the ECJ Opinion 1/94 – Towards Coherence or Diversity', *Legal Issues of European Integration*, vol. 2, p.115.

[62] Pacific settlement of disputes, non-use of force, respect for territorial sovereignty of other States, legal equality of States, etc.

[63] See Franck, T. (1992) 'The Emerging Right to Democratic Governance', *Australian Journal of International Law*, vol. 46, p.86; Marks, S. (2000) *The Riddle of Constitutions*, Oxford University Press, Oxford; Murphy, S. D. (1999) 'Democratic Legitimacy and the Recognition of States and Governments', *International and Comparative Law Quarterly*, vol. 48 No. 3, p.545.

internal security of States reside in the rule of law.[64] Internally, the rule of law that nurtures the State requires adoption by States of internal checks and balances of executive authority to ensure appropriate use of executive power. Externally, it requires that other States regard it as a legal equal with functional capacity in the international legal system. Next in the hierarchy of State needs would be equality needs intended to ensure legal equality of all subjects of the State before the law to ensure basic human rights to all. The need for States to observe basic human rights of individuals including the right to a fair trial, the right not to be arbitrarily arrested, the right to legal representation, and the right not to be treated in an inhuman or degrading manner. Self-actualised States are those States that observed the rule of law, achieved minimum or no crime at all, ensured education and employment for all, etc. A State that failed to realise the near primary need of prohibiting abuse of basic human rights of individuals guaranteed in international conventions[65] and general international law[66] could not be said to have actualised their potential. No serious political party has ever battled in parliamentary or other elections on a manifesto that specifically targeted economic collapse of the State, a weakening of national defence measures, etc.

(b) Determining needs of a State: lessons from Pavlov's theory of classical conditioning

Pavlov's[67] theory of classical conditioning alerts us to the danger of making unwarranted exceptions to the application of rules of law when conduct falls

---

[64] The retaking of Kuwait in 1991 is a fitting example. See in particular Greenwood, C. (1992) 'New World Order or Old? The Invasion of Kuwait and the Rule of Law', *Modern Law Review*, vol. 55 No. 2, p.153.

[65] The 1949 Geneva Conventions which have been ratified by more States (188) than any other Convention except for the Convention on the Rights of the Child (191) each refer to grave breaches under international law, and for which individual criminal liability attaches and for which States have a corresponding duty to prosecute. See Greppi, E. (1999) 'The Evolution of Individual Criminal Responsibility under International Law', *International Review of the Red Cross*, vol. 81 No. 835, pp.531–552. Article 4 of the Genocide Convention provides that: 'persons committing genocide or any of the acts enumerated in article 3 shall be punished, whether they are constitutionally responsible rulers, public officials or private individuals'. Article 5 obligates States to: 'enact, in accordance with their respective constitutions, the necessary legislation to give effect to the provisions of the Convention'.

[66] The United Nations Committee against Torture, itself a creation of the Torture Convention for the purpose of facilitating its implementation, ruled in 1990 that communications submitted by Argentinian citizens on behalf of their relatives who had been tortured by Argentinian military authorities were inadmissible as Argentina had ratified the Convention only after the amnesty laws had been passed. Nonetheless, the Committee held that even before the entry into force of the Convention against Torture, there existed a general rule of international law which obliges all States to take effective measures to prevent torture and to punish acts of torture. See Report of the Committee against Torture, UNGAOR, 45th Session Supplement No. 44, Annex V, pp.109–113; UN Doc. A/45/44 (1990).

[67] See Gerdes, L. C. *et al.* (2nd ed. 1988) *The Developing Adult*, Butterworths, London, pp.54–57.

within their sphere[68] because of the effect that has on people who might in future find themselves considering whether or not to offend against such rules. Pavlov identified a form of learning, which became known as classical conditioning. 'Stated simply, this means that two events which occur in close succession (say governments' abuse of basic human rights of individuals and granting of national amnesty for those crimes) become so associated with one another that they come to have similar meaning and to produce similar behaviour.'[69] There is support for this claim of psychologists both in laboratory experiments[70] and the real life cases in international life. Cassese[71] writes that:

> 'The ... unforeseen – result of the impunity of the leaders and organisers of the Armenian genocide is that it gave a nod and a wink to Adolf Hitler and others to pursue the Holocaust some twenty years later. There are many indications that Hitler and his cohorts were fully aware of the Armenian genocide and that they drew from it lessons suitable for emulating the Turkish model of enacting a "final solution". Adolf Hitler is reported to have said, when debating whether to proceed with his genocidal policies against the Jews, "Who, after all, speaks today of the annihilation of the Armenians?"... Thus, the lack of international response to the Armenian genocide may, in fact, have influenced the development of Nazi ideology.'

Behavioural learning theorists explain human behaviour in terms of a growing constellation of learnt stimulus–response units which fit, like the pieces of an enormous jigsaw puzzle, into a never-completed and ever-changing picture.[72] Radical behaviourists like Skinner insist that personality should be studied in terms of observed behaviour and its consequences only.[73] Thus, State conduct can be described as a mirror of possibilities to both would-be abusers of basic human rights of individuals, and victims of human rights abuses. Both the United Nations Commission on Human Rights and its Sub-Commission on Prevention of Discrimination and Protection of Minorities

---

[68] Kelsen writes that a norm provides a scheme of interpreting human behaviour. Murdering someone of itself is of no legal significance until it falls within the scheme of the norm of homicide. It is this norm that distinguishes murder from manslaughter, etc. See Kelsen, H. (1967) *The Pure Theory of Law*, University of California Press, Berkeley, p.71.

[69] See Gerdes, L. C. *et al.*, note 67 above.

[70] On how little Albert, an 11-month-old baby was conditioned to show fear of white fluffy objects through corresponding presentation of a white rat and an irritating noise, see Watson, J. B. and Raynor, R. (1920) 'Conditioned Emotional Reactions', *Journal of Experimental Psychology*, vol. 3, p.680.

[71] Cassese, A. (1998) 'Reflections on International Criminal Justice', *Modern Law Review*, vol. 61 No. 1, p.1 at p.2.

[72] Gerdes, L. C. *et al.*, note 67 above, at pp.54–55.

[73] See Skinner, B. F. (1953) *Science and Human Behaviour*, McMillan, New York.

write that impunity is one of the main reasons for the continuation of grave violations of human rights throughout the world. In 1990, its Working Group on Enforced or Involuntary Disappearances reported that:

> 'the single most important factor contributing to the phenomenon of disappearances may be that of impunity. The Working Group's experience over the past ten years has confirmed the age-old adage that impunity breeds contempt for law. Perpetrators of human rights violations, whether civilian or military, will become all the more brazen when they are not held to account before a court of law.'[74]

The United Nations's Economic and Social Council reports that impunity enjoyed by Chilean security forces is 'the cause, and an undoubted encouragement in the commission of multiple violations of fundamental rights'.[75] Amnesty can serve therefore to undermine law's efficacy and integrity. Prosecution on the other hand not only upholds law's integrity, but also establishes an authoritative record of abuses that can withstand the challenge of revisionism. Scharf writes that the most authoritative rendering of the truth is possible only through the crucible of a trial that accords full due process.

> 'Criminal trials can generate a comprehensive record of the nature and extent of violations, how they were planned and executed, the fate of individual victims, who gave the orders, and who carried them out. . . . If a society is condemned to repeat its mistakes when it has not learned the lessons of the past, then it is more likely to do so when it fails to take steps to establish an authoritative record that can endure the test of time and resist the forces of revision.'[76]

Prosecutions also serve to restore victims' dignity, and to prevent resort to acts of revenge by victims denied due process, what Cassese[77] calls 'primitive justice'. Revenge is motivated by the need of victims to exact retribution and to draw attention to the denied historical fact. The execution by Haiti lynch mobs in 1986 of soldiers, members of the Tontons Macoutes, and others suspected of involvement with brutalities committed by the Duvalierists[78] is a real example of resort to 'primitive justice' where the State system has not provided due process.

---

[74] *United Nations Commission on Human Rights: Report on the Consequences of Impunity*, UN Doc. E/CN.4/1990/13, para.344.

[75] UN General Assembly report of the ECOSOC, UN Doc. A/38/385 (1983).

[76] Scharf, M. P. (1996) 'Swapping Amnesty for Peace: Was There a Duty to Prosecute International Crimes in Haiti?' *Texas International Law Journal*, vol. 31 No. 1, p.1 at p.13.

[77] Cassese, A. (1998) 'Reflections on International Criminal Justice', *Modern Law Review*, vol. 61 No. 1, pp.1–10 at p.1.

[78] See Scharf, M. P., note 76 above, at p.14.

CONCLUSION

Internal security of the State, as we have seen, requires that the standard of the rule of law applies consistently both to protect individuals and to preserve law's integrity. The needs of State doctrine so understood does not approve granting of national amnesty to governments that have abused basic human rights of individuals. Both considerations of security of State and aspiration to democratic government of the State do not appear to favour granting of national amnesty to previous governments that violated basic rights of individuals. The pursuit of democracy privileges instead due process and equality of all individuals before the law. Amnesty on the other hand emphasises inequality of individuals before the law in that offences that must be prosecuted are placed beyond the crucible of the rule of law.

Besides, granting national amnesty to agents of a previous regime alleged to have violated basic human rights of individuals is itself an assertion of new meanings of justice and of rights which are opposable to universal understanding of those concepts. Nothing, it appears, entitles a State on its own to shift established and commonly held positions in international law. For this to happen, customary international law requires settled practice that manifests a belief that this practice is rendered obligatory by the existence of a rule of law requiring it.[79] The International Court of Justice has highlighted conditions that oppose the emergence of a new norm of customary international law. These include circumstances where:

> 'The facts brought to the knowledge of the Court disclose so much uncertainty and contradiction, so much fluctuation and discrepancy . . . in the official views expressed on various occasions . . . [where] there has been so much inconsistency in the rapid succession of conventions . . . ratified by some States and rejected by others . . . [where] the practice has been so much influenced by considerations of political expediency in the various cases that it is not possible to discern in all this any constant and uniform usage, accepted as law.'[80]

---

[79] *North Sea Continental Shelf Cases (Federal Republic of Germany v Denmark; Federal Republic of Germany v The Netherlands)* ICJ Rep (1969) p.3 para.77.
[80] *Asylum Case (Columbia v Peru)* ICJ Rep (1950) p.266.

4

SCHIZOPHRENIC STATE PRACTICE: TO PROHIBIT OR TO AUTHORISE NATIONAL AMNESTY LAWS?

INTRODUCTION

The previous three chapters arrived at the conclusion that there are not sufficient policy, legal or theoretical arguments to justify national amnesty laws that purport to expunge criminal and/or civil liability of agents of a prior regime alleged to have violated basic human rights of individuals. Nonetheless, State practice shows that on the one hand, States continue to declare[1] national amnesty laws that purport to expunge criminal and/or civil liability of agents of a prior regime alleged to have violated basic human rights of individuals, and on the other, to reject[2] such amnesties by legally pursuing beneficiaries of those amnesty laws wherever they may be – resulting in a schizophrenic pattern of the international community's thinking on this matter. Therefore, the question whether national amnesty laws that purport to expunge criminal and/or civil liability of agents of the State alleged to have violated basic human rights of individuals are legal or illegal under international

---

[1] Hayner writes that since publication of the report of the United Nations Commission on the Truth for El Salvador in the spring of 1993, there has been a marked increase in interest in truth commissions: Hayner, P. B. (1994) 'Fifteen Truth Commissions – 1974 to 1994: A Comparative Study', *Human Rights Quarterly*, vol. 16 No. 4 pp.597–655 at p.598.

[2] Lippmann writes that the United States government has filed a number of denaturalisation actions seeking to deprive alleged Nazi war criminals of their American citizenship as a precursor to deportation proceedings. In 1987, the Office of Special Investigations of the United States Department of Justice determined that President Kurt Waldheim of Austria, the former Secretary General of the United Nations, had assisted or participated in Nazi sponsored persecutions and was ineligible to enter the United States: Lippmann, M. (1998) 'The Pursuit of Nazi War Criminals in the United States and in Other Anglo-American Legal Systems', *California Western International Law Journal*, vol. 29 No. 1 pp.1–100 at p.50.

law also begs the question whether current State practice of accepting some
such national laws and rejecting others is indicative of a nascent norm of
customary international law prohibiting or authorising such national amnesty
laws.[3] If it is indicative of the former, then it becomes necessary to inquire
whether the emerging ban is regional or general, comprehensive or partial;
and if it is partial what exceptions are permissible to the rule, and under what
circumstances. The purpose of this chapter is twofold. The first is to examine
the theoretical undercurrents that underlie the conduct of States of accepting
some and rejecting other national amnesties granted to agents of a previous
government alleged to have violated basic human rights of individuals. The
second is to assess the impact of such national amnesty laws on the unending
interaction between State discretion that asserts sovereign independence and
international constraint of exercise of that sovereignty. In the wider context
of this book, this chapter builds on the effort to determine a theoretical model
that explains and reconciles the limits of State discretion in international law
with international constraint on State sovereignty when regard is had to the
subject of national amnesty laws that purport to expunge criminal and/or civil
liability of agents of a prior regime alleged to have violated basic human
rights of individuals. The critical question is whether the international community's overwhelming endorsement of South Africa's amnesty law of 1995
on the one hand, and its outright rejection of El Salvador's amnesty law of
1987[4] on the other, theoretically can be accounted for. What makes Zimbabwe's declaration of amnesty following the Lancaster House Settlement[5]
acceptable to the international community, but not Chile's political settlement
that replaced Senator Pinochet's military dictatorship with civilian rule in
1990?[6] Analysis of this question will be examined from three perspectives:

(1) human rights as individual property of victims[7] that has enduring legal
    status and consequences;
(2) the theory of justice as fairness,[8] and the requirement that a community's
    previously agreed standards for the determination of legally acceptable

---

[3] Customary international law itself is problematic. Writers remain divided over its formula and
its attributes. See Chigara, B. (2001) *Legitimacy Deficit in Custom: A Deconstructionist Critique*,
Ashgate, Aldershot, Chap. 1.
[4] Decree No. 805, passed by the Legislative Assembly on 27 October. 1987, provides in Article 1
that 'Full and absolute amnesty is granted in favor of all persons, whether nationals or foreigners,
who have participated directly or indirectly or as accomplices, in the commission of political
crimes or common crimes linked to political crimes or common crimes in which the number of
persons involved is no less than twenty, committed on or before October 22 current year.'
[5] 1979.
[6] Chile's 1978 amnesty law imposed by decree during military rule, prevented prosecution of individuals implicated in certain criminal acts committed between 11 September 1973 and 10 March
1978 the first period of Pinochet rule when a state of siege was in force and repression was harshest.
[7] See Chap. 1 above.
[8] Ibid.

and unacceptable conduct in the community must be upheld all the time in order to lend legitimacy to the community's system; and

(3) State practice capable/incapable of resulting in the creation of a new norm of customary international law.

Because the question of validity under international law of national amnesty laws that purport to expunge criminal and/or civil liability of agents of a prior regime alleged to have violated basic human rights of individuals raises also emotive issues of sovereignty and non-interference in internal affairs of other States,[9] regard should be had to potential motivations of States' assertions of legality or illegality under customary international law of other States' claims. Assertions of this character have the potential to abolish previous rights, or to create a new right where none existed.[10]

STATE ASSERTIONS OF EMERGING NORMS OF CUSTOMARY LAW AND THEIR MOTIVATIONS

Determination of what motivates States to assert as opposable to established or to emerging norms of customary international law, conduct of other States has been the subject of much study. The benefit theory asserts that States individually and collectively rely on international law to set up minimum order and agreement necessary for their very existence. Therefore, law enhances each nation's independence and security.

'by general law or particular agreement, one nation gets others to behave as it desires. . . . Both general law and particular agreement avoid the need for negotiating anew in every new instance; both create justified expectation and warrant confidence as to how others will behave.'[11]

This benefit extends also to recognition of each State's internal and external independence as well as to the inviolability of State territory.[12] The benefit theory is premised on the principle of tacit power. No matter how big or small, wealthy or poor, mighty or weak a State might be, when it wraps itself up in the flag of law, it compels other States to subordinate themselves to law

---

[9] As illustrated by attempts in 1998 to extradite Senator Pinochet from Britain to Spain to answer charges of torture and murder while head of State of Chile. For comment, see Woodhouse, D. (ed.) (2000) *The Pinochet Case: A Legal and Constitutional Analysis*, Hart Publishing, Oxford.

[10] The joint declaration of the United States of America and Russia on the use of outer space in 1967 led to what Bin Chen calls instant custom. See Bin Chen (1998) 'The Importance of Custom and the Process of its Formation in Modern International Law', *James Cook University Law Review*, vol. 5, pp.27–45.

[11] Henkin, L. (1979) *How Nations Behave*, Columbia University Press, New York, p.29.

[12] See Jennings, R. and Watts, A. (eds) (9th ed. 1992) *Oppenheim's International Law*, Longman, London, pp.679–680.

in return. This is more the case today than in previous times particularly because of the international political currency purchased when a State professes itself to be democratic.[13] But partaking of the confidence bred by law obliges the benefiting State not to frustrate the legitimate expectations of others. Mighty and wealthy States too need protection of the law because even they can not guarantee dictation to other States. Therefore, all States have a physiological obligation to engage in the reciprocal, compensating game. Moreover, even the rich and powerful States must seek legitimacy and acceptance of their policies by other States.[14] 'Sometimes even they seek protection in the law from the will of majorities and the "tyranny of the weak". And they may agree to limit themselves in order to achieve corresponding limitations on competing powerful nations.'[15] Thus, the reason why States appear to accept some national amnesties granted to agents of a previous government alleged to have violated basic human rights of individuals and to reject others may be compensatory in nature. But compensating for what? The benefit theory recommends at least two possible answers. One, that if in future they themselves declare a similar amnesty, their declaration shall not be challenged. Two, that the conservative influence of the law to maintain order and stability may be upheld. In particular the *laissez-faire* character of the international political system on which international law has been predicated will be sustained. However, neither of these justifications suffices where public office has been applied to abuse basic human rights of individuals. Lord Browne-Wilkinson in *Ex parte Pinochet Ugarte (No. 3)*,[16] stated that although a former head of State enjoys immunity *ratione materiae* in relation to acts done by him as head of State as part of his official functions as head of State, he did not have immunity from prosecution against charges of torture because it could not be said that the commission of a crime which is an international crime against humanity and *jus cogens* is an act done in an official capacity on behalf of the State.

> 'Finally, and to my mind decisively, if the implementation of a torture regime is a public function giving rise to immunity *ratione materiae*, this produces bizarre results. Immunity *ratione materiae* applies not only to ex-heads of State and

---

[13] There is debate even on whether international law has progressed from insisting in the aftermath of the Second World War on the right to self-determination and abandonment of colonies and protectorates or non-self governing territories to the requirement of democratic governance. See Marks, S. (2000) *The Riddle of All Constitutions*, Oxford University Press, Oxford, Chap. 4, discussing the significance of democratic governance.

[14] Development of customary norms on the law of the sea is checkered with the United States and often also Japanese resistance to more generally held positions. See generally Churchill, R. R. and Lowe, A. V. (1991) *Law of the Sea*, Manchester University Press, Manchester, pp.5–10.

[15] Ibid. p.31.

[16] [1999] 2 WLR 827, HL.

ex-ambassadors but to all State officials who have been involved in carrying out the functions of the State.'[17]

Secondly, order and stability are visited upon victims of crimes against humanity only when the disorder and instability that resulted in their victimisation by State authority is subjected to due process of the law. Victims' dignity is justified only when those alleged to have breached it are consequently prosecuted for those breaches in accordance to previously established law. Merely turning the page without prosecuting offenders, as the Constitutional Court of South Africa insisted upon in the *AZAPO Case* in pursuit of what it called '*ubuntu* but not . . . victimisation',[18] empowers further agents of apartheid alleged to have violated basic human rights of individuals and humiliates the victims of those crimes even further. National amnesty laws that purport to expunge criminal and/or civil liability of agents of a prior regime alleged to have violated basic human rights of individuals aggravate victims' loss and deepens their mistrust in the law and its application. South Africa's amnesty law of 1995 appears to achieve this by attempting to edit life's uneditable record. Article 20(10) of the Promotion of National Unity and Reconciliation Act 34 provides that:

> 'Where any person has been convicted of any offence constituted by an act or omission associated with a political objective in respect of which amnesty has been granted in terms of this Act, *any entry or record of the conviction shall be deemed to be expunged from all official records and the conviction shall for all purposes, including the application of any Act of Parliament or any other law, be deemed not to have taken place . . .*'[19]

Thus, the victim gets no protection whatsoever under the law while the wrongdoer receives protection of the law to the extent that even they do not have to declare for employment purposes that previous to the amnesty law they may have been convicted of murder, torture or some similar crime against humanity. Under this law, even official records must be edited to cancel guilt of the wrongdoer for all time. In fact, the victim is stripped of all previously declared rights. This approach is similar to that of condemning the sheep for being the wolf's victim, while taking all the trouble necessary to cleanse the wolf of any blood stains that resulted from its vicious attack of the sheep.[20] The Constitutional Court of South Africa ruled that Article 20 properly applied gives the result that:

---

[17] Ibid. at p.846.
[18] Quoting from the epilogue of the Interim Constitution of the Republic of South Africa (1993) as amended by the 1996 Constitution. Case CCT 17/96, para.3.
[19] Emphasis added.
[20] See *AZAPO Case*, Case CCT 17/196, para.9.

(1) the offender can no longer be held criminally liable for such offence and no prosecution in respect thereof can be maintained against him or her;

(2) such an offender can also no longer be held civilly liable personally for any damages sustained by the victim and no such civil proceedings can successfully be pursued against him or her;

(3) if the wrongdoer is an employee of the State, the State is equally discharged from any civil liability in respect of any act or omission of such an employee, even if the relevant act or omission was effected during the course and within the scope of his or her employment; and

(4) other bodies, organisations or persons are also exempt from any liability for any of the acts or omissions of a wrongdoer which would ordinarily have arisen in consequence of their vicarious liability for such acts or omissions.[21]

Insistence on a *laissez-faire* analogy of the international political system that postulates overriding inter-State activity at the expense of inter-State interaction of private individuals is problematic. Negotiation of conventions triggered by inter-State activity of private persons (both legal and physical) and the setting up of *ad hoc* tribunals[22] to facilitate legal resolution of international crimes imputed to individuals *qua* individuals demonstrates the private individual's indomitable effect on international life. Inter-State interaction of private individuals and private enterprise has intensified beyond expectation of even the most exaggerated imagination previously made. Often, reality makes a mockery of governments' effort to control the relatively prompt, easy and efficient interchange of goods, ideas, values and beliefs among private individuals across national borders and continents. Therefore, the benefit principle alone could not justify acceptance by other States of national amnesty laws granted by a successor government that purport to expunge criminal and/or civil liability of agents of a prior regime alleged to have violated basic human rights of individuals because, at the outset, it requires compromising justification of victims' predetermined legal rights for the forlorn hope that democratic governance will follow, accompanied by all the promises that notion appears to promise. That in turn nullifies previously agreed standards of a society's norms together with the rights and duties that they carry. It is as if victims never had any human rights that had both legal validity and recognised legal sanctions against anyone breaching them. If it is recognised that they had legal rights, then by not attaching to those rights previously established legal consequences to the breach of those same rights, victims' rights are set at

---

[21] Ibid. para.7.
[22] ICTY, ICTR, and the United Nations sponsored Independent Special Court for Sierra Leone. See Security Council Resolution 1315 of 2000.

zero,[23] a position rejected by the Inter-American Court of Human Rights in *Masacre Las Hojas v El Salvador*,[24] but endorsed by the Constitutional Court of South Africa in the *AZAPO Case*.[25] In the former case, the Inter-American Court examined the legality of El Salvador's amnesty law of 1987 and upheld the petitioner's claims that:

(1) The amnesty enjoyed by those responsible for the Las Hojas massacre of 22 February 1983 constitutes an ongoing and gross violation of human rights committed by the Salvadoran government.

(2) The amnesty law undermines the essence of the system of justice in El Salvador and the process of creating the necessary conditions for peace and democracy.

(3) The *Las Hojas Case* presents an issue of critical importance regarding the guarantee of human rights in El Salvador, in that the question of impunity of the perpetrators is an essential part of the case.

The court concluded that the El Salvador government should declare that:

(1) The massacre on 22 February 1983, of approximately 74 people by members of the Salvadoran security forces near Las Hojas, Sonsonate, El Salvador, was carried out in a premeditated fashion by Salvadoran Armed Forces, with the participation of members of the Civil Defense.

(2) By not bringing any successful prosecution against members of its forces implicated in the massacre the government of El Salvador had improperly used an amnesty law in violation of its international obligations under human rights law.

(3) The massacre referred to constitutes violations of the right to life (Article 4), the right to personal security and integrity (Article 5), the right to due process (Article 8) and the right to due judicial protection (Article 25), set forth in the American Convention on Human Rights.

(4) The government of El Salvador has failed to comply with the obligation imposed upon it by Article 1 of the American Convention, to guarantee the free and full exercise of human rights and fundamental guarantees of all persons subject to its jurisdiction.

In the *AZAPO Case* the Constitutional Court of South Africa rejected the applicant's claim that because policies of the previous apartheid administration were breached by the practice of agents of the State of unlawfully murdering and maiming within the scope and in the course of their employment leading activists during the conflict,[26] the court should declare unconstitutional section

---

[23] For a fuller discussion, see Chap. 2 above.
[24] Case 10.287, Report No. 26/92, IACHR OEA/Ser.L/V/II.83 Doc. 14 at 83 (1993).
[25] Case CCT 17/96.
[26] Case CCT 17/96, para.8.

20(7) of the Promotion of National Unity and Reconciliation Act 34 of 1995. The section provides that no person who has been granted amnesty in respect of an act, omission or offence shall be criminally liable in respect of such act, omission or offence and no body or organisation or the State shall be liable, and no person shall be vicariously liable, for any such act, omission or offence. While the court unreservedly decorated them as fundamental rights: the right to life, and the right not to be subjected to torture of any kind; and while it declared also that, when those rights are violated, victims of such violations have the right to obtain redress in the ordinary courts of law, and those guilty of perpetrating such invasions are answerable before such courts both civilly and criminally, it concluded that '*An amnesty to the wrongdoer effectively obliterates such rights.*'[27] If as discussed in preceding chapters of this book,[28] the rights breached are the legal property of victims *qua* individuals, it is difficult to see how without the consent of victims,[29] amnesty of one government to a previous government obliterates victims' legal title to their property so that government can then discount the legal consequences that attach to the wrongdoer for violation of that title, unless analysis is extended also to the dynamics of modern governance and, in particular, to the relationship between the executive, the judiciary and the law making, law unmaking and law identifying processes.[30]

Closely linked to the idea that State acceptance or rejection of emerging norms of customary international law is motivated by States' need to secure future support of those States closely affected by the nascent norm is the notion that State conduct proceeds principally from States' perception of international law as nothing more than a formal and tactical tool relied upon by governments to justify their actions – the diplomatic tool theory.[31] This view is fanned strongest by foreign policy makers who argue that international law's sole purpose is to formalise consequent diplomatic practices. Thus, as a servant of diplomacy international law could not impose 'significant restraint on a nation's freedom to pursue important national interests as it sees them'.[32] Support for this view is abundant. First, the view that an international political system predicated on State sovereignty is inherently resistant to regulation by law[33] appears to countenance sacrifice of private individuals' legal rights

---

[27] Ibid. para.9. Emphasis added.

[28] See Chaps 1 and 2 above.

[29] A point stressed by the claimant in the *AZAPO Case*, Case CCT 17/96, para.8.

[30] Discussed in Chap. 7 below.

[31] See Henkin, L. (1979) *How Nations Behave*, Columbia University Press, New York, pp.2–4.

[32] Ibid. p.3.

[33] Henkin writes that 'Often, the absence of control by international law is purposeful, and many would say desirable: for States, too, there is an area of "privacy", i.e. autonomy, that is not the law's business.' Ibid. p.37.

where they are opposable to State interests. This point is emphasised every time a new government decides not to give effect to a State's previously recognised laws prohibiting murder, torture, kidnapping, forced disappearances, and instead grants amnesty to agents of a prior regime that are alleged to have committed those crimes in pursuit of particular political outcomes. Secondly, international and regional human rights treaties abound that carry derogation clauses and 'claw-back' clauses that have the potential to strip the individual of any positive human rights previously granted. This complicity of States to establish treaties that herald and declare the sanctity of human dignity on the one hand, and to retract those declarations in the same treaties on the other[34] favours the State interest perspective of international law over other perspectives.[35] But as we have already noted above, the State interest argument neglects completely the extent to which private individuals and private enterprise of different States, continents and cultures affect State conduct by their rapid, steadfast and often easy exchange of goods, beliefs, ideas and aspirations. Thus, the effort continuously to portray State interest as the ultimate basis upon which State conduct is predicated facilitates undermining of previously declared positive legal rights of victims of agents of a previous government. It facilitates also rejection of previously agreed legal consequences that must follow violation of basic human rights of individuals, setting the rights of victims at zero.

Another view is that States obey international law because it is law – the positive law theory. Having recognised and accepted the function of international law States no longer question why rules exist. Rather, their concern becomes whether the rule in question is a valid rule of the legal system, that is, is it recognised as a rule of the legal system by the secondary rules of recognition of the legal system? If it is, then affected States ought to comply with it. From this perspective collective conduct of States manifests their legal rights and duties under international law. Thus, current State practice of accepting some and rejecting other amnesties granted by governments to agents of a previous regime alleged to have violated basic human rights of individuals should be assessed only against relevant laws of the international legal system. According to this theory granting of national amnesty laws that purport to expunge criminal and/or civil liability of agents of a prior regime alleged to have violated basic human rights of individuals violates applicable customary international law. However, granting of amnesty in itself creates no legal problem where it predates the current regime of international law that regulates that sphere of international life. But where that amnesty law comes after

---

[34] When the individual most needs them to be upheld, and the State is most likely to violate those rights.
[35] These include positivism, reciprocity, etc.

creation of the international regime forbidding it, that amnesty becomes an issue under international law.[36] But that in itself is not an issue because the idea that human beings have rights as humans is a staple of contemporary world discourse. Vincent writes that:

> 'International conventions, both global and regional, state it, at length and in relation to a large number of rights. People speaking for States proclaim it. Groups other than States assert it in its collective form, sometimes as a way of becoming States themselves, sometimes as a bid for recognition of their group-ness by States Non-governmental organisations make its observance their *raison d'être*. Individuals in *extremis* appeal to it. Reporters presume it. And scholars try to make sense of it, the more so as more use is made of it in the world they seek to understand it.'[37]

Merrills writes[38] that for a long time States made few attempts to use international law as anything other than an instrument for delimiting their sovereign competencies. But greater interdependence of States and also of their nationals, both physical and legal, has necessitated application of international law to promote and preserve their common interests. Thus, identification of these common interests of States facilitates examination of the interaction of international law's constraint on States' discretion that asserts sovereignty. The common interest theory[39] suggests that States accept or reject nascent norms of customary international law depending on their potential to affect their common interests. Because no State effectively can control events beyond its

---

[36] See *Barbie Case*, France Court of Cassation (Criminal Chamber) 20 December 1985, 78 ILR 125 at p.126. The arrest of Senator Pinochet in Britain on charges of torture during his reign of Chile in the 1970s is one example of application of this principle. See *R. v Bow Street Metropolitan Stipendiary Magistrate and Others, ex parte Pinochet Ugarte (No. 3)* [1999] 2 WLR 827, HL; Chigara, B. (2000) 'Pinochet and the Administration of International Criminal Justice', in Woodhouse, D. (ed.) *The Pinochet Case: A Legal and Constitutional Analysis*, Hart Publishing, Oxford, pp.115–128. Further support of this view can be drawn from the practice of the United Nations to set up *ad hoc* international tribunals to try leaders alleged to have committed crimes against humanity. On 24 May 1999 the International Criminal Tribunal for the Former Yugoslavia indicted President Slobodan Milosevic of Serbia and his officials Milan Milutinovic, Nikola Sainovic, Dragoljub Ojdanic and Vlajko Stojiljkovic on charges of crimes against humanity and violations of the laws or customs of war. See *The Prosecutor of the Tribunal v Slobodan Milosevic and Others* www.un.org/icty/indictment/english/mil-ii990524e.htm. On 4 September 1998 Jean Kambanda, former Prime Minister of the Interim Government of Rwanda from 8 April 1994 to 17 July 1994, was found guilty of crimes against humanity, genocide and other crimes and sentenced by Trial Chamber I of the International Criminal Tribunal for Rwanda to life imprisonment. Kambanda, Jean (ICTR-97–23-S). See www.ictr.org/ENGLISH/cases/kambanda/index.htm.

[37] Vincent, R. J. (1986) *Human Rights and International Relations*, Cambridge University Press, Cambridge, p.7.

[38] Merrills, J. (2nd ed. 1981) *Anatomy of International Law: A Study of the Role of International Law in the Contemporary World*, Sweet and Maxwell, London, p.58.

[39] See ibid. pp.58–69.

frontiers, international law provides an instrument with which States can achieve together what none can achieve individually. The problem of pollution, for instance, and the better quality of life campaigned for by many today clearly demonstrates that individual national action alone cannot guarantee success. Potential environmental disaster resulting from among other things reckless damage to the lithosphere and unimaginative exploitation of marine life recommends concerted international agreement on measures targeted at protecting and preserving the lithosphere on the one hand, and responsible use and enjoyment of marine resources on the other, and not individual national strategies for dealing with these global problems. Both these areas have become the subject of much international regulation through treaty and development of customary international law. Protection of basic human rights of individuals is another area where States by their reaction to situations of abuse increasingly show commitment to uphold the standards enshrined in several international and regional human rights treaties since the launch in 1948 of the Universal Declaration of Human Rights. The recent creation by the United Nations of the senior post of United Nations Human Rights Commissioner is a clear illustration of the seriousness with which the organisation regards human rights. Although prohibition of intervention in internal affairs of a sovereign State has been codified in numerous universal[40] and regional[41] treaties, and although the principle that no State may without consent of the target State intervene in internal affairs of the target State enjoys popular

---

[40] Article 8 of the Montevideo Convention on Rights and Duties of States of 1933 provides that: 'No State has the right to intervene in the internal or external affairs of another': Convention on the Rights and Duties of States, 26 December 1933, Montevideo, 165 LNTS 19; PAUTS 37. The United Nations Declaration on Principles of International Law Concerning Friendly Relations and Co-operation among States of 1970 states that: 'No State or group of States has the right to intervene, directly or indirectly, for any reason whatsoever, in the internal or external affairs of any other State. Consequently, armed intervention and all other forms of interference or attempted threats against the personality of the State or against its political, economic and cultural elements, are in violation of international law': Declaration on Principles of International Law Concerning Friendly Relations and Co-operation among States in Accordance with the Charter of the United Nations (1970) Annex to UNGA Res. 2625 (XXV). This declaration is frequently referred to by States and international tribunals as a codification of contemporary international law. See Reisman, M. (1988) 'Old Wine in New Bottles: The Reagan and Brezhnev Doctrines in Contemporary International Law and Practice', *Yale Journal of International Law*, vol. 13, p.171 at p.191. For allowable exceptions to this rule, see Jennings, R. and Watts, A. (eds) (9th ed. 1992) *Oppenheim's International Law*, Longman, London, pp.439–451.

[41] Article 18 of the Charter of the Organisation of American States provides that: 'No State or group of States has the right to intervene, directly or indirectly, for any reason whatever, in the internal or external affairs of any other State': Charter of the Organisation of American States and 1967 Protocol, 30 April 1948, Bogota, 119 UNTS 4; PAUTS 1. Article 3(1) of the Charter of the Organisation of African Unity of 1964 states that: 'Member States affirm and declare their adherence to the principle of non-interference in the internal affairs of States': Charter of the Organisation of African Unity, 25 May 1963, Addis Ababa, 479 UNTS 39; (1964) 3 ILM 1116.

appeal in international law, it is also the case that the welfare of private citizens in any State is no longer the preserve of the host State alone.[42] In spite of the view that the treatment by a State of its own nationals does not ordinarily and in the absence of specific treaty provisions involve any question of international law and falls exclusively within the domestic jurisdiction of the State,[43] it is now widely accepted that widespread abuse of individuals' basic human rights by a State is a legitimate concern of the international community.[44] President Sadam Husseini's treatment of Iraqi Kurds particularly before and after the Gulf War of 1990, and President Milosevic's treatment of Kosovors of Albanian origin both attracted the severest international penalties any State can possibly experience for violating basic human rights of individuals. Oda writes that under customary international law, no State can make a claim on behalf of an alien injured by his own country. *'However, the community of States has increasingly realised that the welfare of the individual is a matter of international concern irrespective of his nationality.'*[45]

Thus, the value of the anachronistic shield extended to the idea of sovereignty in Article 2.7 of the United Nations Charter itself is now questionable.[46] The United Nations Charter lists as one of its core purposes the promotion and observance of human rights and fundamental freedoms for all without distinction as to race, sex, language, or religion.[47] The Charter exhorts member States to take joint and separate action in co-operation with the organisation in order to actualise universal respect for and observance of human rights.[48] Commentary on the meaning of this provision is replete with disagreement. One view is that this provision imposes a general duty on

---

[42] On theories of non-interference, see Varouxakis, G. (1997) 'John Stuart Mill on Intervention and Non-Intervention', *Millennium Journal of International Studies*, vol. 26 No. 1, p.57; Ryan, C. M. (1997) 'Sovereignty, Intervention, and the Law: A Tenuous Relationship of Competing Principles', *Millennium Journal of International Studies*, vol. 26 No. 1, p.77.

[43] Oda, S. (1968) 'The Individual in International Law', in Sorensen, M. (ed.) *Manual of Public International Law*, Macmillan, London, p.495.

[44] See Wheeler, N. J. (2001) 'Humanitarian Vigilantes or Legal Entrepreneurs: Enforcing Human Rights in International Society', in Jones, P. and Caney, S. (eds) *Human Rights and Global Diversity*, Frank Cass, London, p.139 at p.140.

[45] Oda, S., note 43 above, at pp.495–496. Emphasis added. On the argument that the justification of human rights abuse based on the old conception of sovereignty no longer suffices, see also Captori, F. (1986) 'Human Rights: The Hard Road Towards Universality', in Macdonald, R. St J. and Johnston, D. M. (eds) *The Structure and Process of International Law*, Sweet and Maxwell, New York, p.977.

[46] Article 2.7 reads: 'Nothing contained in the present Charter shall authorise the United Nations to intervene in matters which are essentially within the domestic jurisdiction of any State or shall require the Members to submit such matters to settlement under the present Charter; but this principle shall not prejudice the application of enforcement measures under Chapter VII': United Nations Charter, 26 June 1945, San Francisco, UKTS 67 (1946), Cmd 7015; 1 UNTS xvi.

[47] Article 1.3 of the UN Charter.

[48] Article 56 of the UN Charter.

member States to respect human rights.[49] Another view is that because the United Nations Charter does not specify the rights to be protected, member States cannot accept any definite obligation in the field of human rights. If regard is had of subsequent United Nations documents[50] on this subject, then the former view appears to be the better interpretation.

Notwithstanding the prohibition to intervene in matters that belong to the domestic jurisdiction of a State contained in Article 2(7) of the United Nations Charter,[51] the various organs of the United Nations have on several occasions considered alleged violations of basic human rights of individuals and acted on their findings. Relying on its authority to discuss any matters within the jurisdiction of the United Nations Charter, the General Assembly of the United Nations has always deplored human rights violations whenever they occurred. The execution by Nigeria of nine human rights activists on 10 November 1995 met with such condemnation. South Africa's long and dreary era of apartheid is catalogued by a number of condemnatory General Assembly and Security Council resolutions.[52]

Increasingly, resort to the Human Rights Committee of the United Nations (HRC) by individuals seeking redress for perceived human rights violations by their governments also demonstrates the weakening of monolithic perceptions of sovereignty and a strengthening of the idea of shared sovereign competence. Established under Article 28 of the International Covenant on Civil and Political Rights, the HRC has competence to determine claims regarding violations of rights granted under that Covenant. Although decisions of the HRC are merely recommendatory,[53] international opinion on a State is often influenced strongly by the outcome of such recommendations where they have occurred. In recent times, economic assistance to developing countries has often been linked to each target country's human rights record. There is also a case for saying that the increasing workload of the HRC reflects its own

---

[49] See e.g. the judgment of the ICJ in *Sei Fuji v State of California* (1952) 19 ILR 312.

[50] Universal Declaration of Human Rights 1948; International Covenant on Civil and Political Rights 1966; International Covenant on Economic, Social, and Cultural Rights 1966; and other regional conventions.

[51] Nothing contained in the present Charter shall authorise the United Nations to intervene in matters which are essentially within the domestic jurisdiction of any State. United Nations Charter, 26 June 1945, San Francisco, UKTS 67 (1946), Cmd 7015; 1 UNTS xvi.

[52] Resolution 917(X) of 6 December 1955; Resolution 1663(XVI) of 28 November 1961; Resolution 1761(XVII) of 6 November 1963.

[53] See as examples, *Carlton Linton v Jamaica* (Communication No. 255/1987), UN Doc. CCPR/C/46/D/255/1987; (1994) IHRR, vol. 1 No. 1, p.73, paras 9 and 10; *Arvo Karttunen v Finland* (Communication No. 387/1989), UN Doc. CCPR/C/46/D/387/1989; (1994) IHRR, vol. 1 No. 1, p.78, paras 8 and 9; *Peter Chiiko Bwalya v Zambia* (Communication No. 314/88), UN Doc. CCPR/C/48/D/314/1988; (1994) IHRR, vol. 1 No. 2, p.84, paras 6.7, 7, and 8; *Lenford Hamilton v Jamaica* (Communication No. 333/1988), UN Doc. CCPR/C/50/D/333/1988; (1994) IHRR, vol. 1 No. 3, p.60.

success, which might also be taken as acceptance by States of its supervisory role on the implementation of the rights guaranteed in appropriate international instruments.

The Regional Human Rights regimes for Europe, Africa, and the Americas all recognise the individual's right to pursue action for alleged human rights violations in institutions beyond national frontiers. The pre-requirement in all three systems that claimants should first exhaust all domestic remedies prior to petitioning external tribunals does not take away the individual's right to seek redress against a State beyond its own borders. Article 25(1) of the European Convention on Human Rights[54] states that: 'The Commission may receive petitions from any person, non-governmental organisation or group of individuals claiming to be the victim of a violation by one of the High Contracting Parties of the rights set forth in this convention.' Article 44 of the American Convention of Human Rights[55] provides that:

'Any person or group of persons, or any non-governmental entity legally recognised in one or more member States of the organisation, may lodge petitions with the Commission containing denunciations or complaints of violation of this Convention by a State party.'

Articles 55 and 56 of the African Charter on Human and Peoples' Rights[56] allow individuals similar rights. For some[57] these regimes confer on individuals only procedural rights and not the more meaningful substantive rights, that is, the right to initiate against the State proceedings before an international body. Cassese writes that this right is usually limited to forwarding a complaint: the complainant is not allowed to participate in international proceedings.

'Once the international body has pronounced upon the alleged violation, the applicant is left in the hands of the accused State: cessation of, or reparation for the wrongful act will substantially depend on its good will.'[58]

With the exception of the Council of Europe the international bodies responsible for hearing these petitions are generally not judicial in character. Therefore, the outcome of the whole process is not a judgment proper, but a mild act containing the views or recommendations of the body, usually a commission.[59]

---

[54] 87 UNTS 103; ETS 5; UKTS 38 (1965), Cmnd 2643.
[55] American Convention on Human Rights, 22 November 1969, San Jose, PAUTS 36; (1970) 9 ILM 673.
[56] African Charter on Human and Peoples' Rights, 26 June 1981, Banjul, OAU Doc. CAB/LEG/ 67/3/Rev 5; (1982) 21 ILM 59.
[57] See Cassese, A. (1986) *International Law in a Divided World*, Clarendon Press, Oxford, p.100.
[58] Ibid.
[59] Ibid.

The fact is, that these so-called 'procedural rights' obtain to individuals *qua* individuals. The effect on the development of international law of the exercise of these procedural rights is yet to be fully assessed. Suffice it to say that as individuals seek to enforce so-called limited procedural rights, a new dynamic in international law is created between the procedural rights on the one hand, and the substantive rights that they attach to on the other. Potentially, this dynamic yields implied or purposive rights for the individual against the State. Therefore, the view that the non-judicial nature of the commissions that hear these disputes compromises the derivative rights initially granted to individuals, and subsequently the capacity of the individual as a subject of international law, namely other subjects of the system, appears misplaced. Further, there is no record of States refusing to comply with the recommendations of these commissions. States are often quick to accept commission recommendations although implementing them sometimes takes considerable delay. In particular developing countries appear keen to comply in order to create a pro-human rights image of their governments. Granting of amnesty to agents of a prior regime alleged to have violated basic human rights of individuals opposes the common interest of States to promote a culture of universal human rights for three reasons. First, amnesty is contrary to Rawls' theory of justice as fairness in that it robs previously set legal standards of a community of any legitimacy, killing off public confidence in the positive legal rights that any government will tell them they have. Secondly, although declaration of amnesty evidences acknowledgement that basic human rights of individuals have been violated in breach of positively recognised laws, privileging a political resolution of those violations and breaches over a legal resolution by granting amnesty to authors of those same breaches sets victims of those breaches apart from other people who, when their rights are breached, obtain legal justification. In this sense amnesty attacks the very commonality that States claim to be their main link. Thirdly, victims' rights are set at zero regardless of many claims of international law that individuals have numerous positive rights. This makes a mockery of the claim by many that 'Human rights is the idea of our time'.[60]

This diverse range of possible explanations why States accept or reject nascent norms of customary international law combines the scepticism of foreign affairs scholars, the realism of policy makers, and the legalism of international lawyers. But none of these possible accounts singularly could justify State conduct in each case, nor should they be regarded as being mutually exclusive to one another. On the contrary, they each appear to articulate and to emphasise a particular issue from a series of issues that a State must have regard to whenever it has to decide whether to support or to reject a nascent

---

[60] See McGoldrick, D. (1991) *The Human Rights Committee: Its Role in the Development of the International Covenant on Civil and Political Rights*, Clarendon Press, Oxford, Introduction.

norm of customary international law. Because all law making involves the cycle of proposal, debate, negotiation, compromise and final agreement, any of these possible accounts of State motivation to rejection or acceptance of emerging norms of customary international law could dominate the others during the cycle. However, that does not result in an absolute negation or exclusion of the other possible factors. At municipal level, for instance, there usually is a forum for engaging and completing the law creation process – often a parliament. At international level this process occurs in a more loosely structured and often slow and fortuitous manner,[61] involving only those States interested in creation of a rule.[62] Nonetheless, the same course of proposal, debate, compromise and final agreement is much in evidence. Because the State is itself an impersonal entity, diplomats and other government officials are almost always the medium through which State-business is channelled.[63] Thus, diplomats and policy makers are prone to emphasise only national interest as the basis of inter-State relations. Of course national interest is intrinsic to States' assertions of legality and illegality under international law. Even national law making itself manifests State interest in that States are generally assumed to create only those domestic laws most suited to their purposes. However, this does not justify cynicism about international law because as Harris observes:

> 'questions of international law are invariably treated as legal questions by foreign offices which conduct our international business, and in the courts, national or international, before which they are brought; legal forms and methods are used in diplomatic controversies and in judicial and arbitral proceedings, and authorities and precedents are cited in argument as a matter of course. It is significant too that when a breach of international law is alleged by one party to a controversy, the act impugned is practically never defended by claiming the right of private judgment, which would be the natural defence if the issue

---

[61] 'the process of making customary law is informal, haphazard, not deliberate, even partly unintentional and fortuitous, the resulting law may also suffer these qualities.' Ibid. p.34.

[62] For instance, international law on the non-use of nuclear energy in outer space has been influenced to a great extent by the 1963 treaty between Russia and the United States banning nuclear weapon testing in the atmosphere, in outer space and underwater – see Cheng, B. (1965) 'United Nations Resolutions on Outer Space: Instant International Customary Law', *Indian Journal of International Law*, vol. 5, p.23; while State participation in the negotiation of the United Nations Convention on the Law of the Sea (1982) was overwhelming, and ratifications thereafter placing the Convention in the elite category of 'most ratified treaties'. For further analysis, see Chigara, B. (2000) 'The International Tribunal for the Law of the Sea and Customary International Law', *Loyola of Los Angeles International and Comparative Law Review*, vol. 22 No. 4, pp.433–452.

[63] In the *North Sea Continental Shelf Cases*, the ICJ stated that telegrams exchanged between foreign ministers of different governments could be adduced as evidence of their respective countries' position on the matter discussed in those exchanges: ICJ Rep (1969) p.3.

concerned the morality of the act, but always by attempting to prove that no rule has been violated.'

To a large extent, international law proceeds from States' relations one with another. According to the Permanent Court of International Justice (PCIJ):

'International law governs relations between independent States. The rules of law binding upon States emanate from their own free will as expressed in conventions or by usage generally accepted as expressing the principles of law and established in order to regulate the relations between these co-existing independent communities or with a view to achievement of common aims.'[64]

It provides a framework for the regulation of State conduct. Without this framework of rules, diplomacy alone would not prevail. Principally, States create rules that confer rights and duties in particular situations in order to distinguish acceptable conduct from unacceptable conduct among them. One consequence of greater interdependence of States is that custom's constitutive process has become drawn out where universal norms are intended. Within that formative or nascent phase, the basis of State conduct is not strictly legal as there is no ascertainable rule to refer to. However, much international law proceeds also from States' concern for recognition and observance of human rights.[65]

IDENTIFICATION AND APPLICATION OF THE LAW

Sources of law of many nations have in recent years embraced international jurisprudence in both private and public law. European Union Directives are now a recognised source of binding law in member States' domestic law. South Africa's *grundnorm,* the Interim Constitution of South Africa (1993) as amended by the Constitution of 1996 (the Constitution), directed the Constitutional Court of South Africa in its effort to give legal effect to the Constitution to have due regard to international law and to jurisprudence of comparable foreign case law. Article 35(1) provides that: 'In interpreting the provisions of this Chapter a court of law shall promote the values which underlie an open and democratic society based on freedom and equality and shall, where applicable, have regard to public international law applicable to the protection of rights entrenched in this Chapter, and may have regard to comparable foreign case law.' By Article 231(4) 'the rules of customary international law binding on the Republic, shall unless inconsistent with this Constitution or an Act of Parliament, form part of the law of the Republic'. This direction makes

---

[64] *Lotus Case (France v Turkey)* PICJ Rep (1927) Series A, No. 10, p.254.
[65] See Lapidoth, R. (1992) 'Sovereignty in Transition', *Journal of International Affairs*, vol. 45, p.325.

curious the court's decision in the *AZAPO Case*[66] that section 20(7) of South
Africa's amnesty law of 1995 is unconstitutional for two main reasons. First,
South Africa like all States is bound by norms of general international law
regardless of its adherence to the doctrine of incorporation[67] by which international conventions and treaties become binding only after reception into
national law through legislative authority.[68] The second is that the crimes of
torture, inhuman and degrading treatment were considered crimes against
humanity and therefore carried universal jurisdiction regardless of where they
had been committed long before the Torture Convention (1984). '. . . the
objective was to ensure a general jurisdiction so that the torturer was not safe
wherever he went. . . . The purpose of the Convention was to introduce the
principle *aut dedere aut punire* – either you extradite or you punish.'[69] In this
sense, the Torture Convention also codified customary international law. But
section 20(7) inhibits victims of agents of apartheid from prosecuting criminally or civilly agents of apartheid that breached their basic human rights. It
also precludes the possibility of anyone else being found vicariously liable for
the agents' actions after grant of amnesty by the Committee on Amnesty.[70]
This appears to be inconsistent with customary international law which made
apartheid a crime against humanity and ordered that 'inhuman acts resulting
from the policies and practices of apartheid and similar policies of racial
segregation and discrimination are crimes violating the principles of international law'[71] which should be prosecuted.[72] This prohibition of apartheid and

---

[66] Case CCT 17/96, paras 7–8.

[67] See Greenwood, C. (1992) 'New World Order or Old? The Invasion of Kuwait and the Rule of
Law', *Modern Law Review*, vol. 55 No. 2, p.153.

[68] By that rule international conventions and treaties do not become part of the municipal law
enforceable at the instance of private individuals in national courts until after incorporation into
municipal law by legislative enactment. See *AZAPO Case*, Case CCT 17/96, para.26. This rule
commands wide practice. See also *R v Secretary of State for the Home Department, ex parte
Brind and Others* [1991] 1 AC 696 at pp.761G–762D, HL.

[69] *R v Bow Street Metropolitan Magistrate, ex parte Pinochet Ugarte (No. 3)* [1999] 2 WLR 827.
For further commentary, see Chigara B. (2000) 'Pinochet and the Administration of International
Criminal Justice', in Woodhouse, D. (ed.) *The Pinochet Case: A Legal and Constitutional Ana-
lysis*, Hart Publishing, Oxford, pp.115–128.

[70] *AZAPO Case*, Case CCT 17/96, paras 6–7. The Committee on Amnesty in South Africa is one
of three Committees of the Truth and Reconciliation Commission set up by the Promotion of
National Unity and Reconciliation Act 34 of 1995. The Committee on Human Rights Violations
which conducts inquiries pertaining to gross violations of human rights during the material
period and the Committee on Reparation and Rehabilitation whose ultimate responsibility is to
recommend to the President suitable reparations for victims of gross violations of human rights
are the other two.

[71] See UNGA Res. 3068 of 1973 which adopted the International Convention on the Suppression
and Punishment of the Crime of Apartheid. See also Jennings, R. and Watts, A. (eds) (9th ed.
1992) *Oppenheim's International Law*, p.507.

[72] See Article I(2) of the International Convention on the Suppression and Punishment of the
Crime of Apartheid (1973).

criminalisation of its consequent inhuman baggage, coupled with the direction of the Constitution of South Africa that the Constitutional Court should have due regard to applicable international law, makes the court's determination questionable. Besides, section 20(10) of the amnesty law of 1995 limits the application of the amnesty to crimes associated with a 'political objective'. Even if it were supposed that the amnesty law was valid under international law, the question whether the torturing, murdering and maiming of activists against apartheid were political crimes does not appear sufficiently to have been considered by the Constitutional Court. Therefore, the court's decision is vulnerable to the criticism of extending beyond what Parliament intended to be the jurisdiction of section 20(10) of the amnesty law of 1995. Motala[73] argues that by implication section 20(10) does not regard apartheid as a political offence even though international law which the Constitutional Court is directed to have regard to previously described it as a crime against humanity. Therefore, breaches of basic human rights of individuals in pursuit of the policy of apartheid properly belong with international crimes that can not be expunged by an amnesty law.

MAKING AND UNMAKING OF LAW IN THE INTERNATIONAL LEGAL SYSTEM

International law appears unequivocal that war crimes, crimes against humanity and crimes committed in the furtherance of apartheid are crimes against mankind in general. Granting of national amnesty to perpetrators of any of these crimes appears to be inconsistent with international law whether or not national assemblies direct their courts and tribunals to have resort to international law when considering cases where these crimes are alleged. Therefore, current State practice of accepting some and rejecting other national amnesty laws that purport to expunge criminal and/or civil liability of agents of a prior regime alleged to have violated basic human rights of individuals points to either the law making process or the law unmaking process in the international legal system. In particular it raises the question whether States have engaged the process of custom towards a rule on acceptable and unacceptable national amnesty laws for crimes against humanity committed by agents of a prior regime in pursuit of particular political outcomes. Conversely, it raises also the question whether States might have engaged the reverse process of undoing previously established norms of customary international law. In his separate opinion, Judge Alvarez stated that:

---

[73] See Motala, Z. (1995) 'The Promotion of National Unity and Reconciliation Act, the Constitution and International Law', *Comparative and International Law Journal of Southern Africa*, vol. 28, p.338.

'Customs tend to disappear as the result of the rapid changes of modern international life; and a new case strongly stated may be sufficient to render obsolete an ancient custom. Customary law, to which such frequent reference is made . . . should be accepted only with prudence.'[74]

Custom, by which is meant the process by which norms of customary international law are created, continues to attract debate[75] partly because of imprecision of its enabling provision – Article 38(1)(b) of the Statute of the International Court of Justice (ICJ)[76] – and partly because of disagreement among judicial bodies and among writers as to the material evidences of custom, namely State practice and *opinio juris sive necessitatis.*[77] Determination of these elements has been made difficult by practice of the ICJ and other international tribunals of inaugurating new norms to which the label 'customary international law' is attached without any effort whatsoever to justify that event with reference to the requisite State practice and *opinio juris sive necessitatis.*[78] Nonetheless, it is accepted that the process of custom is evidenced by State practice accompanied by a belief of legal obligation.[79] Applied to State practice of accepting some and rejecting other national amnesty laws that purport to expunge criminal and/or civil liability of agents of a prior regime alleged to have violated basic human rights, the question may first appear as simply one of numerical balancing of acceptances and rejections, and giving verdict for the majority. The ICJ considered the effect of divergent practice in the *North Sea Continental Shelf Cases* and concluded that numerous practice alone does not in its aggregate result in the requisite *opinio juris sive necessitatis* because two conditions must be satisfied before a norm of customary international law can be said to have formed. First, not only must the material acts evidence

---

[74] Dissenting opinion, *Anglo Norwegian Fisheries Case (United Kingdom v Norway)*, ICJ Rep (1951) p.116 at pp.148–149.

[75] See continuing work of the International Law Association Committee on the Formation of General International Law, International Law Association, Report of the Sixty-seventh Conference held at Helsinki, Finland (1996) pp.623–646. See also Chigara, B. (2000) 'The International Tribunal for the Law of the Sea and Customary International Law', *Loyola of Los Angeles International and Comparative Law Review*, vol. 22 No. 4, August 2000, pp.433–452, especially notes 35 and 38.

[76] See generally Higgins, R. (1994) *Problems and Process: International Law and How We Use It*, Clarendon Press, Oxford, p.18.

[77] See generally Harris, D. J. (5th ed. 1998) *Cases and Materials on International Law*, Sweet and Maxwell, London, pp.23–45.

[78] For commentary, see Mendelson, M. H. (1989) 'The Nicaragua Case and Customary International Law', *Coexistence*, vol. 26, p.85; Mendelson, M. H. (1995) 'The Subjective Element in Customary International Law', *British Yearbook of International Law*, vol. 66, p.177.

[79] See *North Sea Continental Shelf Cases*, ICJ Rep (1969) p.3 paras70–77. See also Corbett, P. E. (1925) 'The Consent of States and the Sources of the Law of Nations', *British Yearbook of International Law*, vol. 6, p.20; Allot, P. (1977) 'The People as Law Makers: Custom, Practice, and Public Opinion as Sources of Law in Africa and England', *Journal of African Law*, vol. 21, p.1.

settled practice, they ought also to be characteristic of, or to be manifest in a manner that demonstrates belief that that practice:

'is rendered obligatory by the existence of a rule of law requiring it. . . . The States concerned must feel that they are conforming to what amounts to a legal obligation. The frequency, or even habitual character of the acts is not in itself enough. There are many international acts . . . which are performed almost invariably but which are motivated only by considerations of courtesy, convenience or tradition, and not by any sense of legal duty.'[80]

Divided state practice on whether national amnesty laws that purport to expunge criminal and/or civil liability of agents of a prior regime alleged to have violated basic human rights of individuals are valid under international law points to the process of custom – the process that creates norms of customary international law. At the end of it might emerge a norm either prohibiting or authorising national amnesty laws that purport to expunge criminal and/or civil liability of agents of a prior regime alleged to have violated basic human rights of individuals. *Settled practice* and *legal fashion* are cardinal to the process of custom. In practice determination of settled practice on the one hand, and of legal fashion on the other, raises two separate issues. The first refers to the quality of settled practice of States required. The second refers to the values upheld in the choice either to submit alleged perpetrators of crimes against humanity to the due process of law or to deny that victims had positive basic human rights that carried legal significance.

(a) Settled practice of States regarding crimes that offend all of humanity

The first recorded trial of crimes against humanity dates back to the fifteenth century trial at Bresach of a war criminal accused of trampling underfoot the laws of God and of humanity.[81] More recently, the Nuremberg and Tokyo proceedings of 1946, and ongoing proceedings of *ad hoc* international criminal tribunals established by United Nations Security Council Resolutions to try persons alleged to have committed crimes against humanity in the former Yugoslavia (International Criminal Tribunal for Yugoslavia[82] (ICTY)) and in the territory of Rwanda (International Criminal Tribunal for Rwanda,[83] (ICTR)), and the establishment of a United Nations sponsored Special Court to try persons alleged to have committed crimes against humanity in the

---

[80] ICJ Rep (1969) p.3 para.77.
[81] See Chigara, B. (2000) 'Pinochet and the Administration of International Criminal Justice', in Woodhouse D. (ed.) *The Pinochet Case: A Legal and Constitutional Analysis*, Hart Publishing, Oxford, p.115 at p.119.
[82] See Security Council Resolution 827 of 1993, (1993) 32 ILM 1203.
[83] See Security Council Resolution 955 of 1994, (1994) 33 ILM 1600.

territory of Sierra Leone[84] all point to settled practice in international law of legally resolving cases of crimes against humanity. Conclusion of the Rome Statute of 1998 which is intended to set up a permanent international criminal court provides further evidence of the international community's resolve to punish and not to pardon offences that offend all of humanity as violation of basic human rights of individuals does. The issue by the Spanish Court in Madrid on 16 October 1998 of an international warrant of arrest alleging charges of crimes against humanity against Senator Pinochet[85] and the issue on 11 April 2000 by an investigating judge in Belgium of an international warrant of arrest for the Acting Foreign Minister of the Democratic Republic of Congo on charges of 'grave violations of international humanitarian law'[86] also indicate unrelenting and committed effort of States to bring to due process persons alleged to have committed crimes against humanity. Often, developing countries rebuke such practice as extended imperial domination of former colonies by their former colonisers who refuse to regard them as equals. Nonetheless, problems arise when, as formalists require, codification is attempted of the precise effect and application of the norms gathered from all this practice. In its Draft Articles on State Responsibility[87] the International Law Commission (ILC) whose functions include codification of customary international law for the progressive development of international law refers in Chapter III to offences that constitute serious breaches of essential obligations to the international community. These are crimes that impact the whole of humanity. Their impact is not limited to the State where they occur. In a sense, Article 41 could be said to be a codification of *opinio communitatis* in that it targets 'serious breach by a State of an obligation owed to the international community as a whole and essential for the protection of its fundamental interests'. Thus, commission by agents of a State of high crimes such as torture and genocide – acts that offend all of humanity – could not possibly be a matter of national but international contingency. Therefore, resolution of such offences is beyond the remit of national amnesty laws. If this is correct then, national amnesty laws that purport to expunge criminal and/or civil liability of agents of a prior regime alleged to have violated basic human rights of individuals contravene international law. But as the British government's response[88] to

---

[84] See Security Council Resolution 1315 of 2000 authorising the setting up of Special Court with jurisdiction to try charges of crimes against humanity, war crimes and other serious violations of international humanitarian law, as well as crimes under relevant Sierra Leone law committed within the territory of Sierra Leone.

[85] *See R v Bow Street Metropolitan Stipendiary Magistrate and Others, ex parte Pinochet Ugarte (No. 3)* [1999] 2 WLR 827, HL.

[86] See ICJ Press Release 2000/32.

[87] International Wrongful Act of State (2000) A/CN.4/L.600, p.14.

[88] ILC Draft Articles on State Responsibility: Comments by the United Kingdom, 28 February 2001 (FCO Annual Academic Seminar Distribution), paras 9–10.

the ILC's 'Draft Articles on Internationally Wrongful Act of a State' argues, difficulty of clarity arises from the use of insular words in the ICL's codification of *opinio communitatis*:

> 'The first difficulty lies in knowing what would constitute a "serious breach". Accepting that international law recognises a category of obligations *erga omnes*, owed to all States and in the performance of which all States have a legal interest . . . the content of that category is far from settled. Given the significance of this category of *erga omnes* obligations in the context of countermeasures, this point has very considerable practical importance.
>
> This uncertainty is not resolved by the addition of further criteria in draft article 41. The requirement that the breach be "serious" (i.e. involve "gross or systematic failure") is understandable; but quite rightly not all serious breaches fall within the category. The serious breach must also risk "substantial harm" to the "fundamental interests" protected by the *erga omnes* obligation, which must be fundamental interests of the "international community as a whole"; and the obligation must be "essential" for the protection of the interest. Every one of those conditions introduces a further element of uncertainty into the operation of the provisions. While every definition gives rise to doubts over borderline cases, the doubts here are so extensive as to render draft article 41 of little practical value as a definition of the category of breaches.'

But difficulty with definitions is not a new phenomenon. In fact from the moment of law, lawyers, for whom language is their stock in trade, have had to contend with this difficulty as part of their territory. Whether the ILC was merely codifying customary international law, or progressively developing the law, the crucial point is that boldly the ILC declared that the international community prohibits offences that offend against all of humanity and crimes that attack the interests of the international community. In draft Articles 4–11, the ILC identifies conduct that may be attributed to the State so as to make the State vicariously liable for the acts of its agents, something ruled out by the South African amnesty law of 1995 and other national amnesty laws. This includes conduct of:

(1) any State organ acting in that capacity;
(2) any entity which is not an organ of the State but which is empowered by the law of that State to exercise elements of the governmental authority;
(3) a person or group of persons if the person or group of persons was in fact acting on the instructions of, or under the direction or control of, that State in carrying out the conduct;
(4) a person or group of persons if the person or group of persons was in fact exercising elements of governmental authority in the absence of default of the official authorities and in circumstances such as to call for the exercise of those elements of authority;
(5) an organ placed at the disposal of a State by another State;

(6) an insurrectional movement, which becomes the new government of a State; and

(7) not listed above but which a State adopts as its own conduct.

This broadening of actors whose conduct may be attributed to acts of State underlines international law's commitment to plug hitherto outstanding black holes in the protection of international interests, including promotion of a universal culture of human rights, prohibition of terrorism, and others. It also makes it difficult to see how national amnesty laws that purport to expunge criminal and/or civil liability of agents of a prior regime alleged to have violated basic human rights of individuals could still be justified under international law. In fact, it has the potential of triggering a whole range of legal actions by those alleging human rights violations by present or previous agents or personnel of the State. These draft articles are consistent also with customary international law practice of submitting to due process persons alleged to have violated basic human rights of individuals.

(b) Values recognised by practice of State deference to declarations of national amnesty laws that purport to expunge criminal and/or civil liability of agents of a prior regime alleged to have violated basic human rights of individuals

When persons alleged to have violated basic human rights of individuals are not brought to account for those charges in a court of law, the positive legal rights of their victims are set at zero. It is as if victims never had any recognised positive human rights. However, numerous legal precedents and numerous international conventions declaring the inviolability of human dignity particularly since the end of the Second World War suggest that victims have positive legal rights *qua* individuals. South Africa's Constitutional Court gave reasons why victims of apartheid should not hope for legal punishment of agents of apartheid that perpetrated against them or against their loved ones torture, kidnapping, murders and other crimes against humanity. The court's justifications are a fitting object of analysis because they not only indicate what the international community appears to accept as an exception to the common view that perpetrators of crimes against humanity ought to be subjected to the due process of law.[89] First, the Constitutional Court reasoned that 'Much of what transpired in this shameful period is shrouded in secrecy and not easily capable of objective demonstration and proof. Secrecy and

---

[89] South Africa's amnesty law of 1995 is often hailed as a prudent and constructive way forward. See 'National Reconciliation: Is Truth Enough?' *The Economist*, 26 August 2000, pp.72–73. See also Rotberg, R. I. and Thompson, D. (eds) (2000) *Truth v Justice: The Morality of Truth Commissions*, Princeton University Press, Princeton.

authoritarianism have concealed the truth in little crevices of obscurity in our history. Records are not easily accessible, witnesses are often unknown, dead, unavailable or unwilling.'[90] This argument implies immutability to three propositions that are at best flimsy. The first is that the norm among criminals is not to attempt to conceal their tracks at all. The second is that concealment of offence is a tactic known only to agents of the State. The third is that South Africa's investigative authority lacks both the professionalism and competence required to investigate successfully crimes against humanity committed under apartheid. The fact though is that most criminals deliberately seek to conceal their guilt. Therefore, the court's claim that the veil of secrecy surrounding the apartheid era is impenetrable is misleading. What the post-apartheid crime investigating authority might have achieved had it been charged with investigation of the crimes in question will never be known because of the court's presumption of an impenetrable veil of secrecy. Constitutional Courts mandated to determine human rights violations of a previous regime should not simply throw their arms up in the air and say that national crime investigating agencies could never catch up with the culprits because gathering of evidence simply is insurmountable. That endears corruption rather than efficiency. Instead the crime investigating authority is robbed of learning and developmental opportunities purchased only by pursuit of those rare hard cases. Preventing it from investigating what appear to be difficult cases has the strong potential to foster in the whole nation belief that crimes of State are beyond investigation so long as appearances of secrecy are sufficiently communicated by the State while the crimes are being committed. Even worse, the Constitutional Court lurches first for plan 'B' – not to investigate at all because it is impossible, before any attempt has been made at plan 'A' – to investigate and prosecute violation of basic human rights of individuals. The law is of greatest assistance to victims of abuse of public office when the authors of their suffering are subjected to the due process of law, and of no service at all to them when the offenders are insulated by a later amnesty law from prosecution for those breaches. Commenting on the law and politics of Senator Pinochet Ugarte's trial in the United Kingdom in 1998, Byers writes that, 'In terms of empowerment, the law was of greatest assistance to Pinochet's individual victims, and to the human rights organizations that took up their case – both on its merits, and as a means of further developing the law.'[91]

Secondly, the Constitutional Court reasoned that giving agents of apartheid that violated basic human rights of individuals opportunity to confess and to

---

[90] *AZAPO Case*, Case CCT 17/96, para.17.
[91] Byers, M. (2000) 'The Law and Politics of the Pinochet Case', *Duke Journal of Comparative and International Law*, vol. 10, p.415, at pp.440–441.

seek amnesty from prosecution[92] would assuage victims' yearning for truth about what happened to their loved ones,[93] and transform their 'anger and grief into a mature understanding' conducive to the creation in South Africa of 'the emotional and structural climate essential for the reconciliation and reconstruction which informs the very difficult and sometimes painful objectives of the amnesty articulated in the epilogue'.[94] This argument is based on the false assumption that merely giving victims of human rights abuse information about who violated their human dignity or that of their loved ones is sufficient in itself. Thus, that act is imbued with the wonder of instantly engineering in victims a sense of finality which does not care or even yearn for some form of judicial signification of the legal character of the rights violated. By that act and that act alone, victims suddenly become filled with angelic compassion for their torturers and those that maimed, disappeared and murdered their loved ones. Victims clothe themselves with divine forgiveness that unites them in rejection of earthly legal signification of their legal rights. Such an assumption falsely characterises truth bodies or truth commissions as judicial with court-like competencies. The fact is that none of the truth commissions on record was ever resourced to the extent that ordinary national courts are, nor was any of them intended to replace judicial action against perpetrators. Hayner writes that neither victims nor societies at large have understood them to replace judicial action in those countries where truth commissions have been put in place.[95] Therefore, the assumption that merely giving victims of human rights abuse information about who violated their human dignity or that of their loved ones is sufficient in itself overestimates the utility of truth commissions in addressing State terror. Tutu's experience as Chair of South Africa's much publicised Truth and Reconciliation Commission led him to remark that most of those that testified before the commission 'lied like it was going out of fashion'.[96] This is not heartening for a procedure whose hallmark was marketed as disclosure (knowledge on the part of victims) of what perpetrators did (truth about individuals' involvement in violating basic human rights of others). Even if mere disclosure of the truth could be said to have the wondrous qualities of contentment of the victims, it could not be said that a commission lacking in judicial authority would deliver the relevant truth. Therefore, both the quantity and quality of the 'truth' accessed

---

[92] From the Committee on Amnesty, one of three committees established by the 1995 amnesty law of South Africa.

[93] *AZAPO Case*, Case CCT 17/96, para.18.

[94] Ibid. para.17.

[95] Hayner, P. B. (2001) *Unspeakable Truths: Confronting State Terror*, Routledge, New York, p.87.

[96] Tutu, D. (1999) *No Future Without Forgiveness*, Rider, London.

by the Commission will determine the extent of the success of South Africa's attempt to deal with State terror in that way. The invention of truth commissions demonstrates emergence of a parasitic tradition to Rawls' pragmatic of justice as fairness for all, which subjects to judicial outcomes all violations of codes of conduct of agents of society previously established under an imaginary veil of ignorance. The truth commission tradition compels victims and families of victims of State terror to remember themselves and their loved ones respectively as worthless in the eyes of the law even if they were illegally murdered, disappeared, tortured or maimed both under national laws and under international law. Human beings on earth still yearn for the substance of justice and not for the shadow of it cast over their heads by truth commissions.

Very worrying in the Constitutional Court of South Africa's ruling is the court's reasoning that:

> 'The human rights criminals are fellow citizens, living alongside everyone else, and they may be very powerful and dangerous. If the army and the police have been the agencies of terror, the soldiers and the cops aren't going to turn overnight into paragons of respect for human rights. Their numbers and their expert management of deadly weapons remain significant facts of life. . . . The soldiers and police may be biding their time, waiting and conspiring to return to power. . . . If they are treated too harshly – or if the net of punishment is cast too widely – there may be a backlash that plays into their hands.'[97]

It represents the reverse of the argument that there is a need to empty wounds of all the old infection before healing can start.[98] The law's intervention in these circumstances ought not only to initiate healing of wounds, but also to anaesthetise and to destroy for all time in a nation's fabric any propensity to apply civil authority to the service of human rights abuse. The argument that this is impossible in some cases because if you tried to clean out all of the infection you would be left with nothing is laughable not only because its outcome sets victims' rights at zero, but also because it suggests that systems cannot be fathomed yet that can both uphold prior recognised legal rights of victims by investigating and submitting to the due process of law those alleged to have applied public authority to violate rights of others, and direct at the perpetrators sanctions that do not threaten to stampede to a halt the ordinary life of the State. That argument poses challenges to penal strategies for dealing with 'sensitive criminals', and not with the fundamental question whether those criminals should not at all be made accountable at law for their illicit

---

[97] Ibid. para.31.
[98] Hayner, P. B. (1994) 'Fifteen Truth Commissions – 1974 to 1994: A Comparative Study', *Human Rights Quarterly*, vol. 16, p.597 at p.610. For weaknesses in this argument, see Chap. 1 above.

conduct. In Britain at least, the question has practically rehearsed itself in the context of shortage of holding places for prisoners. An approach maintained by successive governments has been to create sanctions that the offender discharges without actually going to prison where she or he would require the kind of services in short supply. Thus, the legal system has developed penal measures[99] that include tagging, community punishment and rehabilitation orders, community sentences, community punishment orders, compensation orders, curfew orders, etc. This approach not only rejects acquiescence with clear breaches of a society's established code of conduct, but also accommodates the society's constraints. Granted that some of the persons alleged to have violated basic human rights of individuals under apartheid have specialist skills and training, community orders in the community of their victim(s) over an extended period could both rehabilitate them in the new South Africa and justify the rights of victims which they breached. Instead of walking away from this challenge by confusing ecclesiastical law with positive law of the State, South Africa and other affected States might yet discover models that reconcile their precarious circumstances with the overwhelming need legally to recognise and to justify victims' rights.

However, the Constitutional Court of South Africa's argument entrenches further the view that agents of the State who commit crimes against humanity can go scot free if collectively they appear to threaten the new regime with disruption of its agenda if ever it attempts to submit them to the due process of law. Therefore, the new order is raised on fear of criminals whose power is maintained while the victims' basic human rights are constrained both before and after the change of government. Indeed the greater the threat of disruption the criminals manifest, the better their chances of never having legally to account for their breaches of their community's previously determined codes of conduct. Even the Constitutional Court itself appeared to fear the criminals' potential to disrupt its function should it rule otherwise. This is lamentable because by giving this impression, the court sensitises citizens to fear of the police force and national defence forces for all time. It also desensitises both these departments of State from any sense of legal or moral responsibility for what they do. In its Comments on Haiti (1995) the United Nations Human Rights Committee expressed serious concern that:

> 'failure to screen and exclude human rights violators from service in the military, the police force and the judiciary, will seriously weaken the transition to security and democracy. The Committee is also concerned that human rights violations by members of the armed forces, agents of security services, and members of

---

[99] See generally, Elliot, C. and Quinn, F. (2nd ed. 1998) *English Legal System*, Longman, London, pp.256–287.

former paramilitary groups still occur. The Committee notes with particular concern the lack of full and effective control by civilian authorities over the military.'[100]

If other professions inspired similar fear in public institutions and the public itself, what use would any declaration of rights be? For instance, if doctors threatened to give only partial treatment to patients coming from communities that previously sued their health authorities for negligent medical care, or if civil engineers threatened to pollute further any waterways complained about by the public, and they actually got for their threats legal indifference of the courts because judges were scared that if they insisted on these professions rising to the required minimum standard of care, they actually might carry out their threats and many more people would die, the law would be like saltless ash. Law premised on fear of how sections of society might react if they were told that they were violating previously established rules of the society is not worthy of its name. Rawls writes that justice is evidenced by practice of principles, which 'free and rational persons concerned to further their own interests would accept in an initial position of equality as defining the fundamental terms of their association. These principles are to regulate all further agreements; they specify the kinds of social cooperation that can be entered into and the forms of government that can be established.'[101] Therefore, neither threat of violence of criminals, nor nannying by the courts of a State's investigative authorities should be used as excuses for not enforcing society's previously established legal rights and duties.

(c) Values stressed by international treaties on crimes against humanity

International treaties that regulate conduct falling within the sphere of crimes against humanity include the London Charter of 1946,[102] the Convention on the Prevention and Punishment of the Crime of Genocide 1948[103] (Genocide Convention), the Convention against Torture and Other Cruel, Inhuman or Degrading Treatment or Punishment 1984[104] (Torture Convention), the International Convention against the Taking of Hostages 1979[105] (Hostages Convention), the Statute of the ICTY, the Statute of the ICTR, and the Statute of the ICC. To varying degrees these treaties criminalise and outlaw, in some

---

[100] UN Doc. CCPR/C/79/Add.49 (1995).
[101] Rawls, J. (1994) 'The Main Idea of the Theory of Justice', in Singer, P. (ed.) *Ethics*, Oxford University Press, Oxford, p.362.
[102] UKTS 4 (1945); UNTS 251.
[103] UKTS 58 (1970); UNTS 277.
[104] (1984) 23 ILM 1027.
[105] UKTS 81; (1979)18 ILM 1456.

cases under specific circumstances and in other cases generally, crimes against peace, war crimes, and crimes against humanity;[106] acts of genocide, conspiracy to commit genocide, direct and public incitement to commit genocide, attempt to commit genocide and complicity in genocide;[107] murder, extermination, enslavement, deportation, imprisonment, torture, rape, persecutions on political, racial and religious grounds, and other inhuman acts.[108] To this list, the Rome Statute setting up the ICC adds crimes of apartheid and enforced disappearance of persons.[109] Further it criminalises rape, sexual slavery, enforced prostitution, forced pregnancy, enforced sterilisation, or any other form of sexual violence of comparable gravity.[110] To be classified as crimes against humanity, these crimes ought to have occurred under particular circumstances. The ICTY requires that the acts complained of ought to have been directed against any civilian population and ought to have occurred in the crucible of an armed conflict.[111] It does not matter that that particular conflict was internal or international. Both the ICTR and the Rome Statute require that these acts evidence also a widespread or systematic attack directed against any civilian population,[112] though the Rome Statute goes further to require 'knowledge of that attack[113] . . . and pursuant to or in furtherance of a State organisational policy to commit such attack'.[114] Prosecution and punishment of these offences is privileged over acquiescence of truth commissions and amnesty laws.

Article 4 of the Genocide Convention appears to prohibit for all time national amnesty laws that purport to expunge criminal and/or civil liability of agents of a prior regime for crimes enumerated in Article 3 of the Convention. 'Persons committing genocide or any of the other acts enumerated in article 3 shall be punished, whether they are constitutionally responsible rulers, public officials or private individuals.' The emphasis is on non-discriminatory punishment. This follows from the fact that human rights are positive legal rights for all humans by virtue of being human. Therefore, all breaches must, without discrimination, have legal resolutions. Article 1 privileges legal resolution of crimes against humanity above politically expedient amnesties. 'The

---

[106] Article 6 of the London Agreement of 8 August 1946 which established the International Military Tribunal 'for the trial of war criminals whose offences have no particular geographical location': Article 2 of the Agreement.
[107] Article 3 of the Genocide Convention.
[108] See Article 5 of the ICTY and Article 3 of the ICTR.
[109] See Article 7(1)–(3).
[110] See Article 7(1)(g) and (2)(f).
[111] See Article 5.
[112] See Article 3 of the ICTR.
[113] See Article 7(1).
[114] See Article 7(2)(a).

Contracting Parties confirm that genocide, whether committed in time of peace or in time of war, is a crime under international law which they undertake to prevent and punish.' The customary international law ban on genocide which is supported by the requirement at all times to punish offenders regardless of whether or not the States concerned recognised the Genocide Convention (1948) is articulated by the ICJ in its advisory opinion on reservations to the Genocide Convention.[115]

> 'The origins of the Convention show that it was the intention of the United Nations to *condemn and punish genocide* as "a crime under international law" involving a denial of the right of existence of entire human groups, a denial which shocks the conscience of mankind and results in great losses to humanity, and which is contrary to moral law and to the spirit and aims of the United Nations. The first consequence arising from this conception is that the principles underlying the Convention are principles which are recognised by civilised nations as *binding on States, even without any conventional obligation.*'

Thus, the law is posited from a criminal law perspective, targeting individuals yet focused on their role as agents of the State.[116] Similar insistence on legal resolution of cases of State terror and atrocity is to be found also in the Torture Convention (1984) which comprehensively defines torture in Article 1 as:

> 'any act by which severe or suffering, whether physical or mental is intentionally inflicted on a person for such purposes as obtaining from him or a third person information or a confession, punishing him for an act he or a third person has committed or is suspected of having committed, or intimidating or coercing him or a third person . . . when such pain or suffering is inflicted by or at the instigation of or with the consent or acquiescence of a public official or other person acting in an official capacity.'

Article 2 mandates legal resolution of all cases of torture without exception by directing State Parties to 'take effective legislative administrative, judicial or other measures to prevent acts of torture in any territory under [their] jurisdiction'.[117] It prohibits in the strongest language derogation from legal resolution of cases of torture. 'No exceptional circumstances whatsoever, whether a state of war or a threat of war, internal political instability or any other public emergency, may be invoked as a justification of torture.'[118] Responsibility for torture is placed squarely at the feet of the perpetrator, and

---

[115] ICJ Rep (1951) p.16 at p.23. Emphasis added.
[116] See Schabas, W. A. (2000) *Genocide in International Law*, Cambridge University Press, Cambridge, p.3.
[117] See Article 2(1).
[118] See Article 2(2).

not at the organisation or institution they were associated with or whose policies they advanced. 'An order from a superior officer or a public authority may not be invoked as a justification.'[119] State Parties are directed to ensure that all acts of torture are offences under their criminal law,[120] and to make these offences punishable by appropriate penalties.[121] Insistence on judicial resolution of all cases of torture is perhaps underlined by Article 5 which directs State Parties to take such measures as may be necessary to establish their jurisdiction over offences of torture.[122] 'Each State Party shall likewise take such measures as may be necessary to establish its jurisdiction . . . in cases where the alleged offender is present in any territory under its jurisdiction and it does not extradite him . . .'[123]

Similarly, the Hostages Convention (1979) directs State Parties to adopt necessary measures to establish jurisdiction over any of the offences set in the Convention.[124] Like the Genocide Convention and the Torture Convention, the Hostages Convention insists on the principle *aut dedere aut punire*.[125] Article 4 enjoins States to co-operate in the prevention of the offences set forth in Article 1 by:

(1) taking all practicable measures to prevent preparations in their respective territories for the commission of those offences within or outside their territories, including measures to prohibit in their territories illegal activities of persons, groups and organisations that encourage, instigate, organise or engage in the perpetration of acts of taking of hostages, and
(2) exchanging information and co-ordinating the taking of administrative and other measures as appropriate to prevent the commission of those offences.

Article 2 directs each State Party to make the offences set forth in the Convention 'punishable by appropriate penalties which take into account the grave nature of those offences'.

It appears that international treaties applicable to the circumstances purportedly covered by national amnesty laws that purport to expunge criminal and/or civil liability of agents of a prior regime are united in prohibiting political resolution of those breaches. Instead, they insist on legal resolution of those cases. They ascribe enduring legal significance to previously declared positive human rights of individuals. They outlaw discriminatory prosecution

---

[119] See Article 2(3).
[120] See Article 4(1).
[121] See Article 4(2).
[122] See Article 5(1).
[123] See Article 5(2).
[124] See Article 5(1).
[125] See Article 5(2).

of violation of human rights perhaps because it is inconsistent with international aspirations of a universal culture of human rights.

(d) Values stressed by customary international law

Harris writes that the Genocide Convention (1948) probably represents customary international law.[126] In *Ex parte Pinochet Ugarte (No. 3)* the House of Lords stated that 'the systematic use of torture was an international crime for which there could be no immunity even before the Convention came into effect and consequently there is no immunity under customary international law for the offences relating to torture . . .'.[127] The House of Lords ruled also that official duties of the State which qualified for immunity from prosecution under international law did not include murder, torture, disappearing of political opponents and commission of other grave violations of basic human rights of individuals.[128] The Nuremberg proceedings declared also the principle that it is not sufficient a defence to a charge of crimes against humanity that the accused was merely carrying out superior orders.[129] That fact does not free the accused from personal responsibility, but may be considered in mitigation of punishment. It appears that customary international law insists on individual responsibility for crimes against humanity and denies government agents appeal to act of State doctrine and sovereign immunity from those of their acts that can not be said to be official duties of the State. The record number of *ad hoc* international tribunals established recently to try crimes against humanity committed in the territories of Rwanda, Yugoslavia and Sierra Leone, coupled with adoption in Rome in 1998 of the Statute of the proposed permanent International Criminal Court, collectively privilege legal resolution of cases of violation of basic human rights of individuals. By rejecting the defences of superior orders and act of State where agents of a previous regime are charged with grave breaches of basic human rights of individuals, customary international law asserts enduring legal significance of basic human rights of individuals. It upholds also validity of previously established laws of the community, what Rawls calls justice as fairness.[130] For these reasons, Dugard[131] is correct to argue that from the perspective of international

---

[126] Harris, D. J. (5th ed. 1998) *Cases and Materials on International Law*, Sweet and Maxwell, London, p.747, n.4.

[127] [1999] 2 WLR 827 at p.829.

[128] Ibid. at p.846.

[129] See judgment of the Nuremberg International Military Tribunal (1947), *American Journal of International Law*, vol. 41, p.172.

[130] See Chap. 1 above.

[131] Dugard, J. (1997) 'Is the Truth and Reconciliation Process Compatible with International Law? An Unanswered Question', *South African Journal on Human Rights*, vol. 13 No. 2, p.258 at p.262.

law, the *AZAPO* decision 'is disappointing because it fails to address adequately the question whether conventional and customary international law oblige a successor regime to punish the officials and agents of the prior regime for violations of international law and thus gave support to the constitutional challenge advanced by the applicants'.

Values stressed by international treaties on crimes against humanity + Values stressed by customary international law + Values underlying national amnesty laws = International constraint on right to declare national amnesty for crimes against humanity. Therefore, national amnesty laws defy a strong presumption under international law that all grave breaches of basic human rights of individuals must have a judicial and not a political resolution. Current State practice of condoning some national amnesty laws that expunge any wrongdoing of agents of a previous regime alleged to have violated basic human rights of individuals, and of rejecting other national amnesty laws compels analysis of the interaction of state discretion and international constraint if a theory grounding this practice is going to be reached.

CONCLUSION

This chapter considered potential motivations of States' acceptance or rejection of other States' claims under customary international law. Any State that grants national amnesty to agents of a previous regime alleged to have committed serious breaches of human rights law makes the claim that it has discretion so to do under international law. Whether States possess that discretion is an area of contest because of State practice of rejecting some national amnesties and accepting others. The theory that States will accept another State's claim if it is in the accepting State's interest so to do in recognition of its need of that other State's support in the future when its own claims may be in dispute does not appear to apply to the question of national amnesty laws that purport to expunge criminal and/or civil liability of agents of a prior regime because no benefit can be had from opposing norms *jus cogens*, and from encouraging impunity in aspiring democracies. Besides, settled practice of States stretching from as far back as the fifteenth-century trial at Bresach of a war criminal alleged to have trampled underfoot the laws of God and humanity, to the setting up in 2000 of a United Nations sponsored Special Court for the trial of people alleged to have committed in Sierra Leone crimes against humanity, suggests that national amnesty for crimes against humanity may no longer be an option under international law. If it is an exception to the norm, the conditions under which that exception applies are perhaps what by their varying practice States are debating through the medium of custom – the process by which norms of customary international law are created.

The chapter also examined the values espoused by the practice of accepting national amnesty laws that purport to expunge criminal and/or civil liability of agents of a prior regime alleged to have committed grave breaches of human rights law. These values appear to be opposed to the usual claim that national amnesty laws facilitate transition from authoritarian rule to democratic practice. They include respect for and subservience to threats of violence accredited to agents of the previous regime that should be submitted to the due process of law; denying efficacy at law of previously declared human rights standards and the setting of victims' human rights at zero; and desensitisation to guilt of institutions of law and order of a State. Unless more exacting reasons can be made for authorising State discretion to grant amnesty to agents of a previous government alleged to have violated basic human rights of individuals, no exceptions should be made to the general ban on such national amnesty laws.

The chapter considered also the view that States obey international law because it is law. Having recognised and accepted the function of international law, States no longer question why rules exist. Rather, their concern becomes whether the rule in question is a legitimate rule of the legal system. If it is, then affected States ought to comply with it. From this perspective collective conduct of States manifests their legal rights and duties under international law. Thus, current practice of States of accepting some and rejecting other amnesties granted by governments to agents of a previous regime alleged to have violated basic human rights of individuals should be assessed only by what applicable laws of the international legal system there are. The practice of granting or accepting national amnesty laws that purport to expunge criminal and/or civil liability of agents of a prior regime alleged to have violated basic human rights of individuals appears to be inconsistent with norms *jus cogens*.[132]

---

[132] Discussing the three different definitions of crimes against humanity, see Chesterman, S. (2000) 'An Altogether Different Order: Defining Crimes Against Humanity', *Duke Journal of Comparative and International Law*, vol. 10, p.307.

5

AMNESTY, STATE DISCRETION AND INTERNATIONAL CONSTRAINT: WHAT MODEL?

INTRODUCTION

The previous chapter concluded that national amnesty laws that purport to expunge criminal and/or civil liability of agents of a prior regime alleged to have violated basic human rights of individuals defy a strong presumption under international law that all grave breaches of basic human rights of individuals must have a judicial and not a political resolution. It showed that values stressed by international treaties and customary international law on crimes against humanity and on grave breaches of human rights point to a severe constraint by international law on the sovereign right of States to declare national amnesty laws for such offences. This chapter examines the place if any of national amnesty laws that purport to expunge criminal and/or civil liability of agents of a prior regime alleged to have violated basic human rights of individuals as an exception to that general prohibition.

STATE DISCRETION VERSUS *OPINIO COMMUNITATIS*

Opinio communitatis refers to those values widely supported by the international community for the achievement of particular goals. Such support sometimes manifests itself through various forms before regulatory measures have occurred, which may compel States to engage the appropriate norm creating processes for the creation of norms that recognise those vital values of the international community. Non-binding United Nations General Assembly (UNGA) resolutions, declarations of heads of governments and concerted efforts of non-governmental organisations to achieve particular outcomes are all good reference points of *opinio communitatis* because all these agents are channels through which streams of international aspirations are aggregated at international level. Work of non-governmental organisations (NGOs) such as Amnesty International, Rights Watch and Interights to expose human rights violations is tacitly approved by some and openly supported by many. There is clear hesitation in the international community to let NGOs play a leading role in setting international agendas that determine or further international values for the simple reason that while governments can claim to represent views of those that elected them, NGOs can make no such claim. Nonetheless, their role in ensuring compliance of States with those commitments that they have reached and publicised is apparent. Lee writes that *opinio communitatis* is realised through UNGA resolutions when those resolutions establish what rules of international law States support widely.[1] Because shared aspirations properly pursued result in shared goals, it appears that man is condemned to interdependence and as a consequence of that to inter-protection. If those that we depend upon are destroyed for a lack of protection that we could have offered, their destruction threatens our own survival. The philosophy that shared responsibility is a necessary element for the conduct of a common life has an ardent advocate in Brierly who writes that:

> 'Modern science has given us vastly increased facilities and speed of communications, and modern commerce has created demands for the commodities of other nations which even the extravagances of modern economic nationalism are not able to stifle. If human affairs were more wisely ordered, and if men were clearer-sighted than they are in seeing their own interests, it might be that this inter-dependence of the nations would lead to a strengthening of their feelings of community. But their interdependence is mainly in material things, and though material bonds are necessary, they are not enough without a common social consciousness; without that they are as likely to lead to friction as to friendship. *Some sentiment of shared responsibility for the conduct of a common life is a necessary element in any society, and the necessary force behind any system of law; and the strength of any legal system is proportionate to the strength of such a sentiment . . .'*[2]

---

[1] Lee, R. (1995) 'Rule Making in the United Nations: Opinio Communitatis', *New York University Journal of International Law and Politics*, vol. 27 No. 33, p.571 at p.573. For a list of UNGA resolutions said to reflect *opinio communitatis*, see ibid. pp.574–575.

[2] See Harris, D. J. (5th ed. 1998) *Cases and Materials on International Law*, Sweet and Maxwell, London, pp.1–2. Emphasis added. Writing that: 'All men are interdependent. Every nation is an heir of a vast treasury of ideas and labour to which both the living and the dead of all nations have contributed. Whether we realize it or not, each of us lives eternally "in the red". We are everlasting debtors to known and unknown men and women. When we arise in the morning, we go into the bathroom where we reach for a sponge which is provided for us by a Pacific islander. We reach for soap that is created for us by a European. Then at the table we drink coffee which is provided for us by a South American, or tea by a Chinese, or cocoa by a West African. Before we leave for our jobs we are already beholden to more than half of the world', see King, C. S. (1983) *The Words of Martin Luther King*, Fount, London, p.18.

However, conflict between, on the one hand, *opinio communitatis* and, on the other, State determination to regulate their domestic sphere in uncomplying fashion is abundant.[3] President Bush's decision to abandon the 1997 Kyoto Protocol which calls for countries to agree legally binding targets for curbing heat-trapping greenhouse gases, mainly carbon dioxide from burning fossil fuels, goes against international opinion that this reduction is painful in the short term but necessary. President Bush's argument that he would not go along with international wisdom if that meant hurting both the American economy and American workers met with near universal condemnation. The *Observer*[4] reports that protests against the United States erupted across European capitals, with calls for boycotts against United States oil companies. President Bush also faced mounting opposition at home. Britain's Deputy Prime Minister John Prescott accused the United States of 'free-riding' on the rest of the world and sitting in 'glorious isolation'. Efforts of States to institute national amnesty laws that seek to expunge criminal and/or civil liability of agents of a prior regime alleged to have violated basic human rights of individuals often meet with international judicial and political opposition.

Often, States that resort to amnesty laws that purport to expunge criminal and/or civil liability of agents of a prior regime alleged to have violated basic human rights of individuals as a means of addressing their horrific past manifest a desperate wish to move away from that past, and to establish a more peaceful and secure future for all. But often, such desperation evidences also governmental anxiety and nervousness that generate needless confusion over what standards to apply to that horrific past. South Africa's Interim Constitution (1993) as amended by the 1996 Constitution (the Constitution), itself a legal document, recommends mingling of ecclesiastical and positive law traditions in dealing with criminal wrongs that are the legacy of apartheid. Premised on the need to forgive rather than to seek retribution, South Africa's amnesty law (1995) incorporates into positive law God's law of forgiveness.

> 'Put on therefore, as the elect of God, holy and beloved, bowels of mercies, kindness, humbleness of mind, meekness, longsuffering; Forbearing one another, and forgiving one another, if any man have a quarrel against any: even as Christ forgave you, so also do ye.'[5]

Putting aside an inherent assumption of the ecclesiastical tradition, that everyone in the concerned State subscribes to, or is sympathetic to Christian teaching,[6]

---

[3] *Observer*, Sunday 1 April 2001.
[4] Ibid.
[5] *King James* Holy Bible 3 Colossians 12–13.
[6] The *raison d'être* of Tutu's thesis in *No Future Without Forgiveness* (1999) is that humanity is fulfilled when victims of human rights abuses put forgiveness before their own right to pursue perpetrators in law courts.

it appears extravagant for any nation caught up in such circumstances to allow international opinion to affect determination of what option to pursue for three reasons.

First, concerned States are eager speedily to separate their grim past from their tomorrows. Perhaps only they are best placed to identify the country's vision of the future and to unite it with various streams of sentiment and thought circulating within the populace. In particular, they are perhaps best placed to determine how crimes attributable to agents of a prior government should be dealt with.

Secondly, history may judge harshly the concerned State if it squanders the opportunity decisively to fathom a political process that offers an escape route from the path of bitterness and counter-recriminations to that offering stability, peace and respect for human rights and the rule of law. Rule of law does not denote here Aristotle's 'rule of reason'. Rather, it denotes Montesquieu's notion of presence in the State structure of institutional restraints that prevent governmental agents from oppressing the rest of society.[7] The escape route theory recommends abandonment of investigation and prosecution of persons for offences of a previous government where it is likely to endanger the new political agenda. Its proponents usually refer to the need to 'heal the wounds of the nation' and to 'steer the nation to economic and social stability'. For this reason, national strategies for dealing with the horror of the past should be privileged over international ones. If the concerned State chooses to seize the opportunity and to apply it to extinguish discord from its lips, no one else, it appears, should challenge that choice.[8] This argument was rehearsed several times over in Britain following Spain's request on 16 October 1998 for extradition of Senator Pinochet Ugarte on charges of murder and torture alleged to have been committed by him while head of State of Chile.[9] It is an argument whose strength is not diminishing. In response to Carla Del Ponte's, the United Nations chief war crimes prosecutor, request to extradite Slobodan Milosevic to The Hague where he is charged with committing crimes against humanity during his presidency of Yugoslavia, Vojislav Kostunica, the new President and friend of Western countries, stated first that Yugoslavia did not recognise the tribunal's jurisdiction, and secondly that Milosevic would be

---

[7] See Dyzenhaus, D. (1999) 'Recrafting the Rule of Law', in Dyzenhaus, D. (ed.) *Recrafting the Rule of Law: The Limits of Legal Order*, Hart Publishing, Oxford, p.1.

[8] Tutu argues that they have 'remarkably short memories' those that think otherwise because they forget that negotiated settlements, particularly South Africa type ones, evidence divine intervention. Tutu, D. (1999) *No Future Without Forgiveness*, Rider, London, p.25.

[9] See Chigara, B. (2000) 'Pinochet and the Administration of International Criminal Justice', in Woodhouse, D. (ed.) *The Pinochet Case: A Legal and Constitutional Analysis*, Hart Publishing, Oxford, p.115.

charged with offences alleged against him in Yugoslavia under Yugoslavia's own laws.[10]

But the escape route theory raises also serious questions about the relationship between law and politics. In particular, the collectivisation of individuals' wounds into national wounds whose care is dictated by governmental rather than concerned individuals' wishes is difficult to sustain normatively. By what process do breaches of individual people's fundamental human rights become wrongs against the State so that government legally becomes competent to pardon those breaches? Devolution of individual strength to the community, which progressively occurred with emergence of State systems and judicial systems, supposed a fairer resolution of disputes between agents of a community and not amnesia, which weaker agents in the primitive setting had always had to accept whenever they had been violated by an agent much stronger than them. Besides, the particular new government may not enjoy the support of the majority of the victims on whose behalf it purports to forgive agents of a prior regime alleged to have made them victims of breach of human rights positively recognised under both national and international law. Individualism is the quintessential product of modernity. 'Modern philosophy, political thought, and economic theory all point toward and revolve around the individual. Modern political and economic institutions like liberal democracy and free-market economy were designed to safeguard and to reward the individual.'[11] The positive law of international human rights that has followed adoption by the United Nations General Assembly in 1948 of the Universal Declaration of Human Rights places incomparable premium on individualisation of the said rights.

In modern parlance States are predicated over some constitution of one sort or another. Some of these constitutions have evolved over a long time and some are much younger than the antique furniture around which they were negotiated. Some are written while others are unwritten. What matters is not the differences a comparison of different national constitutions manifests but the fact that in the contemporary world States use constitutions to constitute both their political climates and legal perspectives. They are the basis for social order. To borrow from Fernandez-Arnesto, 'There is no social order without trust and no trust without truth or, at least, without agreed truth

---

[10] 'War Crimes Prosecutor in Frosty Talks with President', *Guardian*, 24 January 2001. But five months later, Yugoslavia passed a new law to enable it to transfer suspects to the ICTY. See 'Way Cleared for Milosevic Trial', *Sunday Times*, 24 June 2002.

[11] Chaibong, H. (2000) 'The Cultural Challenge to Individualism', *Journal of Democracy*, vol. 11 No. 1, p.127. Discussing the work of the United Nations Human Rights Committee in relation to the right of individuals to communicate directly their grievance to the Committee and not through institutions of a State, see Ghandhi, P. R. (1998) *The Human Rights Committee and the Right of Individual Communication: Law and Practice*, Ashgate, Aldershot.

finding procedures.'[12] It is difficult to think of a State in the modern world that does not have a constitution that provides for processes that are key to establishing certainty. Thus some commentators talk of forensic factual truth that is verifiable and documentable; social truth or the truth of experience that is established through interaction, discussion and debate; and personal truth or the truth of wounded memories.[13] The options on which society depends 'such as mutual respect, adhesion to contracts, obedience to laws, devolution of individual strength to the community – have to be commented on convincing grounds'.[14] For almost all countries of the world, the constitution itself is that commendatory force because it is a legal instrument that provides generally for substantive and procedural management of State affairs, including the enactment of laws. However, the constitution is also a political instrument that embodies and evangelises political aspirations of a nation. Ultimately, it separates the legal from the illegal in matters of the State. It is this tenuous dichotomy of the constitution as a political instrument for the formatting of State institutions on the one hand, and the constitution as the source of legality for the executive and other organs of the State that exercises the relationship between the 'legal' and the 'political' to the extent that separation is possible, desirable and facilitatory to understanding of the question of amnesty laws as previously described. This dichotomy is exacting particularly in situations where the constitution authorising the particular national amnesty laws is itself a change in the basic norm.[15] The Constitution of South Africa is such an example. One political plank in that constitution is section 20(7) which expunges both criminal and civil liability of all agents of the previous regime alleged to have violated basic human rights. This provision is intended to facilitate the political process of 'transcending the divisions and strife of the past, which generated gross violation of human rights, the transgression of humanitarian principles in violent conflicts and a legacy of hatred, fear, guilt and revenge'.[16] It is intended politically to conjure potential for South Africa to escape from the path of bitterness and recrimination. One legal plank in that constitution is section 22 which provides that 'every person shall have the right to have justiciable disputes settled by a court of law or where appropriate, another independent or impartial forum'. In the *AZAPO Case* the claimants identified opposition of the political aspiration of the

---

[12] Fernandez-Arnesto, F. (1998) *Truth, a History and a Guide for the Perplexed*, Black Swan, London, p.3.

[13] See Tutu, D. (1999) *No Future Without Forgiveness*, Rider, London, p.33.

[14] Fernandez-Arnesto, F., note 12 above, at p.3.

[15] See *AZAPO Case*, Case CCT 17/96. The claimants' case centred on the legality of South Africa's amnesty law of 1995 as provided for by the constitution to the extent that it violated Article 22 of the constitution which refers to positive legal basic human rights of individuals.

[16] See epilogue of the Interim Constitution (1993) as amended by the Constitution of 1996.

constitution to transcend divisions and strife of the past (section 20(7)), to the basic positive legal right of all individuals in South Africa to exercise the right to have justiciable disputes settled in a court of law (section 22). The claimants argued that the consequences of section 20(7) were inconsistent with the legal guarantees of section 22 of the Constitution of South Africa to the extent that:

(1) the Amnesty Committee was neither 'a court of law' nor 'an independent or impartial forum' and that
(2) the committee was not authorised to settle 'justiciable disputes', it having authority merely to decide whether amnesty should be granted in respect of a particular act, omission or offence.[17]

When provisions of the constitution result in a tension between positive legal rights of individuals on the one hand, and political aspirations of the government on the other, there arises a need to reconcile the two. The constructivist approach suggests that the conception of justice in periods of political change is extraordinary and constructivist. Thus, justice 'is alternately constituted by, and constitutive of, the transition. The conception of justice that emerges is contextualised and partial: What is deemed just is contingent and informed by prior injustice.'[18] This approach creates semantic and conceptual problems with the nature of justice. It is when we start to talk about shades of justice and to qualify justice with superlatives and adjectival phrases that we embrace in whole, that there is a risk of confusing the content of that which is signified by 'justice'. We risk jeopardising legitimacy of vital concepts when we transform them by adding to them lexical nuances that change totally their content, and yet insist that they are still consistent with their formerly established notions. Add a little pink to red paint or a little blue to white paint and still try to pass it off as originally described. This violation of concepts violently accentuates as justice that which is not consistent with previously established notions of justice.[19] Even more, it risks compromising enjoyment in all communities, basic standards of human rights and civility aspired for by the authors of the Universal Declaration of Human Rights[20] which was adopted by the United Nations General Assembly on 10 December 1948. Constructivist notions of justice that do not acknowledge the violence they inflict on the idea of justice previously held are notoriously problematic. They imply that the standards of

---

[17] *AZAPO Case*, Case CCT 17/96, para.8. Tutu writes that, 'When it came to hearing evidence from victims, because we were not a criminal court, we established facts on the basis of a balance of probability.' Tutu, D. (1999) *No Future Without Forgiveness*, Rider, London, p.33.
[18] Teitel, R. G. (2000) *Transitional Justice*, Oxford University Press, Oxford, p.6.
[19] The libertarian notion of justice is premised on adherence to legal norms established by a community under a veil of ignorance. See Chap. 1 above.
[20] UN Doc. A/811.

justice that we hanker for ourselves in the West are beyond the purview of others that are located geographically farther away from us. They lend themselves to the service of forces bitterly opposed to creation of a universal human culture of human rights that is often traced back to the adoption of the Universal Declaration of Human Rights in 1948. Since then, numerous international and regional conventions and treaties have been concluded whose sole mission is to bring to fruition that universal culture of human rights. Governmental and non-governmental human rights groups daily work to advance this culture in all corners of the world. On the need to guard against retrogressive conformism, Martin Luther King Jr writes that:

> 'The hope of a secure and livable world lies with disciplined nonconformists, who are dedicated to justice, peace, and brotherhood. The trailblazers in human, academic, scientific, and religious freedom have always been nonconformists. In any cause that concerns progress of mankind, put your faith in the nonconformist!'[21]

Justice is properly understood as fairness.[22] Fairness occurs when a community's previously set standards are applied whenever conduct of agents of that community falls within their sphere of operation. Selective application of previously established standards corrodes legitimacy of the rules themselves because predictability is lost about when they will be applied and when they will not; and consistency is lost too about their application. Standards of fairness that are context specific as opposed to context unspecific lose iterability. *Iterability* refers to a *signifier's* ability to signify repeatedly in a number of different contexts. Linguists[23] write that we benefit from using signs if, and only if, they are separable from our intent; and if, and only if, they mean, whether we intend it or not, what they mean. In this sense, language as a series of symbols of communication *signifies* only if it can escape the actual present meaning it had to the person who used it. Therefore, justice means justice only if it does not have to be modified to suit contexts that add on to it superlatives or any other form of qualifier. Otherwise, it becomes *incommensurate*. *Incommensurate* signifiers have mistakable, often confusing meanings.

Thirdly, the norm on self-determination[24] appears to guarantee governments the right to pursue within their territories policies that are consistent

---

[21] King, M. L. Jr (1981) *Strength to Love*, Collins Fount Paperbacks, Philadelphia, p.26.

[22] For discussion of Rawls' theory of justice as fairness, see Chap. 1 above.

[23] See Derrida, J. (1982) *Margins of Philosophy* (translated by Alan Bass), University of Chicago Press, Chicago, p.317.

[24] See UN Res. 1514 (XV) of 14 December 1960. The declaration, in conjunction with the United Nations Charter, supports the view that self-determination is now a legal principle. It is credited with accelerating the pace of the process of decolonisation witnessed after the Second World War. See also Cassese, A. (1995) *Self-determination of Peoples: A Legal Appraisal*, Cambridge University Press, Cambridge.

with their perceived political destiny. But as one of the principles of the United Nations often credited with asserting in the field of human rights the rights of national groups,[25] it would be perverse to suggest that it confers on governments the right to choose for their people the path of injustice and human rights abuse over that of justice and respect for human rights. Ultimately it is that choice that distinguishes legitimate governments from illegitimate ones in modern international law.[26] However, desperation, anxiety and pressure that attend the concerned State's immediate context, coupled with hope, even blind hope of strands of its population on what will be achieved, and how soon that will be, make intervention of international opinion necessary. Moreover, international opinion could not be regarded as a total outsider, it having shared in the nation's horrific past by encouraging and supporting the concerned nation's restorative forces' struggle against tyranny.[27] State practice suggests that the concerned State's previously suspended membership of the international community is restored immediately the rule of law and respect for human rights are restored to the fore of governmental policy.[28] Restoration to the international community of the formerly recalcitrant State commits the State to applicable standards of customary international law whose regime on protection of basic human rights of individuals is compelling.[29] Thus, what

---

[25] See Brownlie, I. (4th ed. 1995) *Basic Documents in International Law*, p.307: 'although its precise ramifications are not yet determined, the principle has great significance as a root of particular legal developments'.

[26] See Roth, B. R. (2000) *Governmental Illegitimacy in International Law*, Oxford University Press, Oxford, pp.1–16. The question today is whether international life is indicative of a nascent customary norm requiring democratic governance. See Marks, S. (2000) *The Riddle of all Constitutions: International Law, Democracy, and the Critique of Ideology*, Cambridge University Press, Cambridge, pp.101–120.

[27] The work of the United Nations' Diplomatic Mission to end civil wars for majority rule in Rhodesia, South Africa, Namibia and several other places is well documented. Economic and cultural sanctions imposed on governments of those countries by the Security Council of the United Nations during their disturbances are well documented.

[28] 'After the election we South Africans found that the coming of democracy and freedom to our land served to open doors that had previously been slammed shut. Now the international community that had treated us as a pariah State threw open its arms to us. We were welcomed back into the Commonwealth in a deeply moving ceremony and church service in Westminister Abbey in London, when the new South African Flag was carried into the sanctuary to join those of other Commonwealth lands. The sporting world, which had in most cases boycotted us, put out the red carpet of welcome.' Tutu, D. (1999) *No Future Without Forgiveness*, Rider, London, p.6.

[29] Arguing that the idea that the consent of States forms the source of the court's jurisdiction is a mischievous attempt to clothe the doctrine of consent with a cloak bigger than its stature, see Chigara, B. (2001) *Legitimacy Deficit in Custom: A Deconstructionist Critique*, Ashgate, Aldershot, p.44. The Statute of the International Court of Justice bestowed once and for all time jurisdiction of the court over all contentious cases. States merely recognise that jurisdiction when they accept to refer to the court their disputes. Further, arguments that new members of the United Nations should be handed a clean slate so that they can pick and choose what pre-existing rules they will be bound by have not changed practice on the matter. The occasion of taking up membership with the United Nations is itself a demonstration that the new member accepts the common rules of the organisation regardless of the fact that it did not have the opportunity to contribute to their creation.

might first appear as international intervention in inquiring about how a State addresses atrocities of a prior regime is actually mere affirmation by the international community that the formerly errant State has been restored fully into the community of nations based on its desire and acceptance to uphold international human rights law. For this reason, the international community is well placed to seek to affect what a State emerging from authoritarian rule does regarding human rights abuses of the tyrannical regime. It is perhaps determination of the rules of engagement between the particular State and the 'outside world' that concerns us here because that issue links up with the wider question whether international law authorises or prohibits national amnesty laws that purport to expunge criminal and/or civil liability of agents of a prior regime alleged to have violated basic human rights of individuals. Attribution theory alerts us to the equivocal tensions unleashed when the 'outsider' or 'bystander' intervenes to direct the action of one involved in a particular situation – the 'insider' or 'active participant'.

ATTRIBUTION THEORY AND INTERNATIONAL LAW AS THE 'BYSTANDER' WHERE EXPRESSION OF STATE DISCRETION CHALLENGES *OPINIO COMMUNITATIS*

Attribution theory deals with how people make causal explanations about how they answer questions beginning with 'why?' For instance, why expunge human rights abuse offences of apartheid and not prosecute them? If apartheid is a crime against humanity[30] is the Truth and Reconciliation Commission the answer to its legacy in South Africa? Attribution theory deals also with the quality of information used to arrive at causal inferences, and with what people do with this information to answer causal questions.[31] In this sense attribution theory is about 'the processes by which man "knows" his world and, more importantly, *knows that he knows*, that is, has a sense that his beliefs and judgments are veridical'.[32] Kelley locates the basis of the attributor's claims on the amount of information available to them and identifies two categories of attributors, namely, multiple and single observation attributors. The multiple observer premises his thesis on the several opportunities had to observe and to respond to the co-variation between an observed effect and its possible causes while the single observer relies on limited experience to arrive at a causal explanation. For instance, a couple's causal attributions to

---

[30] See International Convention on the Suppression and Punishment of the Crime of Apartheid, GA Res. 3068 (XXVIII) (1973).
[31] See Kelley, H. H. (1973) 'The Process of Causal Attribution', *American Psychologist*, vol. 28, p.107.
[32] Ibid.

breakdown of their marriage on the one hand, and the couple's neighbours' attributions based on what they perceived of the couple usually are irreconcilable. Any couple has more information than anyone else does on the state and quality of their own relationship. They are perhaps their own best counsellors on how to preserve or save their marriage from collapse. The neighbours' attributions as to what may have caused a couple's marriage to fall apart is coloured with their own prejudices, expectations and attitudes towards marriage failure. Further it is limited only to what they may have empirically observed of the couple. But not all of the probable co-variants to the collapse of the marriage are susceptible to empirical observation. For instance, the fear of the mind that x which reminds a party to the marriage of unpleasant experience y may have been central to the decision to end the couple's relationship, rather than say blatant philandering of one of the couple, although x by its very nature is not vulnerable to empirical observation. In short, not all the factors known to the active participant are amenable to the bystander. If we accept that the government granting amnesty to agents of a prior regime alleged to have violated basic human rights is the knowledgeable 'insider' to the concerned State's material affairs, then international opinion on amnesty takes the place of the bystander when the question is asked about how a State addresses atrocities of a prior regime. However, this is an imperfect characterisation of the actors. Given that the United Nations Charter's biggest concern is the maintenance of peace and security in the world, no situation can ever be said to be distant or remote from the international community, particularly if it involves violation of peace and security of a community. Therefore, it may be harsh to regard it as a mere bystander and outsider to the atrocities that are the subject of the amnesty. Because of its interest in the peace and security between and within nations, the United Nations is equipped with knowledge of the concerned State's affairs that is superior to that of the ordinary bystander. But possession of knowledge that is superior to that of a bystander alone does not equate the United Nations with the active participant itself – the State in terms of affinity to the issues involved. In our example, perhaps the United Nations fits the description of a marriage counsellor, to whom the couple took their problems. But only a foolhardy marriage counsellor would claim that they ever establish 'everything there is to know' about their clients to enable them a definite attribution and not a tentative one on why the couple's marriage might have failed. In fact, honest and humble counsellors will confess the difficulty involved in any attempt to isolate the reason why a couple's marriage might have failed. In short, the counsellor's view of the concerned marriage is never as sharp and as clear as that of the couple itself. Besides, a counsellor does not prescribe to the couple to quit or not to quit the marriage. Their function is limited to giving advice with the final decision-making resting with the couple itself. Relations between ethnic groups in any State are much more complex than relations between a couple so that no matter how detailed the United Nations' knowledge of a particular State may be, its role in counselling a State regarding whether it should grant amnesty to agents of a prior regime alleged to have violated basic human rights of individuals still should be approached with absolute humility. However, questioning of amnesty laws of some countries[33] by both powerful member States of the United Nations, and by treaty based human rights institutions[34] suggests a prescriptive rather than a recommendatory function of the United Nations on the question of national amnesty laws that purport to expunge criminal and/or civil liability of agents of a prior regime alleged to have violated basic human rights of individuals. One reason for this may be that international law does not allow national law to be used as a defence to breach of international standards. Amnesty for breach of basic human rights of individuals benefits directly persons alleged to have violated basic human rights of individuals, and usually comes in the form of a decree or Act of Parliament. When the legality of such a decree or such an Act of Parliament is questioned under the international law of treaties, arguments of attribution theory, however persuasive, fall short. Article 46(1) of the Vienna Convention on the Law of Treaties (VCLT) (1969) provides that:

'A State may not invoke the fact that its consent to be bound by a treaty has been expressed in violation of a provision of its internal law regarding competence to conclude treaties as invalidating its consent unless that violation was manifest and concerned a rule of its internal law of fundamental importance.'

This rule is of much greater antiquity than its treaty origins in that it reflects also customary international law. In 1827 Great Britain could not rely on the absence of domestic legislation as a sufficient justification for its failure to honour its obligations of neutrality in the American Civil War.[35] In *Texaco v Libya*[36] it was stated that a State cannot plead before an international court that its national laws authorised it to conduct itself in a manner that consequently violated international law. The result is that when a State's conduct falls within the sphere of operation of a rule of international law, it must fulfil that obligation regardless of whether its national law authorises or forbids it so to do.[37] But does this automatically rule out national amnesty laws that

---

[33] Peru's, Haiti's, Chile's and El Salvador's amnesty laws have all been severely questioned by political opinion and several judicial bodies, including the Inter-American Court of Human Rights and the United Nations Human Rights Committee.

[34] See Chap. 4 above.

[35] See *Alabama Claims Arbitration* (1872) Moore 1 Int. Arbitration 495.

[36] (1977) 53 ILR 389.

[37] See also, Kelsen, H. (1934) 'The Pure Theory of Law: Its Method and Fundamental Concepts, Part I', *Law Quarterly Review*, p.475; Dixon, M. (3rd ed. 1996) *Textbook on International Law*, Blackstone Press, London, p.79.

purport to expunge criminal and/or civil liability of agents of a prior regime alleged to have violated basic human rights of individuals if those amnesties are constituted by national constitutions such as the Chile and South Africa ones? Not if the amnesty law is of 'fundamental importance'. Paragraph (2) of Article 46 of the VCLT defines national law of fundamental importance as law that 'would be objectively evident to any State conducting itself in the matter in accordance with normal practice and in good faith'. Insistence on application of an objective test to application of this exception to the general rule precludes default resort by States to national laws that are inconsistent with international laws. South Africa's constitution is predicated on the need to reconcile all sections and all ethnic groups of the population. Mahomed stated in the *AZAPO Case* that:

'This fundamental philosophy is eloquently expressed in the epilogue to the Constitution which reads as follows: This Constitution provides a historic bridge between the past of a deeply divided society characterised by strife, conflict, untold suffering and injustice, and a future founded on the recognition of human rights, democracy and peaceful co-existence and development opportunities for all South Africans, irrespective of colour, race, class, belief or sex.

The pursuit of national unity, the well-being of all South African citizens and peace require reconciliation between the people of South Africa and the reconstruction of society.

The adoption of this Constitution lays the secure foundation for the people of South Africa to transcend the divisions and strife of the past, which generated gross violations of human rights, the transgression of humanitarian principles in violent conflicts and a legacy of hatred, fear, guilt and revenge.

These can now be addressed on the basis that there is a need for understanding but not for vengeance, a need for reparation but not for retaliation, a need for ubuntu but not for victimisation.

In order to advance such reconciliation and reconstruction, amnesty shall be granted in respect of acts, omissions and offences associated with political objectives and committed in the course of the conflicts of the past. To this end, Parliament under this Constitution shall adopt a law determining a firm cut-off date, which shall be a date after 8 October 1990 and before 6 December 1993, and providing for the mechanisms, criteria and procedures, including tribunals, if any, through which such amnesty shall be dealt with at any time after the law has been passed.

With this Constitution and these commitments we, the people of South Africa, open a new chapter in the history of our country.'[38]

---

[38] Case CCT 17/96, para.2.

To the extent that the epilogue of the Constitution emphasises thoroughly the need for post-apartheid South Africa to be guided by the spirit of reconciliation, it is difficult to maintain the view that the principle of reconciliation is not a 'fundamental' pillar of the Constitution, and, therefore, a justifiable exception recognised under Article 46 of the VCLT. The Constitution derives its general tenor and complexion from this philosophy. It is its soul and *raison d'être*. It appears, therefore, that where a national amnesty law is attributable to a manifest 'fundamental law' of the State, the concerned State may without incurring international responsibility violate a rule of international law opposable to its domestic law of such importance. Thus, although international law prohibits national amnesty laws that purport to expunge criminal and/or civil liability of agents of a prior regime alleged to have violated basic human rights of individuals, South Africa type national amnesty laws appear to be acceptable exceptions to that prohibition because they are the constitutional basis on which concerned nations predicate themselves. South Africa type national amnesty laws are not a novelty of recent times. Ancient Graeco–Roman traditions applied them in particular situations in spite of their inherent weakness of sacrificing basic human rights. Of course those cultures did not operate under the guidance of the Universal Declaration of Human Rights and the human rights regime that has emerged after it. Examination of how other traditions before us dealt with similar issues provides invaluable and instructive insight into how we should address the same issues in our own time. On the complex nature of traditions, Glenn writes that:

> 'Most of the tradition which has been captured and retained is aimed at the good or well-being of entire communities, and the largest and greatest of traditions have been directed at very large communities, if not humanity in its entirety. *All of these great traditions generate opposition within themselves, aimed at improvement or transformation of the tradition. There may also be competing traditions which provide alternative advice or models for the same community. There are other traditions, however, which do not seek to play a major role for an entire community, and do not seek its good or well-being. They are parasitic traditions, living off a larger one and profiting from its adherents in a way antithetical to their welfare and well-being.*'[39]

Therefore, traditions are neither static nor temporally exclusive, but dynamic and temporally cohabitative with less dominant or more dominant others. As such, reference to other traditions is problematic because it gives the false impression of control of a singular gigantic tradition at any one time. Often, it ignores the interaction of the target tradition with its opposite others. Grasping of the potential effect on our analysis and its conclusions of these issues

---

[39] Glenn, H. P. (2000) *Legal Traditions of the World*, Oxford University Press, Oxford, p.25. Emphasis added.

facilitates achievement of a reliable examination of how others attempted to resolve similar problems. Glenn[40] defines tradition as information. He distinguishes information from its uses and characterises it as non-dominating on us, but advisory. But that offer to us of advice by information does not absolve us from the responsibility of deciding what to do. 'In particular we always have to decide exactly how the advice applies to our particular problem.'[41] This way we are able to live our lives forwards, but relying also on what lies behind us, what the Chinese call 'cherishing the past in order to understand the future'. It is not intended here to consider how every known legal tradition[42] might deal or might have dealt with the issue whether or not to prosecute agents of a prior regime alleged to have violated basic human rights of individuals. The issue is whether we can discover from looking at the Graeco–Roman tradition, the Common Law tradition and the Human Rights tradition the reasons for accepting or rejecting national amnesty laws that seek to expunge criminal and/or civil liability of agents of a prior regime alleged to have violated basic human rights of individuals. The Graeco–Roman tradition is considered because of its antiquity. The human rights tradition that dominates contemporary world politics and seeks to influence every legal tradition in existence is indicative of legal *opinio communitatis*. Because it emerged after considerable domination in different parts of the world of the Judaic tradition, the Christian and Islamic traditions, it reflects in a peculiar way the experiential harvest and synthesisation of all four traditions and any others that may have been linked to them. It is as instructive to the question whether national amnesty laws that seek to expunge criminal and/or civil liability of individuals alleged to have violated basic human rights of individuals are acceptable or not as it is summative of the traditions that helped form it, influence its emergence and recommend it.

GRAECO–ROMAN TRADITION

The occasion and purpose of granting national amnesty were crucial and served to enhance legitimacy of the amnesty. The occasion of instituting an amnesty itself derived from either internal or external circumstances such as party strife or impending invasion by a foreign power. The need among States to be competitive for economic reasons as well as the need to belong to the category of civilised nations predominate concerns of all States in the modern world. South Africa's amnesty law (1995) occasioned by inauguration of a

---

[40] Ibid. p.45.

[41] Ibid.

[42] For detailed analysis of the Chthonic legal tradition, the Talmudic legal tradition, the Islamic legal tradition, the Hindu legal tradition and the Asian legal tradition, see Glenn, note 39 above.

new constitution and intended to facilitate creation of a culture fundamentally different from the previous one manifests these concerns. There are parallels between South Africa's amnesty law (1995) and the amnesty law promulgated by Trasybulus in 403 BC and extended to the Eleusinians in 401 BC in that like the latter amnesty it was designed to 'implant unity and harmony in diverse political factions'.[43] What makes amnesty laws so attractive in spite of their apparent opposition to the emerging universal culture of human rights is their potential to unite a people against outside foes. Dorjahn writes that before the Persian invasion and after the invasion of Chaeronea, Athens granted amnesty to her wayward subjects in order that she might oppose her maximum strength to the dangers threatening from without.[44] South Africa, like all other nations, has to compete in the globalising economy. To be successful, it must be able not only to secure markets abroad for its goods, but also attract foreign investment. Globalisation is compelling all States to prostitute themselves to multinational companies. Often this involves sacrificing workers' rights, particularly trade union rights and relaxing of worker welfare regulations. Political tension and strife are hardly the right incentives for market forces to operate in.

Amnesty was also often imposed from outside by a victorious foe on the vanquished nation for the purpose of restoring to good standing all citizens who might have compromised themselves during the war. Therefore, there is a long history of foreign governments imposing on another State a legal regime for the protection of its own subjects. Ancient Athens is reported to have given six amnesty decrees.[45] Political forgiveness for crimes including treason has a long history too. Nonetheless, longevity of practice alone is no justification. There has to be more than just longevity. There has to be justice. For it is in justice that people have learnt to bury their hope.[46] The quest for justice is explained by current international practice of questioning the legality in international law of amnesty laws that seek to expunge breach of basic human rights of individuals by agents of a previous regime, and of accepting some amnesty laws and rejecting others.

THE POSITIVE HUMAN RIGHTS LAW TRADITION

Among other treaty based United Nations human rights supervisory instruments,[47] work of the Human Rights Committee of the United Nations (HRC)

---

[43] Dorjahn, A. P. (1946) *Political Forgiveness in Old Athens*, AMS Press, New York, p.1.
[44] Ibid.
[45] Ibid.
[46] See Chap. 1 above.
[47] These include the United Nations Committee against Torture, the United Nations Committee on the Elimination of Racial Discrimination and the United Nations Human Rights Commission.

evidences a fundamental decline of monolithic perceptions of sovereignty and a strengthening of the idea of shared sovereign competence in modern international law. Established under Article 28 of the International Covenant on Civil and Political Rights (ICCPR), the HRC has competence to determine claims regarding violations of rights granted under that Covenant.[48] The fact that the ICCPR is one of the United Nations' most widely ratified instruments potentially broadens the reach of the Committee's work and subjects more governments to accountability. The Regional Human Rights regimes for Europe, Africa, and the Americas all accord individuals the right to seek extraterritorial redress for alleged human rights violations.[49] More than half a century after adoption of the Universal Declaration of Human Rights State practice, writings of publicists,[50] judicial decisions of national[51] and international tribunals,[52] and efforts of non-governmental organisations point to affirmation of the view that there are positive legal rights that inhere in the status of being human.[53] Breach of these rights incurs international responsibility. National amnesty laws are incapable without international consent to expunge that responsibility. Because national amnesty granted to agents of a previous regime alleged to have violated basic human rights of individuals seeks both:

(1) to release persons alleged to have violated basic human rights of individuals from civil and criminal liability, and

(2) to set to zero previously declared positive legal rights of individuals,

---

[48] See as examples, *Rodger Chongwe v Zambia* (2000) (Communication No. 821/1998), UN Doc. CCPR/C/70/D/821/1998; *Ameer Keshavjee v Canada* (2000) (Communication No. 949/2000), UN Doc. CCPR/C/70/D/949/2000; *Barry Hart v Australia* (2000) (Communication No. 947/2000), UN Doc. CCPR/C/70/D/947/2000; *Alexander Padilla and Mr Ricardo III Sunga (legal counsel) v The Philippines* (2000) (Communication No. 869/1999), UN Doc. CCPR/C/70/D/869/1999; *El autor v Alemania* (2000) (Communication No. 808/1998), UN Doc. CCPR/C/70/D/808/1998; *Dimitry L. Gridin v Russian Federation* (2000) (Communication No. 770/1997), UN Doc. CCPR/C/ 69/D/770/1997; *Larry Salvador Tovar Acuna v Venezuela* (1999) (Communication No. 739/1997), UN Doc. CCPR/C/65/D/739/1997.

[49] See Chap. 4 above.

[50] Vincent writes that: 'The idea that human beings have rights as humans is a staple of contemporary world politics. International conventions, both global and regional, state it, at length and in relation to a large number of rights. People speaking for States proclaim it. Groups other than States assert it in its collective form, sometimes as a way of becoming States themselves, sometimes as a bid for recognition of their group-ness by States. Non-governmental organisations make its observance their *raison d'être*. Individuals in *extremis* appeal to it. Reporters presume it. And scholars try to make sense of it...' Vincent, R. J. (1986) *Human Rights and International Relations*, Cambridge University Press, Cambridge, p.7.

[51] See *AZAPO Case*, Case CCT 17/96; *Ex parte Pinochet Ugarte (No. 3)* [1999] 2 WLR 827, HL.

[52] *Prosecutor v Tadic* (1997) IHRR, vol. 4, p.645; *Prosecutor v Jean-Paul Akayesu*, Case No. ICTR-96-4-T, Decision of 2 September 1998.

[53] See Milne, A. J. M. (1984) 'The Idea of Human Rights: A Critical Inquiry', in Dowrick, F. E. (ed.) *Human Rights: Problems, Perspectives and Texts*, Gower, Aldershot, p.23.

it is not surprising that so long after the adoption of the Universal Declaration of Human Rights national amnesty laws should be the subject of intense international scrutiny. The universal human rights tradition appears to have become contemporary world society's dominant culture. It fits with Glenn's purposive function of legal traditions, which is to identify and eliminate crime and criminal traditions.[54] It appears that State practice of challenging some amnesty laws and acquiescing with others points to the nascent stage of emergence of customary international law on the subject.[55] By its very nature, the process of custom is slow and cumbersome.[56] When the process of custom on this matter crystallises it is likely that international law will add to the gains of enforcing respect of human dignity developed in the last half-century by prohibiting for all time national laws that grant amnesty to agents of prior regimes that are alleged to have violated basic human rights of individuals. If any, exceptions to the rule will have to be construed very narrowly.

Linking to the constitution or even placing in the constitution such amnesty laws does not suffice to preclude international rejection of the proposed amnesty particularly if it is imposed on the new regime by the offending, outgoing regime.[57] Current practice shows that to gain international approval, national amnesty laws that purport to expunge criminal and/or civil liability of agents of a prior regime alleged to have violated basic human rights of individuals should pass what I shall call the VANPAJR test by which is meant that is should be shown that the national amnesty law:

(1) had been voluntarily adopted by the new regime, and not merely imposed upon it by the offending regime,[58]
(2) constituted a necessary pillar of the State's constitution or was a fundamental policy of the new administration,[59]
(3) was not an affront to contemporary standards and notions of justice in the light of developments since adoption by the United Nations General Assembly of the Universal Declaration of Human Rights and subsequent emergence of a universal culture of human rights,

---

[54] Glenn, H. P. (2000) *Legal Traditions of the World*, Oxford University Press, Oxford, p.25.

[55] Dugard writes that 'The present state of international law on the issue of amnesty is, *to put it mildly, unsettled.*' Dugard, J. (1999) 'Dealing with Crimes of a Past Regime. Is Amnesty Still an Option?', *Leiden Journal of International Law*, vol. 12, p.1000 at p.1015. Emphasis added.

[56] See Chigara, B. (2001) *Legitimacy Deficit in Custom: A Deconstructionist Critique*, Ashgate, Hampshire, p.56, n.102.

[57] Examples include Chile's amnesty which Tutu has described as an amnesty where 'General Pinochet and his officers and government forgave themselves: they alone knew what precisely they had done; they were the accused, the prosecution and the judges in their own case.' Tutu, D. (1999) *No Future Without Forgiveness*, Rider, London, p.30.

[58] On imposed and elective national amnesty laws, see Chap. 1 above.

[59] One from which no exceptions were intended or are permissible.

(4) everything considered, the amnesty was reasonable and did not violate norms *jus cogens*.

The first three requirements are discussed extensively in Chapters 1 and 2 above. For clarity's sake it is necessary to examine here the fourth requirement. It is also necessary to consider advantages to be had from insisting that all national amnesty laws that purport to expunge criminal and/or civil liability of agents of a prior regime alleged to have violated basic human rights of individuals should be codified in a legal instrument such as a constitution or a constitutive Act of Parliament. However, codification of national amnesty laws alone would not make legal under international law national amnesty laws that purported to expunge criminal and/or civil liability of agents of a prior regime alleged to have violated basic human rights of individuals.

(a) Requirement of reasonableness

The requirement of reasonableness in legal frameworks and in the formulation of particular procedural requirements appears semantically positive in that it identifies the law with logic and equality and not bias and subordination. Devolution of individual strength to the community supposes that those elected to exercise public authority on behalf of everyone else will in that effort act reasonably, respecting rules of natural justice and fairness. Only this premise makes less attractive blood feuds – primitive society's fashion of settling disputes among agents of a community. It is the premium for society's insurance against both tyranny and injustice. In *Associated Provincial Picture House Ltd v Wednesbury Corporation*,[60] Lord Greene stated that:

> 'When discretion of this kind is granted the law recognises certain principles upon which that discretion must be exercised, but within the four corners of those principles the discretion, in my opinion, is an absolute one and cannot be questioned in any court of law. What then are those principles? They are well understood. . . . The exercise of such discretion must be a real exercise of discretion. If, in the statute conferring discretion, there is to be found expressly or by implication matters which the authority exercising the discretion ought to have regard to, then in exercising the discretion it must have regard to those matters. Conversely, if in the nature of the subject-matter and the general interpretation of the Act make it clear that certain matters would not be germane to the matter in question, the authority must disregard those irrelevant collateral matters.'

However, application of the requirement of reasonableness is not without difficulty. The plaintiff in that case had challenged the reasonableness of a condition imposed on him in the exercise by the Corporation of discretionary

---

60 [1948] 1 KB 223.

power conferred by statute, very much like the challenge by some victims of apartheid[61] on the reasonableness of the executive's right to grant amnesty that expunges civil and criminal liability of agents of apartheid alleged to have violated basic human rights of individuals. The Court of Appeal stated that:

'It is true the discretion must be exercised reasonably. Now what does that mean? ... It has frequently been used and is frequently used as a general description of the things that must be done. For instance a person entrusted with discretion must, so to speak, direct himself properly in law. He must call his own attention to the matters which he is bound to consider. He must exclude from his consideration matters which are irrelevant to what he has to consider. If he does not obey those rules, he may truly be said, and often is said to be acting "unreasonably". Similarly, there may be something so absurd that no sensible person could ever dream that it lay within the powers of the authority. Warrington L. J. in *Short v Poole Corporation* [1926] Ch. 66, 90, 91, gave the example of the red-haired teacher, dismissed because she had red hair. That is unreasonable in one sense. In another sense it is taking into consideration extraneous matters. It is so unreasonable that it might almost be described as being done in bad faith; and, in fact, all these things run into one another.

... It is true to say that, if a decision on a competent matter is so unreasonable that no reasonable authority could ever have come to it, then the courts can interfere. That I think, is quite right; but to prove a case of that kind would require something overwhelming, and, in this case, the facts do not come anywhere near anything of that kind.'[62]

Whether matters on which discretionary decisions are predicated are relevant to the issue under consideration of a court appears to be a matter of conjecture. In *Associated Provincial Picture House Ltd v Wednesbury Corporation*,[63] it was held that once it is conceded that a reasonable authority exercising similar discretionary authority would also have had regard to such subject-matter as that on which the Corporation had predicated its decision, then the Corporation's determination assails the requirement of reasonableness.[64] Therefore, the question whether an amnesty law is reasonable ultimately depends on an abstraction: the reasonable man test. It is necessary, therefore, to establish the virtues at law of the reasonable man. Jones writes that:

'The reasonable man, being an abstraction, may be imbued with qualities that can rarely be consistently maintained in the real world. He is "free both from over-apprehension and from over-confidence" (*Glasgow Corporation v Muir [1943] AC 448, 457*), he anticipates the negligence of others where experience

---

[61] See *AZAPO Case*, Case CCT 17/96.
[62] [1948] 1 KB 223, *per* Lord Greene MR.
[63] [1948] 1 KB 223.
[64] Ibid.

suggests that it is common (*London Passenger Transport Board v Upson [1949] AC 155, 173*) he remains cool, calm and collected despite a sudden emergency. . . . He is, protested Sir Alan Herbert, devoid "of any human weakness, with not one single saving vice, *sans* prejudice, procrastination, ill-nature, avarice and absence of mind, as careful for his own safety as he is for that of others, this excellent but odious character stands like a monument in our courts of justice, vainly appealing to his fellow citizens to order their lives after his own example." '[65]

National amnesty laws are problematic for another policy reason. They deny victims expression of their humanity. It is as if victims' human dignity was never breached, and if it was, that their particular humanity was of no legal consequence. In this sense national amnesty laws that purport to expunge criminal and/or civil liability of agents of a prior regime alleged to have violated basic human rights of individuals propose application of the unacceptable caste system of ancient India which gave citizens varying levels of human dignity. The victim of human rights violation assumes the status of the lower human group with no right to pursue the perpetrators of the dehumanising treatment complained about in a court of law. In exchange, the victim supposedly is offered a future filled with peace and none of the experiences that led to his victimhood in the first instance. Perhaps this is the first folly to be observed in Sir Alan Herbert's excellent but odious man. He ignores the fact that he cannot guarantee peace to anyone. It has been said that humanity's enduring manifestations include war and peace. That, although we yearn for peace, we are ever ready to go to war. 'As much as peace cannot be realised and maintained by the mere force of decrees and moralistic rhetoric, war cannot be outlawed or abolished by law or politics. In many instances law and politics form part of the causes of war.'[66] This is amnesty's hope and the future's secret. Intrinsic to the requirement of reasonableness is also the requirement that justice must not only be done, but that it must be seen to be done – properly summed up in the notion of natural justice.

(b) Requirement of natural justice

Administrative laws of most jurisdictions insist on observance of requirements of natural justice where exercise of discretionary authority affects a person's rights, property or character;[67] and where it follows a procedure

---

[65] Jones, M. A. (5th ed. 1996) *Textbook on Torts*, Blackstone Press, London, p.146.
[66] Gutto, S. B. O. (1995) 'The OAU's New Mechanism for Conflict Prevention, Management and Resolution and the Controversial Concept of Humanitarian Intervention in International Law', *Proceedings of the African Society of International and Comparative Law*, vol. 7, p.348 at p.349.
[67] *Ridge v Baldwin* [1964] AC 40, *per* Lord Reid.

involving the confrontation of two opposing views in a manner resembling litigation.[68] The duty to act fairly subsumes and underpins the concept of natural justice. Aided by the rule against bias and the requirement of procedural propriety, it consistently targets justiciable outcomes. To use an English law example, it was stated by Lord Diplock in *R v Commission for Racial Equality, ex parte Hillingdon London Borough Council*[69] that whenever decisions are made that affect to their detriment the rights of other persons or curtail their liberty to do as they please, it is presumed that the administrative body should act fairly towards them. Even where an executive body does not need to conduct an adversarial hearing before it reaches a decision, 'it must act fairly'.[70] It is difficult to imagine a harsher governmental requirement in a liberal society than one that curtails the right of victims of human rights abuse to challenge in law courts the authors and perpetrators of their suffering. For this reason, victims' reaction to amnesty laws that expunge both criminal and civil liability of agents of a previous government alleged to have violated their basic rights potentially is a very good indicator of the fairness of the particular amnesty law. The Constitutional Court of South Africa was exercised by a case challenging the constitutionality of the amnesty law of 1995. The case was collectively brought up against the State by four applicants representing one of South Africa's best known civil rights movement – the Azanian People's Organisation (AZAPO), Steve Biko's wife, Churchill Mxenge and Chris Ribeiro. This challenge to the validity of the amnesty law in question was followed with close interest by many that had an interest in the case. The impact of the decision on both local and international resentment of the amnesty law of 1995 remains to be seen. It may have prevented the opening of floodgates of similar challenges. Therefore, the extent of local rejection of South Africa's amnesty law of 1995 may never be known. However, the planning and collaboration of the four applicants in the *AZAPO Case* whose only link was aversion to the amnesty law should not be taken lightly. Dugard[71] writes that 'the amnesty legislation is not accepted by all. Its opaque origins and the understandable desire for retribution that persists in many quarters have made it the most controversial legislation of post-apartheid South Africa.'

The international community's reaction to national amnesty laws that set to zero previously determined positive legal rights of individuals potentially could serve as an indicator of fairness of such amnesty laws. Chile's amnesty

---

[68] *Durayappah v Fernando* [1967] 2 AC 337 at p.349. See also Bradley, A. W., and Ewing, K. D. (12th ed. 1997) *Constitutional and Administrative Law*, Longman, London, p.790.

[69] [1982] AC 779 at p.787.

[70] *Pearberg v Varty* [1972] 2 All ER 62.

[71] Dugard, J. (1997) 'Is the Truth and Reconciliation Process Compatible with International Law? An Unanswered Question', *South African Journal on Human Rights*, vol. 13 No. 2, p.258 at p.260.

decree of 1978 is arguably the most infamous amnesty law of the twentieth century. It has been scorned even by one of amnesty's most fervent advocates, Nobel Prize laureate Desmond Tutu. He writes that: 'I am a strong supporter of the recent extradition proceedings against General Pinochet. It would be quite intolerable that the perpetrator should decide not only whether he should get amnesty but that no one else should have the right to question the grounds on which he had so granted himself amnesty and for what offence.'[72] Decree 2191 of 18 April 1978 expunges criminal and civil liability of agents of the Chilean government for human rights violations occurring between 11 September 1973 and 10 March 1978 – the period when the bulk of crimes were committed.[73] It was not only Spain that wanted to try Chile's Augusto Pinochet for crimes against humanity, but several other European Union member States which joined in Spain's challenge of the Home Secretary's decision not to publish medical reports on which he had based his decision not to extradite Pinochet to Spain. Spanish, Argentinean, German and Ecuadorian courts have already investigated offences alleged to have been committed in Chile and Argentina by military defendants and seized their property.[74]

Judicial decisions of international human rights commissions and tribunals and foreign national tribunals are a good indicator of fairness of amnesty laws. Adjudicators who have not been caught up in the milieu which is the subject of proceedings may be better placed than those who were involved to be objective, impartial and unbiased.[75] The Inter-American Court of Human Rights examined the legality of Chile's amnesty decree of 1978 and concluded that it was incompatible with Chile's human rights obligations under the American Convention on Human Rights.[76] In the *Insunza Bascunan Case* (1990) and in the *Roma Mena Case* (1995) victims challenged the constitutionality of reasonableness of Decree 2191 of 18 April 1978. In both cases, the decree was ruled constitutional and not unreasonable. In the *Masacre Las Hojas v El Salvador*,[77] the Inter-American Court of Human Rights examined the legality of El Salvador's amnesty law of 1987 and concluded that the amnesty enjoyed by those responsible for the Las Hojas massacre of 22 February 1983 constitutes an ongoing and gross violation of human rights committed by the Salvadoran government, and that the amnesty law undermines the essence of the system of justice in El Salvador and the process of creating the

---

[72] Tutu, D. (1999) *No Future Without Forgiveness*, Rider, London, p.30.
[73] See Boister, N. and Burchill, R. (1999) 'The Pinochet Precedent: Don't Leave Home Without It', *Criminal Law Forum*, vol. 10, p.405 at p.407 n.6.
[74] Ibid. at p.441.
[75] See Cassese A. (1998) 'Reflections on International Criminal Justice', *Modern Law Review*, vol. 61 No. 1, p.1 at p.7.
[76] See IACHR Annual Reports (1985/6) at 193; (1997) at 512 and Report No. 25/98.
[77] Case 10.287, Report No. 26/92, IACHR OEA/Ser.L/V/II.83 Doc. 14 at 83 (1993).

necessary conditions for peace and democracy. The court held that the government of El Salvador had failed to comply with the obligation imposed upon it by Article 1 of the American Convention, to guarantee the free and full exercise of human rights and fundamental guarantees of all persons subject to its jurisdiction. In its comments on El Salvador (1994) the Human Rights Committee expressed grave concern over the adoption of the amnesty law, which prevents relevant investigation and punishment of perpetrators of past human rights violations and consequently precludes relevant compensation. In its view, this 'seriously undermines efforts to re-establish respect for human rights in El Salvador and to prevent a recurrence of the massive human rights violations experienced in the past. Furthermore, failure to exclude violators from service in Government, particularly in the military, the National Police and the judiciary, will seriously undermine the transition to peace and democracy.'[78]

In its comments on Peru (1996) the United Nations Human Rights Committee expressed concern at Peru's amnesty law of 14 June 1995. Decree Law 26,479 absolves from criminal responsibility and, as a consequence, from all forms of accountability, all military, police and civilian agents of the State who are accused, investigated, charged, processed or convicted for common and military crimes for acts occasioned by the 'war against terrorism' from May 1980 until June 1995. In the words of the Committee it makes it:

> 'practically impossible for victims of human rights violations to institute successful legal action for compensation. Such an amnesty prevents appropriate investigation and punishment of perpetrators of past human rights violations, undermines efforts to establish respect for human rights, contributes to an atmosphere of impunity among perpetrators of human rights violations and constitutes a very serious impediment to efforts undertaken to consolidate democracy and promote respect for human rights and is thus in violation of article 2 of the Covenant.'[79]

Further, the Human Rights Committee expressed serious concern in relation to the adoption by Peru of Decree Law 26,492 and Decree Law 26,6181, which take away the right of individuals to challenge in the courts the legality of Peru's amnesty laws that benefit agents of the government alleged to have violated basic human rights of individuals. The Committee stressed that national amnesty law cannot modify a State Party's international obligations under the International Covenant on Civil and Political Rights (1966). Although the Committee's comments were directed at Peru's obligations under

---

[78] UN Doc. CCPR/C/79/Add.34 (1994).
[79] UN Doc. CCPR/C/79/Add.67 (1996).

the Covenant on Civil and Political Rights which Peru ratified on 27 April 1978, because of the remit of these decrees, their overall effect raises also serious questions about Peru's legal obligations under the Convention against Torture and Other Cruel, Inhuman or Degrading Treatment or Punishment (1984) which is monitored by the Committee against Torture[80] and which Peru ratified on 7 July 1988. In particular it raises questions about Peru's obligations under Articles 2, 4 and 5 of the Convention. Article 2(1) directs State Parties to 'take effective legislative administrative, judicial or other measures to prevent acts of torture in any territory under [their] jurisdiction'. Derogation from this obligation does not appear to have been contemplated at all. In fact, it appears to have been prohibited. 'No exceptional circumstances whatsoever, whether a state of war or a threat of war, internal political instability or any other public emergency, may be invoked as a justification of torture.'[81] Thus, neither the effects of terrorist activity in Peru, internal disorder and violence nor the right of the State to take firm measures to protect its population against terror can be invoked by the State to justify the use of torture by agents of the State.[82] Article 2(3) places squarely at the feet of the perpetrator, and not on the organisation or institution they were associated with or whose policies they advanced, responsibility for torture. Article 4(1) directs all State Parties to ensure that all acts of torture are offences under their criminal law. Further, State Parties should ensure that these offences are punishable by appropriate penalties.[83] Article 5 directs State Parties to ensure judicial resolution of all cases of torture by taking necessary measures to establish their jurisdiction over offences of torture in cases where the alleged offender is present in any territory under their jurisdiction and they do not extradite him.[84]

---

[80] The Committee against Torture (CAT) is a treaty based instrument established in accordance with Article 17 of the Convention against Torture and Other Cruel, Inhuman or Degrading Treatment or Punishment. The CAT came into being when the Convention against Torture entered into force on 26 June 1987 after being unanimously adopted by the General Assembly of the United Nations. It is therefore one of the most recently established expert supervised bodies that monitor implementation by States of a United Nations Human Rights Instrument (UNHRI). The Committee holds two sessions annually to consider State reports, interstate and individual communications. Where the Committee receives reports that appear to indicate that torture is being systematically practised in the territory of the State Party, it may under an innovative procedure invite that State to co-operate in the examination of the information and submit its observations.

[81] See Article 2(2) of the Convention against Torture.

[82] Acknowledging that Peru was under the plague of terrorist activity, internal disorder and violence, see Human Rights Committee, Comments on Peru, UN Doc. CCPR/C/79/Add.67 (1996).

[83] See article 4(2) of the Convention against Torture.

[84] See Article 5(1)–(2) of the Convention against Torture. For application of this principle, and in particular the particular difficulties its application triggers, see *R v Bow Street Metropolitan Stipendiary Magistrate and Others, ex parte Pinochet Ugarte (No. 3)* [1999] 2 WLR 827, HL.

(c) Codification in official records

Confronted by the biggest election challenge from the united opposition alliance since he came to power in 1980, and with the fastest shrinking economy in the world, in 2000 President Mugabe required that white Zimbabweans must at the very minimum acquiesce with his governing ZANU (PF) Party, and not affiliate themselves with the opposition parties, because to do that would be to 'declare war' on his government that had extended to them a hand of reconciliation at independence rather than penalise them for the evils of apartheid Rhodesia.[85] This situation demonstrates the advantage of codified amnesty laws to uncodified ones. Zimbabwe type national type amnesty provisions are notoriously problematic mainly because they lack juridical force. They do not exist in such legal documents as national constitutions and constitutive Acts of Parliament. They are merely oral declarations of government policy with no legal documents to support their existence. Therefore, their only referral point is the public policy of the government of the day, and it appears that only while that government retains popularity with the electorate. President Mugabe's sudden declaration that whites could not participate in the political process of Zimbabwe unless it was within his ZANU (PF) party meant that he perceived a trading off between himself and all white Zimbabweans. A trading off never before brought into the open and perhaps not contemplated by the unsuspecting white community, that they individually and collectively owed President Mugabe the duty not to support for all time, political parties opposed to his ruling ZANU (PF) party and the duty not to take up membership of those political parties because his ruling ZANU (PF) party had done them a favour at independence from Great Britain in 1980 of not retaliating previous white victimisation of blacks during colonisation. This raises several dilemmas. Morally, it can not be correct to say that only white Zimbabweans benefited from the obvious harvests of reconciliation.[86]

---

[85] At 8pm of Tuesday 4 March 1980, Prime Minister elect of Zimbabwe, Robert Mugabe addressed the nation. Martin and Johnson note that it was a masterly display of statesmanship: 'He spoke of turning swords into ploughshares to rebuild the war-torn nation, *of the need of reconciliation and not recrimination* and he assured the whites that they had a place in the country – as Zimbabweans. He spoke of a coalition with ZAPU and the inclusion of "members of other communities whom the constitution has denied the right of featuring as our candidates" – he followed through by naming Rhodesian Front MP David Smith as Minister of Commerce and Industry, and Denis Norman, head of Commercial Farmers Bureau, as Minister of Agriculture. Mugabe assured his audience that "it is not our intention to interfere with pension rights", a particular concern of white civil servants . . . "Let us deepen our sense of belonging," he concluded, "and engender a common interest that knows no race, colour or creed. Let us truly become Zimbabweans with a single loyalty."' Martin, D. and Johnson, P. (1981) *The Struggle for Zimbabwe*, Zimbabwe Publishing House, Harare, pp.330–331.

[86] Writing that atrocities were committed on both sides during the protracted 16-year civil war for independence of Zimbabwe from Great Britain, see Chigara, B. (2001) 'From Oral to Recorded Governance: Reconstructing Title to Real Property in 21st Century Zimbabwe', *Common Law World Review*, vol. 30 No. 1, n.27.

Therefore, to impose on them the stigma of 'beneficiaries' of that country's policy of reconciliation so that they must be grateful and for that reason give back something determined by their benefactors alone suggests that there was never pursuit of national reconciliation in Zimbabwe, but an 'unspecified and unspoken' deal between President Mugabe and the white community, which only President Mugabe knew everything about, certainly not the white community. That deal was then 'specified and spoken about' when the President declared 20 years later in 2000 that white Zimbabweans were excluded from all future political processes of the country unless otherwise invited so to do by his ruling ZANU (PF) party, under its own terms.[87] President Mugabe stated that he would revoke Zimbabwe's national racial reconciliation policy, adopted at independence in 1980, because whites, backed by Britain and the United States, were trying to destabilise the country. 'Ian Smith and the whites who participated in the massacre and genocide of our people, those who fought against us, we shall try.'[88]

In the absence of constitutional provision of the said amnesty, and absence of constitutive Acts of Parliament, the aggrieved parties have nothing else to fall back on but flimsy evidence of a national amnesty policy that was but an 'unspecified and unspoken' deal between themselves and their President. This scenario offends all known universal notions of justice, freedom and human rights. Legally, the Universal Declaration of Human Rights (UDHR) (1948) which is often credited with setting off the march towards a culture of universal positive human rights holds that:

'Article 19:   Everyone has the right to freedom of opinion and expression; this right includes freedom to hold opinions without interference and to seek, receive and impart information and ideas through any media and regardless of frontiers.

Article 21:   Everyone has the right to take part in the government of his country, directly or through freely chosen representatives.'

In this connection see also Article 19(1)–(3) of the International Covenant on Civil and Political Rights (1966) which Zimbabwe ratified on 13 May 1991; Articles 5(c), 2(a) and 5(a) of the International Convention on the Elimination of All Forms of Racial Discrimination (1965)[89] which Zimbabwe acceded to

---

[87] See 'Mugabe Terror Moves from Farm to Factory to Continue Reign of Terror', *Guardian*, Monday 8 May 2000.

[88] 'Take Me to Court if You Dare, Smith Tells Mugabe', *Guardian*, Friday 27 October 2000.

[89] UKTS Misc. No. 77 (1969), Cmnd 4108. The Committee on the Elimination of Racial Discrimination established under Article 8 of International Convention on the Elimination of All Forms of Racial Discrimination is another treaty based United Nations human rights supervisory instrument that has jurisdiction under Article 14 to receive individual complaints and to seek and collate all the information it deems necessary to assess the complaint. See Communication No. 16/1999: Denmark. 08/05/2000. CERD/C/56/D/16/1999.

on 13 May 1991 and Article 10(1)–(2) of the African Charter on Human and Peoples' Rights (ACHPR) (1981). This stigmatisation of a minority group of the population by declaration of the President denies the group UDHR Article 21 rights. Further, it conflicts with Zimbabwe's obligation under Article 3(1) of the ACHPR which provides that: 'Every individual shall be equal before the law', a fundamental right whose importance is emphasised in the preamble in the following terms: 'fundamental human rights stem from the attributes of human beings, which justifies their national and international protection'. The President's requirement of the white community raises also concerns of a diagnostic nature. It implies that every white Rhodesian was so bad that but for the policy of reconciliation they all would have been condemned to jail if President Mugabe's government had preferred charges against them instead of the policy of national reconciliation at independence.

Whereas governmental policy can be changed at a moment's notice, constitutional provisions and constitutive Acts of Parliament require more than mere notice. In more democratic countries the process of amending or passing of constitutive Acts of Parliament that supersede previous constitutive Acts of Parliament is exacting, arduous and unpredictable. From this perspective, codified amnesty laws provide a fallback measure in situations such as the Zimbabwean one where 20 years later a desperate government imposes on members of the public conditions it considers necessary in order to balance out the score between itself and them. Persons rightly or wrongly accused of owing the government a duty not to do x because the government had earlier on turned a blind eye to their illegal conduct could always invoke that amnesty code to demonstrate that they owe no one a favour, and are as free as anyone else to enjoy all the rights enjoyed by ordinary members of their society, including association with a political organisation of their choice. However, that is not to say that amnesty laws will prevail over international prohibition merely because they are codified. Although they are codified, amnesty laws of the type promulgated in Peru and Chile have suffered both political and judicial rejection of the international community.

(d) Legality of amnesty laws under international law

With persistent and multifarious sources of political condemnation and judicial rejection, Peru/Chile type amnesty decrees fail the checklist on amnesty laws that could be accepted as exceptions to the rule. This is largely because they are imposed by a regime alleged to have violated basic human rights of individuals for the benefit of its own agents. Thus, they fail the test that acceptable exceptions ought to be the unfettered considered choice of the successor government. They also do not appear to represent fundamental policy of successor governments. The incumbent Chilean government has watched the courts strip Pinochet of his immunity after his return from London in 2000 and has carefully set out charges relating to human rights abuses alleged to have been committed while he was head of State. Thus, they fail also the test that such amnesty laws ought to refer to a fundamental policy of the successor government. They attract near universal political opposition, suggesting very strongly that they are an affront to contemporary notions and standards of justice. Thus, they fail the test that they must be consistent with contemporary notions of justice. Everything considered, due to their manifest unfairness, it cannot be said that they are reasonable. Thus, they fail the test of reasonableness.

Adorned by their advocates as the only way forward because of their potential to balance the requirements of justice, accountability, stability, peace and reconciliation,[90] Haiti/South Africa type amnesty laws are difficult to justify under the exception paradigm discussed above. Even though they may easily satisfy the first and second requirements of the checklist, it can not be said that they satisfy the last two requirements. Satisfying the first requirement in itself does not commend much because even where the amnesty is declared by the incoming administration, the United Nations Human Rights Committee is of the view that pre-amnesty human rights violations should still be investigated. In its comments on Haiti (1995), the Committee expressed its concerned over the effects of the Amnesty Act, agreed upon during the process which led to the return of the elected government of Haiti.

> 'despite the limitation of its scope to political crimes committed in connection with the "coup d'etat" or during the past regime, the Amnesty might impede investigations into allegations of human rights violations, such as summary and extra-judicial executions, disappearances, torture and arbitrary arrests, rape and sexual assault, committed by the armed forces and agents of national security services. In that connection, the Committee wishes to point out that an amnesty in wide terms may promote an atmosphere of impunity for perpetrators of human rights violations and undermine efforts to re-establish respect for human rights in Haiti and to prevent a recurrence of the massive human rights violations experienced in the past.'[91]

The argument that perpetrators could not be tried in a court of law for lack of evidence and because the statutes of limitation exclude from investigation and prosecution old cases does not suffice because on a theoretical level, crimes against humanity and crimes that constitute the legacy of apartheid are international crimes that are not constrained by national statutes of limitation. Prosecutions for violations of international law are issues beyond local

---

[90] Tutu, D. (1999) *No Future Without Forgiveness*, Rider, London, p.27.
[91] UN Doc. CCPR/C/79/Add.49 (1995).

contingency.[92] For this reason, there were arguments by some in the Standing Committee on the International Criminal Court Bill [Lords] that on a substantive level, customary international law established by the London Agreement and Charter of the International Military Tribunal (Nuremberg)[93] suggests that there is no time limit to prosecution of crimes of such gravity.[94]

TRUTH AND RECONCILIATION COMMISSIONS AND INTERNATIONAL LAW

Hayner's[95] work shows that effort has been made by some States to use truth commissions and truth and reconciliation commissions to resolve atrocities of a prior regime. Governments that have deployed this strategy have emphasised varying reasons for taking that approach. These include closing the book on the past; facilitating national reconciliation; separating the new government from the previous one that committed the atrocities; and highlighting a new era that emphasises observance of human rights standards.[96] The question is whether such a big requirement as 'marking a new era of human rights observance' is best marked by setting to zero the rights of victims of a government of terror. The question can also be asked whether 'reconciliation' can be born out of perceived fundamental injustice of victims of the reign of terror. If it is correct that prosecutions for violations of international law are issues beyond local contingency,[97] then the Statute of Rome setting up the International Criminal Court has extremely important consequences on the use of truth and reconciliation commissions as a strategy for dealing with violations of basic human rights of individuals. In its consideration of the International Criminal Court Bill [Lords] on 26 April 2001, the Standing Committee considered the implications for truth and reconciliation commissions of the International Criminal Court Bill [Lords]. Concern was expressed that because it is the purpose of the Statute of Rome to signal to dictators around the world that there will be no way out for leaders and their agents that engage in the very serious crimes specified in the statute:

---

[92] Orentlicher, D. (1991) 'Settling Accounts: The Duty to Prosecute Human Rights of Violations of a Prior Regime', *Yale Law Journal*, vol. 100, p.2537 at p.2547.

[93] Nuremberg Rules, in Agreement for the Prosecution and Punishment of the Major War Criminals of the European Axis, 82 UNTS 279.

[94] See also Convention on the Non-Applicability of Statutory Limitations to War Crimes and Crimes against Humanity, GA Res. 2391 (XXIII), Annex, 23 UN GAOR Supplement (No. 18) at 40, UN Doc. A/7218 (1968).

[95] Hayner, P. B. (2000) *Unspeakable Truths: Confronting State Terror and Atrocity*, Routledge/London, London.

[96] Ibid. p.24.

[97] Orentlicher, D. (1991) 'Settling Accounts: The Duty to Prosecute Human Rights of Violations of a Prior Regime', *Yale Law Journal*, vol. 100, p.2537 at p.2547.

'We are, in a sense, saying goodbye to truth and reconciliation commissions. We are putting future dictators and people who are guilty of certain crimes in the same position as the Allied powers deliberately put the leaders of Germany in 1943 by demanding unconditional surrender. The leaders of Germany and Japan knew that there would be no negotiated settlement. One can draw that analogy.'[98]

In support of the Bill, the Minister of State, Foreign and Commonwealth Office thought that the Bill would not curtail use of truth and reconciliation commissions as a device for addressing atrocities of a prior regime. Rather, threat strategy would where necessary be applied in tandem with investigation and prosecution of offences:

'the ICC will not prevent or block future truth and reconciliation commissions. . . . let us look briefly at the example of Sierra Leone. There, a special court that will work alongside the truth and reconciliation commission has been created with international support. The work of the two bodies will be complementary and they will not undermine each other in any way.'[99]

The Minister's comments are at best hopeful that the two strategies are mutually supportive. The fact is that they are not. Truth and reconciliation commissions depend, even as the South African, Chilean and Guatemalan experiences cited in the Minister's comment demonstrate, on the goodwill of those persons alleged to have committed the atrocities while prosecutions depend on the force of law. Truth commissions depend for their operational efficacy on offer of amnesty to those alleged to have violated basic human rights of individuals in exchange for disclosure by them of their involvement in committing atrocities. Punishment and not pardon of those found guilty of acts proscribed by law is the outcome. This functional opposition of the two approaches makes opposable to each other their respective dynamics, making the one the target of the other's effort. The future use of truth and reconciliation commissions in light of the setting up of the International Criminal Court may be in great doubt.

CONCLUSION

This chapter examined the place if any of amnesty as an exception to the general prohibition against amnesty laws that expunge civil and/or criminal liability of agents of a previous regime alleged to have violated basic human rights of individuals. It showed that although recorded amnesty dates as far back as 401 BC, and although the practice of granting amnesty may even be of

---

[98] www.publications.parliament.uk/pa/cm200001/cmstand/d/st010426/pm/10426s02.htm.
[99] Ibid.

greater antiquity than that, current State practice of acquiescing with some
amnesty laws and rejecting others makes questionable and uncertain the legality of amnesty laws that seek to expunge both criminal and civil liability of
agents of a prior regime alleged to have violated basic human rights of individuals. This chapter noted that State practice of challenging amnesty laws of
other countries and acquiescing with others points to three things. The first is
the domination over all other legal traditions that may be in existence of the
human rights legal tradition. The second is the stronghold on national discretion of *opinio communitatis*, what Brierly describes as a sentiment of shared
responsibility for the conduct of a common life that is a necessary element in
any society, and the necessary force behind any system of law, and the source
of strength of any legal system. The United States had a 'quick short sharp'
reminder of the strength of *opinio communitatis* when on 3 May 2001 it lost
its seat on the United Nations Human Rights Commission which it had held
since the creation of the Commission in 1947. Given the United States' 'power
to twist arms' its loss was attributed to 'widespread UN dismay over President
George W. Bush's environmental policies, including on global warming'.[100]
The third is the nascent stage of emergence in international law of customary
law on the matter. It also noted that more than half a century after adoption
of the Universal Declaration of Human Rights, the international community
is eager to question and challenge developments in other countries if they
oppose the growing culture of universal human rights. Therefore, as the process of custom crystallises, it is most probable that a fully fledged binding
norm of customary international law will result that adds rather than subtracts from the gains of the positive human rights law tradition, and prohibits
for all time national amnesty laws that purport to expunge criminal and/or
civil liability of agents of a prior regime alleged to have violated basic human
rights of individuals. The setting up recently of the United Nations Sierra
Leone Court, and adoption of the Statute of the proposed International Criminal Court[101] buttress rather than weaken earlier decisions of the United
Nations to set up *ad hoc* tribunals to prosecute offences against the whole of
humanity committed in the former Yugoslavia and in Rwanda.[102] It argued
that exceptions to the rule would have to be construed very narrowly. An
exception paradigm with a four-point checklist was suggested – the VANPAJR
model. Chile type national amnesty laws, which failed on each of the four
requirements of the VANPAJR model, are not sustainable under international
law. Although South Africa type national amnesty laws satisfy the first two

---

[100] 'US loses seat on Human Rights Body', *Financial Times*, Friday 4 May 2001.
[101] Rome Statute of the International Criminal Court, UN Doc. A/CONF.183/9 (1998).
[102] International Criminal Tribunal for Rwanda, Rules of Procedure and Evidence, UN Doc.
ITR/3/REV.1 (1995) entered into force 29 June 1995.

requirements of the VANPAJR model, they succumb to the last two, making them unsustainable under international law. The next chapter considers the future if any of national amnesty laws that purport to expunge criminal and/ or civil liability of agents of a prior regime alleged to have violated basic human rights of individuals.

6

POSITIVE HUMAN RIGHTS LAW TRADITION: EXCLUSION OF THE NATIONAL AMNESTY LAWS TRADITION?

INTRODUCTION

This chapter examines the scope of the positive human rights law tradition in relation to the national amnesty laws tradition that it dominates. The aim here is to determine the scope, if any, of the national amnesty laws tradition in international law's response to claims by some States of competence to grant amnesty to agents of a prior regime alleged to have violated basic human rights of individuals. It shall be shown that the positive human rights law tradition has diversified and become both encompassing and specialised to make vain any claims that the national amnesty laws tradition is applicable even as an exception to the dominant positive human rights law tradition. Few are the areas of human life, if any, that are still not protected generally or specifically through supervisory United Nations or regional treaty instruments. In fact, some writers refer to over-regulation in the effort of universal and regional organisations to promote and to encourage human rights observance.

PERSISTENT AND INCREASING UNIVERSAL FORCE OF THE UNITED NATIONS VERSUS INCONSISTENT, INTERMITTENT FORCE OF A HANDFUL OF STATES' DECLARATIONS OF NATIONAL AMNESTY LAWS

The United Nations is the universal organisation that is the hub of the positive human rights law tradition. Its constitution, the United Nations Charter (UNC) (1945), is based on the principles of the dignity and equality inherent in all human beings. States Parties to the Charter, basically all nations but one

(Switzerland)[1] have pledged themselves to take joint and separate action, in co-operation with the organisation, to promote and to encourage universal respect for and observance of human rights and fundamental freedoms for all, without distinction as to race, sex, language or religion. This is confirmed in numerous human rights declarations and conventions that the United Nations has sponsored since its creation in 1945. The United Nations General Assembly Declaration on the Right and Responsibility of Individuals, Groups and Organs of Society to Promote and Protect Universally Recognised Human Rights and Fundamental Freedoms (1999)[2] is the latest in a series of United Nations sponsored declarations that enlist support for promotion and observance of basic human rights of individuals. It authorises the broadest range of social agents in the fight against impunity where basic human rights of individuals are at issue. The argument that resolutions and declarations of the United Nations General Assembly (UNGA) are not so significant because they are not binding on States Parties is misleading because it exaggerates the insignificance of these declarations. Steiner and Alston write that:

> 'Of course the declaration will have solemn effects as the formal act of a deliberative body of global importance. Its subject matter, like that of the UDHR, may be of global importance. But when approved or adopted, it is hortatory and aspirational, recommendatory rather than, in a formal sense, binding.'[3]

While the UNC does not confer binding status on UNGA resolutions and declarations, it is often the case that the same resolutions and declarations set off the process of customary international law, resulting in the creation sometimes of both customary norms and treaty norms of international law on their subject-matter. This is illustrated by the process that resulted in the creation of the norm on the prohibition against all forms of racial discrimination. The International Convention on the Elimination of All Forms of Racial Discrimination (1965)[4] has its roots in the UNGA Resolution 1904 of 20 November 1963.[5] Brownlie[6] writes that this resolution, together with Resolutions 1780 (XVII) of 7 December 1962 and 1906 (XVIII) of 20 November 1963 were the precursors of the International Convention on the Elimination of All Forms of Racial Discrimination. This Convention is one of several United Nations sponsored human rights treaties with a treaty based supervisory organ. Therefore, it is of very great significance in the promotion and protection of basic human rights of individuals. Further, in its determination whether a new norm of

---

[1] Nauru, Kiribati and Tonga having joined on 14 September 1999.
[2] A/Res/53/144, 8 March 1999.
[3] Steiner H. J. and Alston, P. (1996) *Human Rights in Context*, Clarendon Press, Oxford, p.123.
[4] UKTS Misc. No. 77 (1969), Cmnd 4108. In force from 4 January 1969.
[5] For text see *American Journal of International Law*, vol. 58, p.1081.
[6] (3rd ed. 1983) *Basic Documents in International Law*, Clarendon Press, Oxford, p.302.

customary international law has emerged, in particular whether there is evidence of *opinio juris*, the International Court of Justice (ICJ) often resorts to UNGA resolutions and declarations.[7] The persistent effort of the United Nations to promote and to encourage universal respect for international human rights law has endeared, empowered and enabled the positive human rights law tradition to eclipse and dominate competing and parasitic traditions, including the national amnesty laws tradition. This contrasts sharply with the procedurally inconsistent and intermittent declaration of amnesty laws by national governments with the forlorn hope that the international community will accept their escape route theory.[8] Besides *de facto* amnesty laws such as the Chile one (1975), truth commissions such as the El Salvador one (1992), truth and reconciliation commissions such as the South Africa one (1995) and reconciliation policies such as the Zimbabwe one (1980) have peculiar dynamics that do not result in a common outcome for individuals concerned. This weakens their opposition to the dominant universal positive human rights tradition, making them parasitic traditions for regulation of violations of basic human rights of individuals by agents of a prior regime and appropriate targets of control of the positive human rights tradition.

THE POSITIVE HUMAN RIGHTS LAW TRADITION ECLIPSES AND COMPELS TO SUBMISSION COMPETING AND PARASITIC TRADITIONS

Allot[9] writes that the law is a mode of the self-constituting of a society. It is that which constitutes and manifests society's common interest and organises the making and application of law. The social function of the international legal system is manifest in its integration of subordinate legal systems through customary international law and treaty law and declarations of the UNGA, sometimes called soft-law. Positive international law's recognition of human rights that derive from the status of being human is the focus of the Universal Declaration of Human Rights (UDHR) (1948) which heralded the dawn of the positive human rights law tradition, and of several other international Conventions and treaties. Its preamble begins: 'Whereas recognition of the inherent dignity and of the equal and inalienable rights of all the human family is the foundation of freedom, justice and peace in the world . . .'. However, the essence of UDHR rights is weakened by the fact that the universe is

---

[7] See *Nicaragua Case (Merits)* ICJ Rep (1986) p.14. Discussing legitimacy deficit in the process of customary international law, see Chigara, B. (2001) *Legitimacy Deficit in Custom: A Deconstructionist Critique*, Ashgate, Aldershot.

[8] See Chap. 1 above.

[9] Allot, P. (1999) 'The Concept of International Law', *European Journal of International Law*, vol. 10, pp.31–50.

no society. It maintains no social structure or system to implement those rights. Despite the social appeal of such metaphors as 'family of man' or 'brotherhood of man' it is no State and has no constitution, no government, no legislature, no courts, no political parties, and no institutions of its own.[10] Therefore, the universal sphere of human rights protection must defer to other spheres, notably the international and the domestic spheres for protection and enjoyment of rights that it recognises as basic human rights that inhere in the status of being human.[11] Although the States that voted for the adoption of the UDHR did not ascribe its resolutions and declarations with legally bind-ing authority,[12] the achievements of the universal sphere should not be be-littled. First, it established the values that underpin *opinio communitatis*.[13] Therefore, it 'may properly be resorted to for the interpretation of the provi-sions of the Charter in the matter of human rights and fundamental freedoms'.[14] Secondly, it bestows superiority and dominance over other traditions on the positive human rights law tradition. Thirdly, it mandates the positive human rights law tradition with securing and safeguarding freedom, justice and peace in the world. For these reasons claims that the national amnesty laws tradi-tion serves to secure national peace and stability and to consolidate national freedom are an attempt to usurp authority of the positive human rights tradi-tion which is handsomely connected to the values that underpin *opinio communitatis*. Therefore, the national amnesty laws tradition must, like all usurpers, subject itself to the wrath of the proper authority – the positive human rights law tradition that dominates the universal, international and domestic spheres.

The international sphere of human rights law is credited with achieving fulfilment of the aspirations of the UDHR. Many rights declared in the Inter-national Covenant on Civil and Political Rights (ICCPR) resemble closely rights declared in the UDHR except that they are amplified in the former instrument. For example, Articles 14 and 15 of the ICCPR which set the minimum requirements for criminal trials appear to be an amplification of Articles 10 and 11 of the UDHR. To borrow from Friedman:

---

[10] Feinberg, J. (1973) *Social Philosophy*, Eaglewood Cliffs, Prentice Hall, p.85.

[11] Analysing the opposition of cosmopolitanism, world citizenship and global civil society to Aristotle's notion of *polis* and his argument that it is not possible to be human outside of the *polis* 'because a man who is incapable of entering into partnership, or who is so self-sufficing that he has no need to do so is not part of a state . . . he must be either a lower animal or a god', see Brown, C. (2000), 'Cosmopolitanism, World Citizenship and Global Civil Society', in Caney, S. and Jones, P. (eds) *Human Rights and Global Diversity*, Frank Cass, London, pp.7–24.

[12] On the recommendatory nature of UNGA decisions see Articles 11 and 12 of the UNC (1945). See also Jennings, R. and Watts, A. (eds) (9th ed. 1996) *Oppenheim's International Law*, Longman, London, pp.1001–1002.

[13] See Chap. 5 above.

[14] See Jennings, R. and Watts, A., note 12 above, at p.1002.

'human rights are a product of international action such as treaty negotiations and conference deliberations. Attempts at international protection have led to "discovery" and endorsement of the rights, bringing them down from the lofty heights of universalism and up from the normative instruments of the domestic sphere. It has largely taken the institutional and political capability of the "primitive", decentralised, pluralistic international community to infuse an operational existence into human rights.'[15]

The international sphere has become the midwife of the positive human rights law tradition. It has amplified UNC and UDHR provisions in several conventions, treaties and conferences, creating in the process treaty based supervisory instruments that monitor States Parties' compliance with protected rights. Examples of these treaties are considered below. The aim is to determine whether the dominant positive human rights law tradition allows the national amnesty laws tradition any space in the determination of the question whether national amnesty laws that expunge civil and criminal liability of agents of a State alleged to have violated basic human rights of individuals are legal or not.

TAMING IMPUNITY FOR VIOLATION OF BASIC HUMAN RIGHTS OF INDIVIDUALS: HUMAN RIGHTS TREATIES EMERGE THAT HAVE SUPERVISORY ORGANS

A deficit of UNGA declarations is that their recommendatory nature deprives them of capacity to create supervisory organs that monitor compliance with each particular recommendation. Because international conventions or treaties are the only way that States can consciously create international law[16] treaties have capacity to create supervisory organs that monitor States Parties' compliance with their obligations under the particular treaty or convention. Certainly, the United Nations' major human rights treaties have treaty bodies[17] that supervise States Parties' compliance with their obligations. This development has helped to draw recognised human rights provisions from the lofty heights of theory into the realm of application, entrenching further the positive human rights law tradition into national practice. An early example of this was the creation of the Committee on the Elimination of Racial Discrimination (CERD) by Article 8 of the International Convention on the

---

[15] See Nelson, J. J. and Green, V. M. (1980) *International Human Rights: Contemporary Issues*, Human Rights Publishing Group, New York, p.29.
[16] See Dixon, M. (3rd ed. 1996) *Textbook on International Law*, Blackstone Press, London, p.23.
[17] Except the International Covenant on Economic, Social and Cultural Rights (1966) whose supervisory mechanism was established by the Economic and Social Council after the Covenant had come into force.

Elimination of All Forms of Racial Discrimination (1965) for the purpose of supervising States Parties' application within their territories of rights protected under the convention.

(a) Monitoring of States Parties' compliance with their obligations under the International Convention on the Elimination of All Forms of Racial Discrimination (1965) by the Committee on the Elimination of Racial Discrimination

The International Convention on the Elimination of All Forms of Racial Discrimination (1965) came into force in 1969. Created to promote and to encourage States to adopt all necessary measures for the speedy elimination of racial discrimination in all its forms and manifestations, and to prevent and combat racist doctrines and practices in order to promote understanding between races and to build an international community free from all forms of racial segregation and racial discrimination,[18] the Convention established in Article 8 the Committee on the Elimination of Racial Discrimination (CERD). It is the first body created by the United Nations to monitor and to review States Parties' compliance with their obligations under a multilateral treaty. Article 9(1) of the Convention directs States Parties to submit to the CERD an initial report within one year of taking up membership of the Convention, on the legislative, judicial, administrative or other measures which they have adopted and which give effect to the provisions of the Convention. Thereafter, States Parties are obliged to submit to CERD periodic reports every two years and whenever else that the CERD so requests. This reporting strategy which is common to all treaty bodies compels States Parties, above all else, to acknowledge a potential human rights problem within their territories, to talk about it, to take measures to address it, and most of all to limit its impact on ordinary lives of ordinary individuals. It is a user-friendly strategy in that governments take the initiative to inform about their positive achievements to a committee that is keen to encourage them to ensure delivery of their Convention commitments.[19] It facilitates also the use of conciliation as a means of

---

[18] See preamble and Article 2 of the International Convention on the Elimination of All Forms of Racial Discrimination (1965).

[19] The European Commission Against Racism and Intolerance publishes periodically examples of 'good practices' to fight against racism and intolerance. See CRI(2000)19 on Fighting Racism and Intolerance in the European Media. Growing jurisprudence of the European Court of Human Rights demonstrates in part, permeation into regional and national institutions values promoted by the International Convention on the Elimination of All Forms of Racial Discrimination (1965) and the CERD to uphold human dignity of all persons. Discussing the Assenov Case, *Assenov and Others v Bulgaria*, No. 90/1997/874/1086, see Goldston, J. A. (1999) 'Race Discrimination in Europe: Problems and Prospects', *European Human Rights Law Review*, Issue 5, pp.462–483.

resolving disputes in the application of the Convention – Article 12. Secondly, Article 11 provides for inter-State complaints. If a State Party considers that another State Party is not giving effect to the provisions of this Convention, it may bring the matter to the attention of CERD. This strategy which is common to other United Nations human rights treaty bodies has the potential to facilitate enjoyment of Convention rights by adding on to the number of watchmen – something that deters anyone deciding whether or not to go against what is the norm. Thirdly, under Article 14(1) the communications procedure enables an individual or a group of persons who claim to be victims of racial discrimination to lodge with the CERD a complaint against a State Party. This is possible only where the State in question has declared that it recognises the competence of the CERD to receive such complaints. O'Flaherty[20] reports that by 1996 just 22 States had made the declaration accepting the Article 14 procedure. These included Algeria, Australia, Bulgaria, Chile, Costa Rica, Cyprus, Denmark, Ecuador, Finland, France, Hungary, Iceland, Italy, the Netherlands, Norway, Peru, Russian Federation, Saudi Arabia, Slovak republic, Ukraine and Uruguay. The potential of this vital tool to ensure protection of Convention rights is wasted on States Parties' shyness to accept it. By Article 14(2) States which have made the declaration may establish or indicate a national body within its national legal order which shall be competent to receive and consider petitions from individuals and groups of individuals within its jurisdiction who claim to be victims of violations of Convention rights if they have exhausted other available local remedies. The potential effect of this accounting strategy which is common to other United Nations human rights supervisory organs is wasted on the requirement that the State complained against must have recognised the CERD's competence so to do. Only those States Parties with exemplary race relations practices would be confident enough to submit themselves to this process. This leaves those States Parties where individuals and groups of individuals that would most benefit from its application unprotected by its capabilities.

Further, although the reporting procedures do not specifically refer to the role of NGOs, and although NGOs may not formally address proceedings, they have tremendous possibilities to inform proceedings. O'Flaherty[21] writes that NGOs may indicate their interest to the Secretariat once a State Party's report has been scheduled for consideration by the CERD. This declaration of interest should be accompanied by as much preliminary information as possible for transmission to the Country Rapporteur and other members. Their final written submissions should be filed with the CERD some weeks before

---

[20] O'Flaherty, M. (1996) *Human Rights and the UN: Practice before Treaty Bodies*, Sweet and Maxwell, London, p.105.
[21] Ibid. at pp.92–93.

the session. Alternatively, NGOs may send their submissions through the Geneva based Anti-Racism Information Service (ARIS), another NGO that facilitates transmission to and from the CERD. ARIS then summarises all the information clearly stating the sources of information forwarded to it and transmits it to CERD.

In keeping with its function of ensuring that rights guaranteed by the Convention are delivered to target individuals, in 1993 the CERD developed an early warning and urgent procedure[22] which enables it to examine State practice on the Convention in circumstances where a report was not pending from the target State Party, and where none was under consideration by the committee. The trigger for this procedure is merely concern of the CERD that there is actual or potential risk of breach of Convention rights by a State Party.[23] Once a State is placed under the early warning and urgent procedure, 'it remains indefinitely on the agenda of the (CERD) . . . and may receive attention at forthcoming sessions'.[24] This procedure potentially adds to the possibility of NGOs affecting the process by which CERD monitors compliance of States Parties' compliance with the Convention. The stigma of permanently being under the watch of the CERD is something that States Parties to the Convention may well wish to avoid. That psychological pressure on States Parties, although unquantifiable in real terms, contributes to the purpose of the Convention to promote human rights and to encourage human rights observance.

(b) Monitoring of States Parties' compliance with their obligations under the International Covenant on Civil and Political Rights (1966) by the Human Rights Committee

The United Nations Human Rights Committee (HRC) is an ongoing institution that gives institutional support to norms of the International Covenant on Civil and Political Rights (ICCPR), thereby allowing for the supervision of States' compliance with their obligations under the Covenant.[25] The Covenant and the first Optional Protocol provide for three separate procedures for supervision of State compliance with the ICCPR. The first is the HRC's duty to receive, study and comment on the reports submitted by States on:

(1) factors and difficulties that affect implementation of the Covenant,

(2) positive development that may have occurred for the period under review, and

---

[22] See UN Doc. A/48/18 Annex 3.
[23] O'Flaherty, M., note 20 above, at p.103.
[24] Ibid. p.104.
[25] See Steiner, H. J. and Alston, P. (1996) *Human Rights in Context*, Clarendon Press, Oxford, p.124.

(3) specific issues of concern that relate to application of provisions of the Covenant.

Upon taking up membership of the ICCPR, States automatically become subject to self-report procedure of submitting periodic reports to the Committee (Article 40(1)(a)). The first or initial report is submitted within the first year of ratification, and thereafter whenever the HRC so requests.[26] All reports are submitted through the office of the Secretary General of the United Nations who transmits them to the HRC for consideration.

Secondly, Article 40(1)(e) establishes the inter-State report mechanism which authorises the HRC to consider allegations by a State Party that another State Party is not fulfilling its obligations under the ICCPR. This promotes the view that international human rights law recognises that the basic human rights of individuals of any one State are not a matter for that State alone to determine, but of all States. States share a common responsibility to protect ICCPR rights of all human beings. Thus, the international community's interest in what happens to human rights of individuals anywhere in the world is a legitimate one. No longer can other States be regarded as attribution theory's bystanders when a State emerging from totalitarian rule decides the question whether or not to prosecute agents of the prior regime alleged to have violated basic human rights of individuals.[27] However, this jurisdiction of the HRC is governed by the principle of reciprocity, that is, that the Committee can only consider this type of communication where both States have declared that they recognise its competence to attend such communications. Thirdly, under the Optional Protocol, the HRC is authorised to attend to communications from individuals that claim to be victims of human rights violation by a State Party to both the ICCPR and the Protocol.[28]

The HRC supervises also States Parties' compliance with the requirement to institute a remedial mechanism for persons whose rights have been infringed.[29] A significant strength of the ICCPR is that it does not limit itself to setting a negative criteria for States not to interfere in certain ways with individuals. It charges States to 'develop and enforce a legal system adequate to respond to claims of violation. . . . duties of States parties are . . . both *negative/hands off* (don't torture) and *positive/affirmative* (provide a legal system to which individuals can have recourse in order to seek remedies for violations)'.[30] Aided

---

[26] For discussion of rules of procedure and HRC strategy in addressing State reports see Ghandhi, P. R. (1998) *The Human Rights Committee and the Right of Individual Communication*, Ashgate, Aldershot, pp.22–29.

[27] Discussing attribution theory, see Chap. 5 above.

[28] Discussing this function of the Committee, see Ghandhi, P. R., note 26 above, at pp.28–29.

[29] See Article 2 of the ICCPR.

[30] Steiner, H. J. and Alston, P., note 25 above, at p.125.

by the emergency procedure developed by the HRC in 1991,[31] this sword and shield approach of the Covenant appears to target for legal sanction breaches of human rights recognised under the ICCPR and to reject also national amnesty laws that seek to expunge criminal and civil liability of agents of a prior regime alleged to have violated basic human rights of individuals and leaving victims with no remedy. Because regulation of this sphere is one of the prime concerns of the positive human rights law tradition, which is also the dominant tradition, the national amnesty laws tradition must succumb to the former tradition. It is a parasitic tradition[32] and an object of attack for the dominant tradition whose purpose is to identify and eliminate crime and criminal traditions.[33] Considerable jurisprudence of the HRC that shows that ICCPR rights are having effect in most States across the world is discussed in Chapters 2 and 5 above.

(c) Monitoring of States Parties' compliance with their obligations under the International Covenant on Economic, Social and Cultural Rights (1966)

The Committee on Economic, Social and Cultural Rights (CESCR) is a subsidiary organ of the Economic and Social Council[34] (ECOSOC). Unlike the supervisory body of the ICCPR, which derives its formal authority from the constituent covenant, the CESCR derives its formal authority from ECOSOC. Created in 1985 following the less than ideal performance of two previous bodies entrusted with monitoring the International Covenant on Economic, Social and Cultural Rights (ICESCR) (1966), the CESCR met for the first time in 1987. The Committee currently convenes twice a year, holding two three-week sessions, generally in May and November/December. All its meetings are held at the United Nations Office at Geneva. The primary function of the CESCR is to monitor the implementation of the ICESCR rights by States Parties. Through dialogue with States Parties it seeks to determine through a variety of means whether or not the norms contained in the ICESCR are being adequately applied by States Parties and how the implementation and enforcement of the Covenant could be improved so that all people who are entitled to the rights enshrined in the Covenant can actually enjoy them in full. The Committee assists governments in fulfilling their obligations under the Covenant by issuing specific legislative, policy and other suggestions and recommendations targeted at facilitating enjoyment of economic, social and cultural rights. Articles 16 and 17 of the ICESCR direct States Parties to

---

[31] See O'Flaherty, M., note 21 above, at pp.45–46.
[32] See Glenn, H. P. (2000) *Legal Traditions of the World*, Oxford University Press, Oxford, p.25.
[33] Ibid.
[34] One of six principal organs of the United Nations.

submit periodic reports to the CESCR within two years of the entry into force of the Covenant for a particular State Party, and thereafter once every five years. In their reports, States are obliged to outline the legislative, judicial, policy and other measures which they have instituted for the period under review to ensure the enjoyment of the rights contained in the ICESCR. States Parties are obliged to provide also detailed data on the degree to which the rights are implemented and areas where particular difficulties have been faced in this respect. The CESCR has assisted the reporting process by providing States Parties with a detailed 22-page set of reporting guidelines specifying the types of information it requires in order to monitor effective compliance with the Covenant. Alston[35] writes that the reporting requirement is not merely a formalistic commitment. Although a large number of States often do not submit reports on time, the reporting mechanism has a number of important functions. 'Among these are the initial review function, the monitoring function, the policy formulation function, the public scrutiny function, the evaluation function, the function of acknowledging problems and the information-exchange function.' In its General Comment No. 1 (1989),[36] the Committee identified seven functional objectives of the reporting obligations under the ICESCR as:

(1) To ensure that a State Party undertakes a comprehensive review of national legislation, administrative rules and procedures, and practices in order to assure the fullest possible conformity with the Covenant.

(2) To ensure that the State Party regularly monitors the actual situation with respect to each of the enumerated rights in order to assess the extent to which the various rights are being enjoyed by all individuals within the country.

(3) To provide a basis for government elaboration of clearly stated and carefully targeted policies for implementing the Covenant.

(4) To facilitate public scrutiny of government policies with respect to the Covenant's implementation, and to encourage the involvement of the various sectors of society in the formulation, implementation and review of relevant policies.

(5) To provide a basis on which both the State Party and the Committee can effectively evaluate progress towards the realisation of the obligations contained in the Covenant.

(6) To enable the State Party to develop a better understanding of problems and shortcomings impeding the realisation of economic, social and cultural rights.

---

[35] Alston, P. (1991) 'The Purposes of Reporting', in *Manual on Human Rights Reporting*, United Nations Centre for Human Rights, United Nations Institute for Training, and Research, pp.14–16.
[36] E/1989/22, Annex III, General Comment No. I (1989), paras 2–9. See also www.uncchr.ch/html/menu6/2/fs16.htm.

(7) To facilitate the exchange of information among States Parties and to help develop a fuller appreciation of both common problems and possible solutions in the realisation of each of the rights contained in the Covenant.

While the ICESCR stresses the importance of group rights such as the right to self-determination of peoples (Article 1), equal rights for men and women (Article 3), protection of the family (Article 10(1)–(3)), parents and guardians (Article (13)(3)), the joint work of the CERD, the Human Rights Committee (HRC) and of the CESCR[37] shows that:

> 'The international human rights program is more than a piecemeal addition to the traditional corpus of international law, more than another chapter sandwiched into traditional textbooks of international law. By shifting the fulcrum of the system from the protection of sovereigns to the protection of people, it works qualitative changes in virtually every component.'[38]

Their effort is augmented by a growing number of treaty supervisory bodies, including the Committee against Torture (CAT), which monitors the Convention against Torture and Other Cruel, Inhuman or Degrading Treatment or Punishment (Torture Convention) (1984); the Committee on the Elimination of Discrimination against Women (CEDAW), which monitors the Convention on the Elimination of All Forms of Discrimination against Women (1979); and the Committee on the Rights of the Child (CRC), which monitors the Convention on the Rights of the Child (1989). The most recent such treaty, the International Convention on the Protection of the Rights of All Migrant Workers and Members of their Families, was adopted in (1990) but is yet to come into force.

Nonetheless, problems exist which question actual commitment of States Parties to enforce the rights that they declare in these conventions. While it has been proclaimed that all human rights are indivisible and universal, international law appears to have adopted different implementation standards for civil and political rights on the one hand and economic, social and cultural rights on the other. The ICCPR directs States Parties to respect and ensure observance of the rights therein (Article 2), while the States Parties to the ICESCR undertake merely to take steps to the maximum of their available resources, with a view to achieving progressively the full realisation of the rights recognised in the Covenant (Article 2(1)). The different commitments

---

[37] For further commentary see Craven, M. (1994) 'Towards an Unofficial Petition Procedure: A Review of the Role of the UN Committee on Economic, Social and Cultural Richts', in Drzewicki, K. *et al.* (eds) *Social Rights as Human Rights: A European Challenge*, Abo Akademi University Institute for Human Rights, Finland, p.91.

[38] Reisman, W. M. (1990) 'Sovereignty and Human Rights in Contemporary International Law', *American Journal of International Law*, vol. 84, p.866.

to civil and political rights which are to be granted immediately, and economic and social cultural rights which are regarded as aspirational goals to be achieved progressively, may lie in the fact that the former are generally characterised as negative rights that are cost free. To discharge their obligations under the Covenant, States merely have to refrain from doing those things that would amount to breach of Convention rights. Of course some civil and political rights, like the right to life (Article 6), require States to take substantial positive action which may be costly. However, the latter positively oblige States Parties to intervene positively by providing goods, services and facilities. Further, and to borrow from Van Bueren, civil and political rights are regarded as:

> 'suitable for judicial proceedings as they are seen as clearly definable rights attaching to a specific individual, whereas economic, social and cultural rights are regarded as more complex and unsuitable for court attention because any judgment in the applicant's favour would entail significant expenditure of resources. It is also widely believed in industrialised States that civil and political rights are concepts untainted by ideology, whereas economic, social and cultural rights are infused with political doctrine.'[39]

The aspirational and committal distinction between economic, cultural and social rights and civil and political rights recognises also the fact that enforcement of human rights occurs in particular contexts, where States have to make priorities because resources required for delivery of these rights are not uniformly distributed across the membership of the United Nations. Therefore, the largely cost free civil and political rights can be insisted upon immediately while the very costly economic, social and cultural rights can be pursued at each member State's own pace according to their capacity. Such a compromise does not suddenly make inferior one set of rights compared to the other, nor does it actually divide the rights referred to. Rather it acknowledges the practical reality of the present world.

(d) Monitoring of States Parties' compliance with their obligations under the Convention against Torture and Other Cruel, Inhuman or Degrading Treatment or Punishment (1984) by the Committee against Torture

The Committee against Torture (CAT) is a multilateral instrument for the supervision of the application of the Convention against Torture and Other Cruel, Inhuman or Degrading Treatment or Punishment (1984). Its main function is to ensure adequate protection for all persons against torture and other cruel, inhuman or degrading treatment or punishment. Established pursuant

---

[39] Van Bueren, G. (1995) *The International Law on the Rights of the Child*, Martinus Nijhoff, London, p.382.

to Article 17 of the Convention it began to function on 1 January 1988. The CAT met for the first time in April 1988 in Geneva and has established firm jurisprudence on the application of the Convention.[40] The CAT has broad powers to examine and investigate and determine State compliance with the Convention. Article 19 of the Convention directs each State Party to submit to the Committee, through the Secretary-General of the United Nations, reports on the measures implemented to give effect to obligations under the Convention. Each State Party must submit the initial report within one year after the entry into force of the Convention for the State concerned. Thereafter, supplementary reports on subsequent developments shall be submitted every four years. Further reports and additional information may also be requested by the Committee. The efficacy of the reporting mechanism has been enhanced by the guidelines given to States by the CAT. Unfortunately many of the countries where gross violation of torture is alleged are still not parties to the Convention, or the acts complained about may not be covered as they may have occurred prior to that particular State's ratifying the Convention. For example, Zimbabwe, which currently appears to have reverted to pre-legal primitive times,[41] and Haiti, Lesotho, the Democratic Republic of Congo (DRC), Yugoslavia, Malaysia, Pakistan and Rwanda, which have all recently been mired in situations most conducive to the practice of torture, are not parties to the Convention and therefore not subject to the State report mechanism of the CAT. South Africa conveniently became a party to the Convention on 10 December 1998. Therefore, the South African government's accountability to the CAT precludes any violations of previous years. Crimes of apartheid can still be considered under general international law.

The CAT has adopted a constructive approach to the actual examination of State reports. Representatives of the States Parties are invited to attend when their reports are considered. Where the CAT decides that a State must supply further information a State representative may attend when the Committee examines such further information. Such a representative should be able to answer questions which may be put to him or her by the Committee and clarify, if need be, certain aspects of the reports already submitted by his or her State. Article 19(3) of the Convention authorises the CAT to make such general comments on the report as it may consider appropriate. In particular the CAT indicates whether it appears to it that some of the obligations of the State have not been discharged as prescribed under the Convention. The CAT forwards its conclusions to the State Party, which in turn may reply to them. This conciliatory approach of the CAT is consistent with the overall objective of the United Nations to promote and encourage respect for observance of

---

[40] See Chap. 5 above.
[41] See 'Mugabe's Army Hands Out Guns', *Guardian*, Sunday 7 May 2000.

human rights of individuals. It achieves State submission to outside monitoring of its own practice in relation to treaty obligations. In a world where economic issues are increasingly determined by global forces, the need of States to appear 'clean' in their record of respect of human rights of individuals is increasingly perceived as a determining factor for foreign investors. Therefore, States are keen to be seen to co-operate with the CAT in fostering within their borders practice that is consistent with their obligations under these human rights treaties.

Article 20 of the Convention against Torture authorises the CAT to receive information and to institute inquiries concerning allegations of systematic practice of torture by States Parties. Confidentiality and co-operation govern this function of the CAT. The fact that it is optional and not compulsory further limits its potential to ensure compliance of States with their obligations under the Convention. The CAT may not exercise Article 20 competence where the target State Party has entered its reservation upon its applicability to it. Where States have accepted the procedure set out in Article 20 the CAT has competence to receive information concerning the existence of the practice of torture. If that information appears reliable and contains well-founded indications that torture is being systematically practised in the territory of a State Party to the Convention, the CAT may do one of two things or both. First, invite that State to co-operate in its examination of the information. Secondly, it may decide to request additional information either from the representatives of the State concerned or from governmental and NGOs as well as individuals to help itself form an opinion. Further, the CAT has competence:

(1) To attend inter-State complaints arising from States Parties that have deposited the declaration specified in Article 21. This authorises the CAT to attend communications in which a State Party alleges that another State party is not discharging its obligations under the Convention.

(2) Under Article 22 to receive communications regarding the violation of one or more of its provisions by a State Party from private individuals or on their behalf in certain circumstances. For the Committee to be able to admit and examine individual communications against a State Party, its competence in that regard must, however, have been expressly recognised by the State concerned. A State Party may at any time declare it recognises the CAT's competence to receive from individuals subject to its jurisdiction or on their behalf, complaints of torture under Article 22. A communication may be submitted by any private individual who claims to be the victim of a violation of the Torture Convention by a State Party which has accepted the competence of the Committee under Article 22. The Committee in closed meeting always examines individual complaints.

This wide range of supervisory competencies enjoyed by the CAT, coupled with the spirit of co-operation under which the CAT must intervene to promote and to encourage States Parties to comply with their obligations under the Torture Convention, and general concern of States to appear to be human rights friendly even for the purposes of wooing foreign investment and foreign aid go a long, long way to protect individuals across the world from torture. It also forges ahead dominance of the positive human rights law tradition and constrains parasitic traditions.

(e) Monitoring of States Parties' compliance with their obligations under the Convention on the Elimination of All Forms of Discrimination against Women (1979) by the Committee on the Elimination of Discrimination against Women

From its earliest days, the United Nations has been concerned with the status of women in a world community aspiring for equality in its broadest sense.[42] In 1946, the United Nations Commission on the Status of Women was established by the ECOSOC to prepare reports and recommendations to the Council on the promotion of women's rights in all spheres of life, and to develop recommendations and proposals for action on urgent problems confronting women. More recently, the same Commission was tasked with monitoring, reviewing and appraising the implementation of the Nairobi Forward-looking Strategies for the Advancement of Women adopted by the 1985 World Conference on Women.[43] Concern for the status of women has been boosted by recent research, which shows that:

(1) women are the majority of the world's poor,
(2) the number of women living in rural poverty has increased by 50 per cent since 1975,
(3) women are the majority of the world's illiterate,[44]
(4) women in Asia and Africa work 13 hours a week more than men and are mostly unpaid,
(5) worldwide, women earn 30 to 40 per cent less than men for doing equal work,
(6) women hold between 10 and 20 per cent of managerial and administrative jobs worldwide and less than 20 per cent of jobs in manufacturing,
(7) women make up less than 5 per cent of the world's heads of State, women's unpaid housework and family labour, if counted as productive

---

[42] See preamble and Article 1(2) of the United Nations Charter (1945).
[43] See www.unhchr.ch/html/menu6/2/fs22.htm.
[44] Estimates suggest that the number rose from 543 million to 597 million between 1970 and 1985.

output in national accounts, would increase measures of global output by 25 to 30 per cent.[45]

The UNGA adopted in 1979 the Convention on the Elimination of All Forms of Discrimination against Women. Premised on the prohibition of all forms of discrimination against women (Article 2), the Convention obliges States Parties to adopt particular positive measures to ensure that women enjoy Convention rights. By Article 17 the Convention establishes the Committee on the Elimination of Discrimination against Women (CEDAW) whose task is to monitor States Parties compliance with their obligations under the Convention. The Convention directs States Parties to submit an initial report within the first year of taking up membership (Article 18(a)) and periodically every four years thereafter, or whenever the CEDAW requests them so to do (Article 18(b)). As we have already seen[46] this strategy is consistent with the United Nations' general strategy of promoting and encouraging human rights observance and with the use of conciliation as a dispute resolution strategy. Article 22 broadens the category of persons or bodies that may submit communications to the CEDAW regarding a State Party's failure to comply with Convention obligations. Again this may serve as a deterrent for States considering violating Convention norms. In spite of problems such as States Parties' failure to submit their reports on time and perhaps over reliance on conciliation and the goodwill of States to comply with Convention rights, supervision of Covenant rights by the CEDAW entrenches further the positive human rights law tradition by focusing specifically on human rights that women must not be denied just because of their sex.

(f) Monitoring of States Parties' compliance with their obligations under the Convention on the Rights of the Child (1989) by the Committee on the Rights of the Child

Premised on the self-report mechanism, offer of technical advice and assistance to States Parties, but with no power to receive complaints, the Committee on the Rights of the Child (CRC), which was established under Article 43 of the Convention on the Rights of the Child (1989),[47] supervises implementation of the Convention. Article 44 directs States Parties to submit reports to the Committee on the steps taken to actualise convention rights and the enjoyment of those rights. The initial report is to be submitted within the first

---

[45] United Nations (1991) *The World's Women 1970–1990: Trends and Statistics*, United Nations Publication.
[46] Above.
[47] Van Bueren, G. (1995) *The International Law on the Rights of the Child*, Martinus Nijhoff, London, p.6.

two years of ratification and periodically thereafter every five years. Reports submitted to the CRC ought to indicate factors and difficulties, if any, affecting the degree of fulfilment of the obligations under the Convention (Article 44(2)). States may request CRC for technical advice or assistance on how to ensure delivery of convention rights to beneficiaries (Article 45(b)). This constructive, collaborative and co-operative approach to implementation of the Convention, coupled with the CRC's authority to involve in its work other specialised United Nations agencies and the United Nations Children's Fund (Article 454(a)), recommends States Parties' facilitatory rather than defensive approach to the Convention.

While shortcomings[48] can not be ruled out in operations where States appear to submit themselves to external supervision of their domestic standards, establishment of the treaty bodies that monitor high contracting parties' compliance with their obligations under the respective human rights conventions and covenants privileges above any other tradition the positive human rights law tradition. It underlines the unacceptability of approaches that seek to condone abuse of basic human rights of individuals. The setting up of the *ad hoc* Yugoslav and Rwanda tribunals in 1993 and 1994 respectively manifests, on the one hand, the charge of the positive human rights law tradition and, on the other, a deficit in the United Nations institutional provisions for enforcement of the human rights norms that it has created.[49] Nonetheless, it is testimony of the fact that under modern international law violation of basic human rights of individuals will not go unpunished. Watts writes that:

> Problems in this area – such as the non-existence of any standing international tribunal to have jurisdiction over such crimes and the lack of agreement as to what acts are internationally criminal for this purpose have not affected the principle of individual responsibility for international criminal conduct.[50]

In this connection, the adoption of the Statute of Rome establishing the International Criminal Court (ICC) (1998) is a much welcome step if ratification by the requisite number of States will result in the actual setting up of the court. On the whole, the setting up of the two *ad hoc* tribunals, the adoption of the Statute of Rome and, more recently, the creation of the United Nations Special Court for Sierra Leone tasked with prosecution of war criminals suggests that it is now settled in international law that the Nuremberg Principles

---

[48] For a more detailed consideration see Van Bueren, ibid. pp.388–399.

[49] Harris writes that these two tribunals are founded upon 'the insecure base of Security Council Resolutions': Harris, D. J. (5th ed. 1998) *Cases and Materials on International Law*, Sweet and Maxwell, London, p.752.

[50] Watts, A. (1994) 'The Legal Position in International Law of Heads of Governments and Foreign Ministers', *Hague Recueil*, 247, p.9 at p.81. Applied also by Lord Browne-Wilkinson in *Ex Parte Pinochet (No. 3)* [1999] 2 WLR 827 at p.846, HL.

regarding war crimes and crimes against humanity are custom wherever abuse of basic human rights of individuals is alleged. The Pinochet saga conducted in England starting in October 1998 and running through to January 2001 when finally the General was allowed to return home on medical grounds, instead of being extradited to Spain where he had been indicted with charges of torture and murders while head of Chile in the 1970s, illustrates international thinking on crimes that affect all of humanity, namely, that they should have a judicial and not a political resolution. Although the historical development of international law appeared initially to focus on the quality and dynamics of inter-State relationships, ultimately it is the individual who is the final beneficiary of the international legal system, a fact made more apparent by the increasing significance of the positive human rights law tradition through treaty bodies, *ad hoc* tribunals and other human rights agencies and organisations. The transformation of the status of the individual in international law is one of the most remarkable developments in international law.[51] This has happened largely through development of the positive human rights law tradition.

(g) Some issues on the monitoring by treaty bodies of States Parties' compliance with treaty obligations

Chapman[52] advocates for a more radical 'violations approach' to the monitoring of State Parties' compliance with their obligations under human rights conventions. This is important because:

(1) Submission of reports by States Parties for review by United Nations established bodies does not on its own mean that effective monitoring will take place.

(2) The exercise of monitoring State compliance is itself complex, exacting, and encumbered with numerous political and methodological prerequisites that the observatory and facilitatory approaches currently at work may not adequately address.

(3) The determination of which of the data that have been systematically gathered are relevant for analysis depends on translating the abstract legal norms into operational standards is an operational act that requires adequate conceptualisation and development to be able to measure implementation or to identify violations.

---

[51] Van Bueren, G., note 47 above, at p.378.
[52] Chapman, A. R. (1996) 'A "Violations Approach" for Monitoring the International Covenant on Economic, Social and Cultural Rights', *Human Rights Quarterly*, vol. 18 No. 1, p.23 at pp.24, 36.

Moreover, States' compliance with reporting requirements to some of the treaty bodies could be better.[53] To assist States Parties that are overdue in reporting, the Committee on the Elimination of Discrimination against Women (CEDAW) has adopted procedures by which States are allowed to combine reports. Because the CEDAW has the shortest meeting time of any treaty monitoring body (two weeks) a considerable backlog of reports has built up. There is now an average of three years between the time a State Party submits a report and the consideration of that report by the Committee. This is itself a disincentive to report and leads to the need for the State to present additional information to update its report.[54] Chapman writes that most of the reports that are submitted are very superficial and appear to be designed to camouflage rather than to reveal problems and inadequacies.[55] Therefore, the quality of advice given by treaty bodies in such cases is almost always hitting below deck. The fact that governments are loath to admit to violations of human rights compels anyone that is interested in the integrity and vitality of human rights review processes to look to alternative sources of information. Of these the work of non-governmental organisations (NGOs) is illustrious. The British Minister of State, Foreign and Commonwealth Office highlighted this in the Standing Committee on the International Criminal Court Bill [Lords] debate on 3 May 2001:

'I refer first to the role of non-governmental organisations . . . On 22 March 2001, in a speech before the United Nations Commission on Human Rights, I said: "I cannot over emphasise the importance of the positive contribution of NGOs to human rights . . . I believe they are our eyes and ears on the ground and the voice of our conscience. It is vital that we all give a hearing to and listen to that voice". Amnesty International, the Medical Foundation for the Care of Victims of Torture, Save the Children and other bodies have been involved in the background work to the clause [clause 49 of the ICC Bill [Lords]]. They are the eyes and ears on the ground and often draw the attention of the world to those victims who suffer as a result of gross war crimes and genocide. I pay tribute to those organisations. Throughout the negotiations on the Rome statute and during the preparation of the Bill, the Government have listened to the voice of NGOs.'[56]

The efficacy of treaty bodies that monitor States Parties' compliance with their obligations under human rights conventions is sometimes compromised by what Cohen[57] calls the classic discourse of official denial of reports of

---

[53] Cataloguing the record of failure to report on time, or to report at all, see O'Flaherty, M. (1996) *Human Rights and the UN: Practice before Treaty Bodies*, Sweet and Maxwell, London.

[54] www.unhchr.ch/html/menu6/2/fs22.htm.

[55] Chapman, A. R., note 52 above, at p.28.

[56] www.publications.parliament.uk/pa/cm200001/cmstand/d/st010503/pm/10503s01.htm.

[57] Cohen, S. (1996) 'Government Responses to Human Rights Reports: Claims, Denials, and Counterclaims', *Human Rights Quarterly*, vol. 18, p.517 at pp.522–534.

treaty bodies. In literal denial, State officials refute that anything of the sort mentioned in the report ever happened. Interpretive denial involves State officials arguing that what actually happened is really something else. Implicatory denial argues that what happened is of no consequence because it is justifiable. Cohen observes a tendency when denial is at play, of linking up the denial chain, starting with literal denial, and if it fails, moving on to interpretive denial, and if that fails, invoking implicatory denial. This has the potential of sapping the determination of litigants who would already have had to exhaust local remedies before engaging extraterritorial human rights bodies. One way of limiting official denial that has the potential of sapping victims' morale is to review the reporting strategies, so that it becomes less attractive for States to engage the denial route in the wake of a report of a treaty body. However, in spite of these difficulties it is indisputable that treaty bodies are impacting enjoyment of respective Convention rights in States Parties' territories.

Efficacy of treaty monitoring bodies could be enhanced if treaty bodies shared good practice targeted at facilitating timeliness and quality of States Parties' reports. This could be achieved for instance by standardisation of guidelines for reporting which would in turn reduce the administrative burden on States Parties. A uniform system of reporting would also increase the speed and efficiency with which the various committees could review and evaluate reports during their annual sessions. Training of government officials responsible for compilation of reports could also benefit monitoring of States Parties' compliance with their obligations. Chapman observes that often reports ignore requests found in conventions' reporting guidelines for specific types of disaggregation in reporting data. She writes that the Committee on Economic, Social and Cultural Rights (CESCR) which monitors State Parties Compliance with the ICESCR 'rarely receives data that differentiate between the sexes or that identify disadvantaged groups and minorities. Instead, countries present national averages that cloak gender differences and the problems of disadvantaged and vulnerable groups.'[58] In this regard, training courses on reporting under all major human rights conventions organised by the United Nations Centre for Human Rights as part of its technical assistance programme are a step in the right direction.

WHAT ABOUT IMMUNITY FOR ACTS DONE IN THE NAME OF THE STATE?

Jurisprudence of the Nuremberg and Tokyo trials, the Yugoslav and Rwanda *ad hoc* tribunals and of national courts, and policies adopted by national

---

[58] Chapman, A. R., note 52 above, at p.28.

assemblies regarding immunity from prosecution of persons alleged to have violated humanitarian law, both point to a narrowing of arguments in favour of pleading act of State doctrine or acting on 'superior orders' as a trigger to immunity. This development has as its centrepiece the ever-growing universal campaign to end the golden era of impunity for human rights abuse that has hitherto flourished.

(a) Immunity of a former head of State

If the position in international law on the immunity of heads of State, both serving and former, was unclear,[59] *R v Bow Street Metropolitan Stipendiary Magistrate and Others, ex parte Pinochet Ugarte (No. 3)*[60] has done much to clarify that position. The act of State doctrine,[61] which emerged from developments in international law that occurred between the seventeenth and nineteenth centuries, applied the representative character theory as the basis of both *personae materiae* and *rationae materiae* immunity. However, while still acknowledging the function of the representative theory, current trends[62] suggest a departure 'from the theory of absolute immunity towards a more restrictive doctrine which distinguishes between the private and public acts of a society by focusing on the nature of a particular act rather than its purpose'.[63] While

---

[59] As asserted by Warbrick, C. and McGoldrick, D. (1999) 'The Future of Former Head of State Immunity after *Ex parte Pinochet*', *International and Comparative Law Quarterly*, vol. 48 No. 4, p.937 at p.938.

[60] [1999] 2 WLR 827, HL.

[61] It is asserted that this doctrine gives effect to the principle that the 'courts of one State do not as a rule, question the validity or legality of the official acts of another sovereign State or the official or officially avowed acts of its agents, at any rate insofar as those acts involve the exercise of the State's public authority, purport to take effect within the sphere of the latter's own jurisdiction and are not in themselves contrary to international law', see Jennings, R. and Watts, A. (eds) (9th ed. 1996) *Oppenheim's International Law*, Longman, London, pp.365–366.

[62] Abandoning the traditional absolute immunity approach and embracing the limited immunity approach, see e.g. the European Convention on State Immunity 1972; the International Law Commission Draft Articles on Jurisdictional Immunities of States and their Property, provisionally adopted in 1986; the United States Holtzman Amendment (1987) which renders ineligible to enter the United States any alien who during the period beginning 23 March 1933, and ending on May 1945, under the direction of, or in association with:

(a) the Nazi government of Germany;

(b) any government in any area occupied by the military forces of the Nazi government of Germany;

(c) any government established with the assistance or occupation or co-operation of the Nazi government of Germany; or

(d) any government which was an ally of the Nazi government of Germany, ordered, indicted, assisted, or otherwise partcipated in the persecution of any person because of race, religion, national origin, or political opinion.

See Lippman, M. (1998) 'The Pursuit of Nazi War Criminals in the United States and in Other Anglo-American Legal Systems', *California Western International Law Journal*, vol. 29 No.1, n.2.

[63] Warbrick, C. and McGoldrick, D., note 59 above, at p.938. See also Jennings, R. and Watts, A., note 61 above, at pp.360–363.

personae materiae is immunity that derives from the status of the person whether as head of State or as diplomatic agent, *rationae materiae* resides in the nature of the act under scrutiny. Warbrick and McGoldrick write that the crucial aspect of immunity *rationae materiae*:

> 'is that the acts in question are deemed not to be the personal acts of the diplomatic agent or head of State. Rather, they are the acts of the State for which the individual cannot be held personally liable. . . . the first condition for the applicability of diplomatic immunity *rationae materiae* is that the act in question be official in its character. An act is official if it is performed by an organ of a State in his official capacity, so that it can be imputed to the State and regarded as an act of State.'[64]

Such acts cannot be imputed to the personal capacity of the head of State. Thus, *rationae materiae* subsists beyond the cessation of official functions of Heads of States.[65] Therefore, it may be necessary as a first step, to ascertain that the criminal acts alleged against a head of State or former head of State are not official acts etched with *rationae materiae* for all time and therefore not prosecutable. Writes Watts:

> 'A Head of State clearly can commit a crime in his personal capacity; but it seems equally clear that he can, in the course of his functions as a Head of State, engage in conduct which may be tainted by criminality or other forms of wrongdoing. The critical test would seem to be whether the conduct was engaged in under the colour of or in ostensible exercise of the Head of State's public authority. If it was, it must be treated as official conduct, and so not as a matter subject to the jurisdiction of other States whether or not it was wrongful or illegal under the law of his own State.'[66]

The question this raises is what amounts to official conduct of a head of State which is etched with *rationae materiae* for all time and therefore not prosecutable, and what does not. In *Ex parte Pinochet Ugarte (No. 3)* Lord Browne-Wilkinson stated: [67]

> 'The question then which has to be answered is whether the alleged organisation of State torture by Senator Pinochet (if proved) would constitute an act committed by Senator Pinochet as part of his official functions as head of State. Actions which are criminal under the local law can still have been done officially and therefore give rise to immunity *ratione materiae*. . . .

---

[64] Warbrick, C. and McGoldrick, D., note 59 above, at p.940.
[65] Ibid. p.941.
[66] Cited in Warbrick, C. and McGoldrick, D. (1999) 'The Future of Former Head of State Immunity after *Ex parte Pinochet*', *International and Comparative Law Quarterly*, vol. 48 No. 4, p.937 at p.942.
[67] [1999] 2 WLR 827 at p.846. Emphasis added.

Can it be said that the commission of a crime which is an international crime against humanity and *jus cogens* is an act done in an official capacity on behalf of the State? I believe there to be strong ground for saying that *the implementation of torture as defined by the Torture Convention cannot be a State function.*'

The strong ground for refuting the view that commission of a crime which is an international crime against humanity and *jus cogens* can be said to be an act done in an official capacity, and on behalf of the State, that Lord Browne-Wilkinson refers to appears to have been furnished in *Ex parte Pinochet Ugarte (No. 1)*[68] by Lord Nicholls who stated that:

'International law recognises, of course, that the functions of a head of State may include activities which are wrongful, even illegal, by the law of his own State or by the laws of other States. But international law has made plain that certain types of conduct, including torture and hostage-taking, are not acceptable conduct *on the part of anyone*. This applies as much to heads of State, or even more so, as it does to everyone else; *the contrary conclusion would make a mockery of international law.*'

The positive human rights law tradition referred to in the *Pinochet Case* prohibits torture of individuals by *anyone* and prohibits extending justifications or even immunity to *anyone* alleged to have practised it. Therefore, there appears to be no scope for application of the national amnesty laws tradition, even as an exception, where torture is alleged. This probably applies too where any offence is alleged that offends against the public order of the international community. Crimes of apartheid that South Africa's Promotion of National Unity and Reconciliation Act 34 (1995) grants amnesty for under particular conditions are crimes that, like slavery, torture, genocide and rape which furthers political objectives, offend against the public order of the international community, and ought therefore to be placed beyond national political contingencies. The enforceability of these offences does not depend on States' membership of treaties or conventions that prohibit them but on their status under customary international law.[69] For instance, torture became a crime against all of humanity before the Torture Convention came into force. *Per* Lord Millet and Lord Phillips *in Ex parte Pinochet Ugarte (No. 3):*

'the systematic use of torture was an international crime for which there could be no immunity even before the Convention came into effect and consequently

---

[68] [1998] 3 WLR 1456 at p.1500. Emphasis added.

[69] Discussing genocide, Ratner and Abrams write that: 'The status of genocide under customary international law is significant because it determines the obligations of all States regarding genocide, whether or not they are party to the Convention.' Ratner, S. R. and Abrahams, J. S. (2nd ed. 2000) *Accountability for Human Rights Atrocities in International Law*, Oxford University Press, Oxford, p.41.

there is no immunity under customary international law for the offences relating to torture.'[70]

The editors of *Oppenheim's International Law*[71] write that: 'in respect of the criminality of genocide the Convention may be regarded as confirming a rule of customary international law', a position confirmed by the International Court of Justice (ICJ) in the *Reservations Case* where it stated that: 'the principles underlying the Convention are principles which are recognised by civilised nations as binding on States, even without any conventional obligation'.[72] In the *Barcelona Traction Case*,[73] the ICJ declared *erga omnes* obligations regarding genocide. Applying this declaration of the ICJ to Article 19 of the Draft Articles on State Responsibility, the International Law Commission remarked that:

> 'It follows, according to the Court, that responsibility engaged by the breach of these obligations is engaged not only in regard to the State which was the direct victim of the breach; it is also engaged in regard to all the other members of the international community, so that, in the event of a breach of these obligations, every State must be considered justified in invoking – probably through judicial channels – the responsibility of the State committing the internationally wrongful act.'[74]

Apartheid has been denounced generally in Article 2 of the United Nations Charter (1945) and the International Convention on the Elimination of All Forms of Racial Discrimination (1965), and more specifically in the Convention on the Suppression and Punishment of the Crime of Apartheid (1973)[75] and also in numerous UNGA declarations and resolutions that condemned apartheid as a violation of legal obligations and *opinio communitatis*. 'There has been a steady increase in the severity of the language in which the condemnation has been phrased: it has gradually come to include reference to it being a "crime against humanity" and a "slavery-like practice".'[76] The customary force of the positive human rights regime that prohibits torture, genocide, slavery, apartheid and crimes against humanity is augmented as we have seen by the treaty regime, and it points to a strong *opinio communitatis* against the national amnesty laws tradition in situations where basic human rights of individuals are at issue. However, opposition of this strong *opinio*

---

[70] [1999] 2 WLR 827 at p.829.
[71] Jennings, R. and Watts, A. (eds) (9th ed. 1996) *Oppenheim's International Law*, Longman, London, p.994.
[72] ICJ Rep (1951) p.15 at p.23.
[73] *Belgium v Spain*, ICJ Rep (1970), p.3 paras 33–34.
[74] *Yearbook of the International Law Commission* (1976) vol. II Part 2, p.99.
[75] UNGA Res. 3068 (XXVIII) (1973).
[76] Jennings, R. and Watts, A., note 71 above, at p.1011.

communitatis even by only a handful of States can be troubling for the overwhelming practice of the majority. On a different matter that is nonetheless
illustrative of difficulties that attend efforts to exclude altogether parasitic
traditions in preference for the dominant one, the opposing State (Norway)[77]
was able to secure for itself rights contrary to the practice of all her neighbours largely on humanitarian grounds.[78] A strict application of the law by
the ICJ might have resulted in severe hardship for the local population that
relied for its survival on fishing in the waterways off the disfigured coast of
Norway.[79] Thus, the ICJ deemed it a necessary inconvenience to give some
recognition to the persistent objector status in the process of customary international law.[80] In the context of national amnesty laws that purport to expunge civil and criminal liability of agents of a prior regime alleged to have
violated basic human rights of individuals, it has often been argued that in
some cases like the Mozambique amnesty law provided at the end of hostilities with RENAMO, the State would grind to a halt if those involved in
perpetration of violations were pursued through the courts. Usually, concerned States lack the human resources and economic muscle and stamina
required to see through the process of prosecuting offences.[81] Therefore, national amnesty laws allow concerned States to focus on the more urgent task
of social, political and economic reconstruction. But if the ICJ's decision in
the *Anglo Norwegian Fisheries Case* appears to lend support to this view, the
treatment by the international community of both Rhodesia and South Africa
in relation to their opposition to the view that apartheid was unacceptable
does not. Neither Rhodesia nor South Africa secured any real advantage from
opposing the dominant universal position expressed in the norm against apartheid. The difficulty these two examples raise is one of distinction. How should
we distinguish significant opposing conduct of a limited number of States
from conduct of a handful of States that is insignificant? In the *Anglo Norwegian Fisheries Case* the livelihoods of a significant section of the Norwegian
population depended on a finding for Norway regardless of whether the legal
question and facts of the case favoured the United Kingdom. For apartheid
Rhodesia and apartheid South Africa restoration of the dignity of non-whites
as equal and free human beings of society depended on the international
community's outright rejection of any significance being attached to Rhodesia

---

[77] *Anglo Norwegian Fisheries Case (United Kingdom v Norway)* ICJ Rep (1951) p.116.
[78] See Evensen, J. (1952) 'The Anglo Norwegian Fisheries Case and its Legal Consequences',
American Journal of International Law, vol. 46, p.609 at p.630.
[79] See Chigara, B. (2001) *Legitimacy Deficit in Custom: A Deconstructionist Critique*, Ashgate,
Aldershot, pp.204–240.
[80] One of three law-creating processes in international law. For discussion see Harris, D. J. (5th
ed. 1998) *Cases and Materials on International Law*, Sweet and Maxwell, London, p.21.
[81] See Chap. 1 above.

and South Africa's persistent objection to the international ban on apartheid. Humanitarian considerations lent themselves to abolition of apartheid and not to support of the two delinquent States. It might appear that where the local population is the beneficiary of State conduct that opposes *opinio communitatis*, that opposition might be acceptable only as an exception to the dominant position. But such an analysis ignores the fact that unlike Rhodesia and South Africa, Norway had not challenged a peremptory norm of *jus cogens*, that is, 'a norm that enjoys a higher rank in the international hierarchy than treaty law and even "ordinary customary" rules'.[82] Therefore, it might be the case that where State conduct challenges norms *jus cogens*, even if the local population stands to benefit, that conduct remains illegal and unacceptable under international law.

Although the customary law force of these norms points to a strong presumption that States that declare national amnesty laws that seek to expunge criminal and civil liability of agents of a prior regime alleged to have violated basic human rights of individuals in reliance perhaps on their non-participation in relevant prohibitive international conventions are still obliged to investigate and prosecute offenders rather than pardon them, the indistinct nature of customary law norms raises the problem of legality of resulting prosecutions. Ratner and Abrams[83] write that the prohibition on assigning guilt for acts not considered as crimes when committed summed up in the maxim *nullum crimen sine lege, nulla poena sine lege*, or 'no crime without law, no punishment without law' also expressed in the prohibition on *ex post facto* laws and prohibition on ambiguous criminal laws oppose application of customary international law norms that do not accurately define the contours of the offences to be prosecuted. This view is shared by Warbrick and McGoldrick who write that establishing that conduct is criminal in customary international law is beset by the uncertainties of the customary law process.[84] Ambiguous laws strike at the heart of any allegation that an act prohibited by law has occurred. While prosecution of crimes against humanity is mandate that is common to both the ICTY and the ICTR, there appears to be in circulation several divergent definitions of that crime around, in spite of it having customary law force.[85] Inconsistency resides also in customary international law's

---

[82] *Ex parte Pinochet Ugarte (No. 3)* [1999] 2 WLR 827 at p.841, *per* Lord Browne-Wilkinson.

[83] (2nd ed. 2000) *Accountability for Human Rights Atrocities in International Law*, Oxford University Press, Oxford, p.21.

[84] Warbrick, C. and McGoldrick, D. (1999) 'The Future of Former Head of State Immunity after *Ex parte Pinochet*', *International and Comparative Law Quarterly*, vol. 48 No. 4, p.937, n.46.

[85] See Chesterman, S. (2000) 'An Altogether Different Order: Defining the Elements of Crimes Against Humanity', *Duke Journal of Comparative and International Law*, vol. 10, pp.307–340. See also Harris, D. J. (5th ed. 1998) *Cases and Materials on International Law*, Sweet and Maxwell, London, pp.743–744.

definition of the crime of genocide.[86] However, in spite of this problem, practice shows that this deficiency of offences defined under customary international law has not weakened them. In fact some of these norms have ascended to the status of *jus cogens* and *erga omnes*. Nonetheless, it is a problem which practitioners and commentators have to bear in mind and one which crystallisation of practice will hopefully resolve.

(b) Acting under superior orders

Since its adoption on 17 July 1998, the Statute of the International Criminal Court (ICC) has been the subject of much comment[87] not least because the United States fears that it will lead to politicised prosecutions of its peacekeepers.[88] Much controversy stems from Article 33 which contrary to established customary international law allows subordinates conditional defence of 'superior orders' to charges of crimes against humanity. Policy considerations and requirements of justice as fairness exert different pulls to the question whether 'orders of a superior' should constitute sufficient defence against a criminal charge under international law of armed conflict or under general international law. At the heart of this question is the issue of military discipline, which requires that orders must be obeyed, and the requirement of justice, that crimes should not go unpunished. In his poem 'The Charge of the Light Brigade', Lord Tennyson appears to sympathise with the predicament of the infantry men caught in the valley of death. 'Theirs is not to reason why? But to do and die!'

The genealogy of Article 33 of the Statute of the ICC shows incomparable instability in the doctrine. Prior to the Nuremberg trials, the question had been debated in the fifteenth century at Bresach during the trial of a war criminal accused of trampling underfoot the laws of God and humanity.[89] By 1906 the law favoured the view that where members of armed forces violate international law under the orders of their commanders, 'the members may

---

[86] See Ratner, S. R. and Abrams, J. S. (2nd ed. 2000) *Accountability for Human Rights Atrocities in International Law*, Oxford University Press, Oxford, pp.41–45.

[87] For a comprehensive discussion of, see Symposium of the European Journal of International Law (1999) 'The International Criminal Court: The US v. the Rest?', *European Journal of International Law*, vol. 10 No. 1, pp.93–144.

[88] For a detailed discussion of American reservations to the Statute of the ICC, see Zwanenburg, M. (1999) 'The Statute of the International Criminal Court and the United States: Peacekeepers under Fire', *European Journal of International Law*, vol. 10 No. 1, pp.124–143; Wedgwood, R. (1999) 'The International Criminal Court: An American View', *European Journal of International Law*, vol. 10 No. 1, pp.93–107.

[89] See Chigara, B. (2000) 'The Administration of International Criminal Justice', in Woodhouse, D. (ed.) *The Pinochet Case: A Legal and Constitutional Analysis*, Hart Publishing, Oxford, p.115 at p.119.

not be punished, for the commanders are alone responsible, and the latter may, therefore, be punished as war criminals on their capture by the enemy'.[90] Trials of war criminals at the end of the First World War preferred the view that:

> 'However, the subordinate obeying an order is liable to punishment, if it was known to him that the order of the superior involved the infringement of civil or military law . . . It is certainly to be urged in favour of the military subordinates that they are under no obligation to question the order of their superior officer, and they can count upon its legality. But no such confidence can be held to exist, if such an order is universally known to everybody, including the accused, to be without any doubt whatever against the law.'[91]

Thus, manifest knowledge of the accused that the order of the superior was illegal prohibited him from executing it, and if he did, he incurred responsibility for his actions. This approach was developed further in the Charter of the International Military Tribunal (IMT) established to try major war criminals at the cessation of hostilities commonly known as the Second World War. Article 8 limits pleas of 'superior orders' to mitigatory considerations in sentencing only. Such pleas are not acceptable to the charge itself.

> 'The fact that the Defendant acted pursuant to order of his Government or of a superior shall not free him from responsibility, but may be considered in mitigation of punishment.'[92]

The IMT Judge Advocate in the Peleus Trial[93] acknowledged the difficulty created by the untempered application of the rule against the defence of 'superior orders'.[94] 'It is quite obvious that no sailor and no soldier can carry with him a library of international law or have immediate access to a professor . . . who can tell him whether or not a particular command is a lawful one.' Nonetheless, the principle was established and affirmed by the UNGA in 1946[95] that the plea of 'superior orders' whether military or administrative only went to mitigating sentence and not to the charge itself.[96] Harris writes that the Nuremberg Principles have the status of customary international law.[97] Cassese writes

---

[90] Oppenheim, L. F. L. (1st ed. 1906) *International Law: A Treatise*, vol. 2, p.264.

[91] *Llandovery Castle Case* (1921), Supreme Court of Leipzig, cited in Garaway, C. (1999) 'Superior Orders and the International Criminal Court: Justice Delivered or Justice Denied?' *International Review of the Red Cross*, vol. 81 No. 836, p.785 at p.786.

[92] Article 8 of the IMT. See Harris, D. J. (5th ed. 1998) *Cases and Materials on International Law*, Sweet and Maxwell, London, p.742.

[93] (1945) 1 War Crimes Reports 12, British Military Court, Hamburg.

[94] See Article 6(c) of the Charter of the IMT.

[95] GA Res. 95 (I) (1946).

[96] The Nuremberg Principles were later formulated by the ILC on the Instruction of the UNGA. See *Yearbook of International Law Commission* (1950) vol. II, p.188.

[97] See Harris, D. J., note 92 above, at p.745.

that under customary international law 'superior orders are *never* a defence to serious violations of international humanitarian law, be they crimes of genocide, crimes against humanity or war crimes, but may only be urged in mitigation'.[98] Both the Statute of the ICTY[99] and that of the ICTR[100] take this view. Does the Statute of the ICC herald therefore a departure from customary international law?[101]

Article 33 of the ICC provides:

'1. The fact that a crime within the jurisdiction of the Court has been committed by a person pursuant to an order of a Government or of a superior, whether military or civilian, shall not relieve that person of criminal responsibility unless:

(a) The person was under a legal obligation to obey orders of the Government or the superior in question;

(b) The person did not know that the order was unlawful; and

(c) The order was not manifestly unlawful.

2. For the purposes of this article, orders to commit genocide or crimes against humanity are manifestly unlawful.'

Under Article 33(1) a person charged with committing international crimes can plead the complete defence of 'acting under superior orders' if he can prove also that any one of the circumstances listed in sub-paragraphs (a)–(c) applied. Thus, where orders are not manifestly illegal, their execution even if it results in international crimes can be justified fully under the defence of 'superior orders'. This does not offer defendants an easy escape route as might first be feared because human rights atrocities to which criminal culpability attaches are patently atrocious so that ignorance can never suffice as an excuse.[102] Moreover, the order of the superior itself would retain illegality, making the superior issuing the order liable to punishment, but not the subordinate who executed the order in good faith, and relying on its legality, 'and in circumstances in which it was not "manifestly unlawful"'.[103] He would have a complete defence entitling him to an acquittal. Nonetheless, the conditional defence of superior orders available to subordinates in the Statute of

---

[98] Cassese, A. (1999) 'The Statute of the International Criminal Court: Some Preliminary Reflections', *European Journal of International Law*, vol. 10 No.1, p.144 at p.156.

[99] See Statute of the ICTY, Article 7(4).

[100] See Statute of the ICTR, Article 6(4).

[101] Arguing that by adopting the conditional liability approach with regard to war crimes, Article 33 of the Statute of the ICC departs from customary international law without sufficient justification, see Gaeta, P. (1999) 'The Defence of Superior Orders: The Statute of the International Criminal Court versus Customary International Law', *European Journal of International Law*, vol. 10 No. 1, pp.172–191.

[102] In this connection see also Ratner, S. R. and Abrams, J. S. (2nd ed. 2000) *Accountability for Human Rights Atrocities in International Law*, Oxford University Press, Oxford, p.137.

[103] Cassese, A., note 98 above, at pp.156–157.

the ICC is contrary to *lex lata* which requires any order to commit an international crime 'regardless of its classification . . . illegal and therefore . . . not to be urged in defence by the subordinate who obeys the order'.[104] This is most surprising in the context of the Statute of the ICC which in Article 8 provides an exhaustive list of the crimes for which the proposed court will have jurisdiction. To borrow from Cassese:

> 'Given this specificity of Article 8, one fails to see under what circumstances the order to commit one of the crimes listed therein may be regarded as being not manifestly unlawful, i.e. if nothing else, it would be manifest in the text of the Rome Statute itself. Therefore, if the subordinate knew the Rome Statute's provisions, then illegality of any order to commit a war crime as defined in the Statute would *ipso facto* be manifest to him.'[105]

The potential danger posed to the developing corpus of international law by this retrogressive step of the Statute of the ICC in providing a conditional defence of 'superior orders' to subordinates falls off if Article 33 is read together with Articles 10 and 22 whose effect is to prevent the Statute from limiting application of norms of international law developed for purposes other than the application of the Statute. This suggests that two bodies of international criminal law might well develop, one Statute based and another not Statute based. How the proposed court might then resolve the question of which law to apply to which case might depend on a number of factors, yet to play themselves out. The danger remains though that one law might accept conditionally the defence of superior orders and the other might not. This might weaken rather than strengthen public perception of the function of the ICC.

(c) The proposed International Criminal Court and amnesty

The Statute of the ICC was adopted by the United Nations Conference of Plenipotentiaries on the Establishment of an International Criminal Court in Rome on 17 July 1998. As of 10 May 2001 only half the number of States required to ratify the Statute for it to come into force had done so. Of those 30 countries only two – Andora and Argentina – had ratified the Statute in the year 2001, indicating perhaps a less than rapid rate of ratification of the treaty. This raises the question why the final effort to set up a court supported both extensively and broadly[106] evidences such travail and hesitancy? An often

---

[104] Ibid. p.157.
[105] Ibid.
[106] One hundred and twenty countries, including all of the United States' allies, voted in favour of adopting the Statute of Rome setting up the ICC. Twenty-one countries abstained, and seven others, namely the United States, China, Israel, Libya, Iraq, Qatar and Yemen, opposed the treaty. Most non-governmental organisations and voluntary organisations had lobbied for adoption of the Statute.

cited reason is the uncertainty among States about whether the ICC might become also a vehicle for vexatious prosecutions generated by mischievous and malign States. Because of that perceived danger, States have become anxious about the extent to which ratifying the treaty as it stands might risk exposing their subjects to undue hardship. Thus, in the determination whether or not to ratify the Statute of Rome in the light of misgivings about the danger that its nationals – particularly its servicemen who play an active role in world security – would be exposed to, the French *Assemblee Nationale* invoked Article 124 of the Statute of Rome, a provision proposed during the negotiation process of the treaty by France itself. That provision gives States that exercise it a seven-year opt-out, when the Statute comes into force, allowing them to observe how the court progresses while exempting their armed forces from the jurisdiction of the court for the offence of war crimes. That question alone, in spite of the safeguard of the pre-trial procedure contained in the Statute that is intended to wash out of the system any bogus allegations, has exercised other States regarding the question whether or not to ratify the Statute.[107]

The question whether indemnity automatically should be granted by the ICC for Article 8 crimes committed either by United Kingdom nationals or on United Kingdom territory exercised[108] the United Kingdom Parliament on 10 May 2001. The House of Commons debated that issue in its consideration of whether or not to pass the International Criminal Court Bill [Lords] intended to give effect to the Statute of the International Criminal Court. The Bill which received Royal Assent on 11 May 2001 was introduced to Parliament on 15 December 2000, and took its second reading on 3 April 2001 and was also debated in Committee.[109] Another stage of its consideration was scrutiny by the Select Committee appointed to report whether the provisions of any Bill inappropriately delegate legislative power, or whether they subject the exercise of legislative power to an inappropriate degree of parliamentary scrutiny. On 7 February 2001 the Select Committee examined government amendments for Committee stage on clause 23 which deals with the consequences of proceedings in the United Kingdom for the arrest and surrender

---

[107] Arguing that that was one reason Parliament should enter reservations to the Statute of Rome, see Mr Maude, House of Commons Debates, 10 May 2001, pp.328, 329, 331, 332. Arguing that there was no real prospect of such a possibility under the Statute of Rome, see Mr Cook, House of Commons Parliamentary Debates, 10 May 2001, p.330; Mr Browne, pp.337, 338.

[108] See new clause 3 tabled as an amendment of the jurisdiction of the proposed ICC by Mr Maude in the final debate on the ICC Bill in the House of Commons. House of Commons Debates, 10 May 2001, p.327.

[109] See House of Commons Standing Committee on the International Criminal Court Bill [Lords] 00/01, 11 April–10 May.

of a person charged with an ICC crime when that person is the subject of State or diplomatic immunity. Clause 23 provides that if that immunity exists because of the accused person's connection with an ICC State, it is no bar to proceedings. However, if the accused person's immunity exists because of his connection with another State, it is a bar unless that State has waived the immunity at the request of the ICC. The government amendment sought to address a situation where a State does not waive immunity in a case where the prosecution is undertaken at the request of the United Nations Security Council, acting under Chapter VII of the United Nations Charter. The Select Committee found that:

(1) The amendment extends section 1 of the United Nations Act 1946 which at present is limited to enabling measures to be applied in the United Kingdom when the Security Council has called upon the United Kingdom to apply those measures to give effect to a decision of the Council. Subsection (1) provides that an Order in Council may make such provision as appears necessary or expedient for enabling those measures to be effectively applied (including provision for the apprehension, trial and punishment of persons offending against the Order). An Order in Council under the Act has to be laid before Parliament after being made but is not subject to parliamentary control. It was under this power that the Rhodesian and Iraqi and Kuwait sanctions were imposed and embargoes placed upon the export of arms to South Africa.

(2) The effect of the amendment to clause 23 is that an Order in Council may remove the immunity of a person charged with an ICC crime in a case where that immunity would not otherwise be affected by the clause.

The Select Committee saw no need to draw the attention of the House to the proposed amendments which would strip immunity from persons in the United Kingdom charged with ICC crimes and whom the Security Council wished to see prosecuted by the ICC. It argued that 'The power in the 1946 Act had been used many times to give effect to Security Council decisions and this is a natural extension of the power'.[110] Inclusion of this amendment in the Bill that received Royal Assent on 11 May 2001 demonstrates a weakening of claims of immunity by persons charged with ICC crimes and a strengthening of the universal effort to stamp out impunity for crimes against humanity.

But the case for immunity in certain cases was made by some in the House of Commons who opposed ratification of a Bill that did not have reservations, which could ensure 'the protections needed for our [British] citizens, especially

---

[110] House of Lords Session 2000–01, 7th Report, Select Committee on Delegated Powers and Deregulation, International Criminal Court Bill [HL] – Government Amendments for Committee Stage, 7 February 2001, pp.3–4.

our armed services personnel'.[111] Exercise of the opt-out mechanism contained
in Article 124 was one way of doing it. They argued that jurisdiction of the
court should be determined from zero for countries like the United Kingdom
that have large populations in comparison to many small countries, and participate extensively in world security and therefore command influence among
other nations; to complete jurisdiction for States that have small populations,
do not participate extensively in world security operations and command
little or no influence in world politics.[112] Those arguments echoed strongly
United States arguments for refusing to adopt the Statute of the ICC at Rome.
The United States had argued that the two-tier jurisdiction of the ICC potentially threatened its servicemen more than any other State in that as the most
powerful military and economic State on earth, it is expected more than any
other country to intervene to halt humanitarian catastrophes around the world.
This renders United States personnel uniquely vulnerable to the unimpeded
jurisdiction of a permanent international criminal court. Thus, the United
States preferred the ICC with jurisdiction consisting of situations referred to
the court by the Security Council – type one jurisdiction. All States would be
compelled to submit to United Nations Charter Chapter VII measures on
action to be taken with respect to threats to the peace, breaches of the peace,
and acts of aggression. The United States opposed the other jurisdiction granted
to the ICC for the reasons stated above. This jurisdiction, in spite of the
mechanisms built into it to thwart politically motivated claims by other countries, appeared to leave open that possibility because it recognised the competence of the ICC to consider claims resulting from situations referred to the
ICC by individual countries or by the ICC prosecutor type two jurisdiction.
Article 15(1) of the Statute of the ICC makes the prosecutor *proprio motu*,
that is, a prosecutor that may initiate investigations on the basis of information on crimes within the jurisdiction of the court. These crimes are listed in
Article 5 as genocide, crimes against humanity, war crimes and aggression.

There is no denying that the international community is made up of diverse
States in terms of size, population wealth, religion, political openness, etc.
Nonetheless, international law is premised on the sovereign and legal equality
of all member States, and not on world influence as the House of Commons
properly observed.

'If we choose to take that reservation, what is sauce for the goose will be sauce
for the gander, and every other country that has signed up to the statute – even
some of those who were dismissed by the Opposition in Committee as being

---

[111] *Per* Mrs Gilillan, House of Commons Debates, 10 May 2001, pp.327 and 310, *per* Mr
Edward Garner, ibid. p.322.
[112] *Per* Mr Blunt, House of Commons Debates, 10 May 2001, p.321.

irrelevant to important international decisions because of their size, population or history – should be able to do the same thing.[113]

Therefore, the reservation which sought to effect indemnity of United Kingdom nationals from jurisdiction of United Kingdom nationals even from Article 8 crimes was rejected. Although the seven-year opt-out mechanism appears to be a residual overtone, the ICC appears to be firmly anchored on the universal human rights laws tradition. This view is buttressed by the fact that the Statute prescribes that there shall be no amendments until seven years after it comes into force. That is long enough for practice premised on the universal human rights culture to entrench itself further, probably killing off any residual overtones of the amnesty laws tradition for crimes against humanity.

In their determination to halt impunity for crimes against humanity some countries have let their zeal outpace collective international thinking on the matter even to the detriment of diplomatic relations with other States. One such example is Belgium which on 8 June 2001 delivered judgment on four Rwandans: two Benedictine nuns, a former professor at the National University of Rwanda, and a factory owner, for alleged breach of international human rights laws during the Rwanda genocide of 1994. The case is unique for two reasons.

First, it marked the first trial under the Belgian Act of Parliament of 16 June 1993[114] on the punishment of grave breaches of international humanitarian law as modified by the Act of 10 February 1999. The purpose of this legislation is to proscribe three categories of grave breaches of international law, namely, genocide, crimes against humanity and grave breaches of humanitarian law and to integrate them into Belgian law. To maintain consistency with international conventions the Act borrows the wording of Article 2 of the Genocide Convention (1948) and of Article 7 of the Statute of the ICC (1998) and of the Geneva Conventions (1949) and their Additional Protocols I and II (1977) to define the acts of genocide, crimes against humanity, and grave breaches of humanitarian law respectively. There are a few exceptions made to the international conventions. First, instead of the 11 offences proscribed under the ICC Statute, the Act limits itself to nine. Secondly, while the Geneva Conventions and their Protocols limit application of 'grave breaches' to international armed conflicts, the Act makes no such distinction between internal and international armed conflicts. This deliberate enlargement of the scope of operation of the relevant norms addresses present reality, which shows that norms of international humanitarian laws are breached as much during internal

---

[113] *Per* Mr Browne, ibid. p.338.
[114] 38 ILM 921–925.

conflicts as in international conflicts. Article 3 of the Act equates culpability
of a facilitator of grave breaches of international humanitarian law with that
of the perpetrator.

Secondly, this was probably the first time members of the jury were presid-
ing not over their peers, but on behalf of another State's peers over offences
allegedly committed outside Belgium. By Article 7 Belgian courts are granted
under the Act universal jurisdiction for proscribed crimes irrespective of where
such breaches have been committed. In the *Benedictine Nuns Case* all four
accused were found guilty of most of the 55 charges put to them. Nonetheless, it is being felt already in Belgium that continued application of this law
as it is, is more likely than not, to 'hobble Belgian international relations . . .
[For instance] A private group has filed charges under the law against Israeli
Prime Minister Ariel Sharon for his role in alleged war crimes against Pales-
tinians by Christian militia in Lebanon in 1982'.[115] Both the Foreign Minister
of Belgium and other diplomats have called for a weakening of the Belgian
universal jurisdiction law. This is not surprising because even the Statute of
the ICC recognises that international criminal jurisdiction operates to complement and not to usurp national jurisdictions. However, the *Eichmann Case*[116]
lends support to the proposition that customary international law accepts that
a State may exercise universal jurisdiction over certain international crimes
committed outside its territorial jurisdiction and not involving its nationals,
either as actors or victims, or indeed its national interest. In such a case the
State acts as the agent of the international community in the prosecution of an
enemy of all mankind in whose punishment all States have an interest. The
principle *aut dedere aut judicare* which obliges States either to prosecute criminals for particular offences or to extradite them to another State for prosecution of those offences appears to emphasise customary notions of universal
jurisdiction for crimes against humanity.

In a case[117] pending consideration of the ICJ at the time of writing, Belgium
sought to apply universal jurisdiction for offences proscribed under the Act
concerning the Punishment of Grave Breaches of International Humanitarian
Law 1993/99 committed in the Democratic Republic of Congo (DRC). It is
not clear whether any of the victims of those offences were in fact Belgian, but
the alleged offender is a Congolese member of Parliament. The ICJ unanimously
rejected on 8 December 2000 Belgium's request that the *Case concerning the*

---

[115] See Keller, L. (2001) 'Addendum to: Belgian Jury to Decide Case Concerning Rwandan Genocide' www.asil.org/insights.htm.
[116] *Attorney-General of the Government of Israel v Eichmann* (1961) 36 ILR 277 at pp.298–
304.
[117] *Case concerning the Arrest Warrant of 11 April 2000 (Democratic Republic of Congo v
Belgium)* www.lawschool.cornell.edu/library/cijwww/ icjwww/idocket/iCOBE/iCOBEframe.htm.

Arrest Warrant of 11 April 2000 (Democratic Republic of the Congo v Belgium) be removed from the list, and found by 15 votes to two that the circumstances, as they now presented themselves to the court, were not such as to require the exercise of its power to indicate provisional measures, as the DRC had wished. That case arose from the issue by a Belgian investigating judge on 11 April 2000 of an international arrest warrant against Yerodia Abdoulaye Ndombasi, Minister for Foreign Affairs of the DRC at the time, seeking his provisional detention pending a request for extradition to Belgium for 'serious violations of international humanitarian law'. On 17 October 2000, the DRC instituted proceedings against Belgium claiming that Belgium's action violated:

(1) The principle that a State may not exercise its authority on the territory of another State and the principle of sovereign equality among all Members of the Organisation of the United Nations, as laid down in Article 2, paragraph 1, of the Charter of the United Nations.
(2) The diplomatic immunity of the Minister for Foreign Affairs of a sovereign State, as recognised by the jurisprudence of the Court and following from Article 41, paragraph 2, of the Vienna Convention of 18 April 1961 on Diplomatic Relations.

The DRC asked the ICJ to order the immediate discharge of the disputed arrest warrant.

These two cases illustrate the rapidity with which some States have acted to prevent any attempt to grant impunity for crimes against humanity regardless of where they were committed. It has been argued that the exercise of universal jurisdiction for extraterritorial charges brought against non-citizens for the killing of non-citizens has no basis in Belgian law except perhaps where the homicide amounts to genocide. Keller[118] writes that universal jurisdiction under the 1993 and 1999 Acts covered homicide only in so far as it constituted grave breaches of the Geneva Conventions and Additional Protocols. Therefore, defendants in the historic *Benedictine Nuns Case* decided on 8 June 2001 could have been charged with those crimes under the Geneva Conventions and Additional Protocols which also relate to accusations of homicide in particular circumstances.

CONCLUSION

The positive human rights law tradition that recognises positive human rights that derive from the status of being human has diversified to become both

---

[118] See ASIL Insight: *Rwandan Genocide [Benedictine Nuns] Case* www.asil.org/insights/insigh72.htm.

encompassing and specialised. Through international commissions and committees that hold governments to their commitments under human rights covenants, treaties and also through the work of national and international *ad hoc* and permanent tribunals, and through the work of non-governmental organisations, the positive human rights law tradition now bestrides the world like a colossus. Sponsored by concerted and consistent effort of the most powerful universal organisation there is – the United Nations – it seeks to uphold the basic dignity of individuals wherever they are. Specialised treaty bodies have been created to supervise State compliance with their obligations under particular human rights covenants and treaties. Besides supervising States' compliance with treaty obligations, these bodies also offer States technical assistance on how to deliver these rights to their intended beneficiaries. Treaty bodies have been created also that supervise States' observance of treaty based rights of specially affected groups like ethnic minorities, women and children. In contrast the national amnesty laws tradition evidenced in the practice of only a handful of States that have legislated to prevent criminal and civil litigation against agents of a prior regime alleged to have violated basic human rights of individuals does not have such a labyrinth of support structures. In fact it is so opposite to the overwhelming *opinio communitatis* that carries the positive human rights law tradition that its unacceptability sticks out like a sore thumb. Whereas the positive human rights law tradition is manifestly growing and developing delivery structures that States appear to co-operate with, the national amnesty laws tradition appears to be receding and without support of non-governmental organisations, inter-governmental organisations and in some cases without support of the majority of their populations. Jurisprudence resulting from the positive human rights law tradition shows that even heads of States or their predecessors cannot claim immunity from prosecution for acts that while clothed under the veil of 'official acts' or 'acts of State' violate basic human rights of individuals. Neither can subordinates claim the defence of 'superior orders' for acts that violate basic human rights of individuals under customary international law. While the Statute of the ICC appears conditionally to allow subordinates the complete defence of 'superior orders' this seems to be inconsistent with established customary international law. We must wait to see how in practice the proposed ICC navigates this and other complexities that appear in its text, if or when it starts operating.

7

CONCLUSIONS

This study examined the legality in international law of a particular type of amnesty, namely national amnesty laws that purport to expunge criminal and/or civil liability of agents of a prior regime alleged to have violated basic human rights of individuals. The question was analysed from several perspectives. The first regarded human rights as property rights with enduring legal consequences. Positive international human rights law ascribes inalienability to these rights because they inhere in the status of being human. As a consequence every person has them. They cannot be misappropriated, obliterated or expunged by government or anyone else. Because that property has enduring legal status, libertarian notions of 'justice as fairness' require that society's previously determined norms that regulate breach of property rights of individuals be upheld all the time for human rights law to manifest, maintain and inspire legitimacy. This perspective rejects the possibility that national amnesty laws could ever be passed that have capacity either to obliterate those property rights or to set them aside. To allow that to happen would offend the character of positive human rights of individuals as they have become known. Contemporary understanding on human rights is firmly anchored on their international origins. Therefore, their application or denial ought to have as its focus an international and not a domestic contingency. Secondly, human rights are legal rights that only holders of title have authority specifically and legally to deal with them. Therefore, such legal title must pass or be transferred from one holder to another before that other can claim to have the capacity to obliterate or to expunge them. Title of victims' positive human rights needs to be shown to have passed from victims themselves to their government before that government can claim to have capacity or authority to grant national amnesty to individuals alleged to have breached those entitlements. Theoretically, how that happens is difficult to explain. If this is correct, then national amnesty laws that seek to expunge criminal and/or civil liability of agents of a prior regime alleged to have violated basic human rights of individuals are a legal fraud which attempt to set to zero basic human rights of individuals and to usurp positive human rights law tradition's universal and international authority to regulate breaches of basic human rights of individuals. Such laws ignore society's previously set standards by which all future conduct of agents should be governed. They also ignore the fact that victims have legal rights that require legal accountability and not political accountability. They attempt to anaesthetise society from its own self-preserving and self-asserting standards.

Secondly, the question whether national amnesty laws that purport to expunge criminal and/or civil liability of agents of a prior regime alleged to have violated basic human rights of individuals are legal under international law was examined from the constraint/discretion dynamic that characterises the relationship between international and national laws. It is commonly assumed that whatever international law does not specifically prohibit States from doing, States have discretion within their jurisdictions so long as they do not offend general international law, particularly norms *jus cogens*. Nonetheless, it is now widely accepted that the way in which a government treats people under its jurisdiction is now a legitimate matter of international scrutiny. In this connection non-governmental organisations such as Amnesty International, Rights Watch and Interights contribute immensely to the monitoring of States' compliance with international human rights standards. More importantly, international human rights conventions have been created that establish treaty bodies that supervise States Parties' compliance with their treaty obligations. States not only submit to these treaty bodies periodic reports on the progress that they have made to ensure delivery of convention rights, but may also request from them technical assistance on how to promote and to encourage human rights observance within their own territories. In addition to the periodic reports, treaty bodies may at their own discretion request a State Party to the convention to supply a report on a matter of specific or general concern. Some of these treaty bodies have authority of States Parties to receive complaints of breach of human rights from individuals. Some treaty bodies are authorised to receive inter-State complaints, that is, complaints by any of the other parties to the relevant convention that another State party to the same convention is not adhering to the norms of the convention. In particular these treaty bodies are concerned that States adopt within their judicial and administrative systems, sufficient and continuing measures for the delivery of the rights recognised under the conventions they enforce. In spite of their obvious weaknesses,[1] and although one might wish that these treaty bodies had more power to intervene, their work manifests a severe restriction by international law on State discretion where human rights of individuals are concerned. This is consistent with the international origin of human rights as they have become known today. Therefore, *opinio communitatis* on the validity of national amnesty laws that seek to humiliate victims of basic human rights abuse by setting to zero their human rights is crucial to an examination of the question whether national amnesty laws that purport to expunge criminal and/or civil liability of agents of a prior regime alleged to have violated basic human rights of individuals are legal under international law. The forward march of the universal human rights culture sparked off by the UDHR (1948) appears to reject political resolution of allegations of breach of basic human rights violations of individuals in favour of a legal one, making national amnesty laws appear unwelcome under international law.[2]

Thirdly, the question was examined from the perspective of conflicting legal traditions. The basis and dynamics of the national amnesty laws tradition were pitted against those of the positive human rights law tradition. The latter tradition, with support of the single biggest universal organisation there is, the United Nations, reflects *opinio communitatis* and clearly dominates this sphere, while the former points to a weak, uncoordinated attempt to usurp universal and international authority of the positive human rights law tradition to promote and to ensure peace, freedom and stability and justice in the world, what Allot describes as the social function of the law.[3]

Arguments made in support of the national amnesty laws tradition reflect misconceptions of either the nature and function of human rights as they have become known in the contemporary world, or of issues raised by the requirement of justice as fairness, or by requirements of social engineering in general. Failure to grasp the fact that although they ultimately are secured, enjoyed or breached in the domestic sphere, human rights as they have become known today are a product of international engineering and not national engineering leads to the misconception that local contingencies and not international ones determine resolution of alleged breach of human rights of individuals by agents of a previous regime. Attribution[4] of knowledge of what is in the best interest of the State declaring national amnesty laws to agents of a prior regime alleged to have violated basic human rights of individuals is bizarre in that it ignores

---

[1] Discussed in Chap. 6 above.
[2] See Chap. 5 above.
[3] See Chap. 6 above.
[4] Discussing attribution theory, and the United Nations wrongly perceived as the outsider, see Chap. 3 above.

the role played by the international community through organs such as the United Nations and other inter-governmental and non-governmental organisations in the effort to rescue the concerned State from totalitarian rule. From these three perspectives national amnesty laws that purport to expunge criminal and/or civil liability of agents of a previous regime alleged to have violated basic human rights of individuals appear to be illegal under international law. Any benefits that national amnesty laws appear to confer are limited, transitory and illusory. In fact, they nurture a backlash capable of undermining in the future the rule of law in the concerned State as the Zimbabwe crisis of 2000 and 2001 threatens.

SUBMISSIONS

Chapter 1 critiqued amnesty and evaluated the validity of the argument that political contingencies must replace judicial ones in the resolution of crimes against humanity and breach of basic human rights of individuals by agents of a prior regime. It examined the resilience of philosophical assumptions on which the idea of amnesty is based in the wake of the international community's effort to create a universal culture of human rights that emphasises juridical and not political resolution of breaches of basic human rights of individuals. It concluded that:

(1) The '*claimed utility*' of national amnesty laws that expunge criminal and civil liability of agents of a prior regime alleged to have violated basic human rights of individuals is at best illusory and that the values said to underpin amnesia to crimes against humanity are both inconsistent and incompatible with international law.

(2) Processes that sponsor amnesia and by which individual policy preferences are aggregated into binding collective decisions of the executive are normatively unjustifiable even to the extent that they oppose two of protagonists' 'virtues' of amnesty, namely, the creation of democratic practice in a formerly totalitarian State and restoration of the rule of law.

(3) The push for amnesia presupposes breach of established standards in society. In this sense amnesia is opposable to established notions of justice. It is unlikely therefore that international law would shoot itself in the foot by sanctioning a process that goes against what it has rejected vehemently through its human rights regime.

Chapter 2 featured an evaluation of the distribution of competencies between national and international law in relation to State practice on amnesty. It showed that increasingly, and with resort to international human rights law and general international law, State practice of trying foreigners for crimes against humanity committed abroad, comments and decisions of treaty bodies that supervise States parties' compliance with their treaty obligations, and setting up by the United Nations of *ad hoc* tribunals and special courts that try individuals alleged to have committed crimes against humanity all favour the review by international law of national amnesty laws that seek to expunge criminal and/or civil liability of agents of a prior regime alleged to have violated basic human rights of individuals. This strengthens the force of the view that declaration of such national amnesty laws, whatever its motivation,[5] is illegal under international law.

If Chapter 2 appeared to adopt a critique of amnesia that is strictly legal – viewing rights as property with legal title that creates exclusive rights and negative duties on others – and if it appeared also to condone use by the international community of its aggregate force to seek out and punish those that offended its morals, Chapter 3 balanced the power dynamic in discourse on the legality in international law of national amnesty laws that purport to expunge criminal and/or civil liability of agents of a prior regime alleged to have violated basic human rights of individuals by considering whether the needs of State doctrine[6] provides any real justification for privileging amnesia over justice. It concluded that it is in the interest of the concerned State that the standard of the rule of law is applied consistently in order to protect legally recognised rights and to preserve law's integrity. It does not appear that the needs of State doctrine so understood encompasses also the granting of national amnesty to agents of a prior regime alleged to have violated basic human rights of individuals. Considerations of both the security of State and of aspiration to democratic government of the concerned State do not appear to favour granting of national amnesty to agents of a prior regime alleged to have violated basic human rights of individuals. The pursuit of democracy privileges instead due process and equality of all individuals before the law. Amnesty on the other hand privileges inequality of individuals before the law in that it places beyond the crucible of the rule of law offences that must be prosecuted. For this reason, it creates a false dawn that simmers with among other things discontentment, disillusionment with the law and a general sense of injustice and resentment of the establishment.

The first three chapters arrived at the conclusion that it is extremely difficult to justify both normatively and theoretically national amnesty laws that seek to expunge criminal and/or civil liability of agents of a prior regime alleged to have violated basic human rights of individuals. Chapter 4 examined therefore why it still is the case that the United Nations acquiesces with some national amnesty laws and rejects others. It examined the theoretical

---

[5] See Chap. 1 above.
[6] On needs of State doctrine, see Chap. 1 above. See also Rawls, J., *The Main Idea of the Theory of Justice*, Oxford University Press, Oxford.

undercurrents that characterise the United Nations' varied approach. It also assessed the impact of such national amnesty laws on the unending inter-action of State discretion, which asserts sovereign independence on the one hand, with international constraint of exercise of that sovereignty on the other. The critical question focused upon was whether the international com-munity's overwhelming endorsement of South Africa's national amnesty law of 1995 on the one hand, and its outright rejection of El Salvador's amnesty law of 1987[7] on the other, theoretically can be accounted for. What makes Zimbabwe's declaration of amnesty following the Lancaster House Settle-ment of 1979[8] acceptable to the international community, but not Chile's political settlement that replaced Senator Pinochet's military dictatorship with civilian rule?[9] The question was considered from three perspectives, namely:

(1) human rights as individual property of victims[10] that has enduring legal status and consequences;
(2) the theory of justice as fairness,[11] and the requirement that a community's previously agreed standards for the determination of legally acceptable and unacceptable conduct in the community must be upheld all the time in order to lend legitimacy to the community's system; and
(3) State practice capable/incapable of resulting in the creation of a new norm of customary international law.

It was established that there is not one, but several factors that may attach acquiescence with, or rejection of, assertion of competence to declare national amnesty to persons alleged to have violated basic human rights of individuals. These were discussed under four models, namely, the benefit model, diplo-matic tool model, positive law model and common interest model. The theory that States acquiesce with another State's exercise of sovereign discretion by granting national amnesty to agents of a prior regime alleged to have violated basic human rights of individuals if it is in the acquiescing State's interest so

---

[7] Decree No. 805, passed by the Legislative Assembly on 27 October 1987, provides in Article 1 that 'Full and absolute amnesty is granted in favor of all persons, whether nationals or foreigners, who have participated directly or indirectly or as accomplices, in the commission of political crimes or common crimes linked to political crimes or common crimes in which the number of persons involved is no less than twenty, committed on or before October 22 current year.'

[8] Which Martin and Johnson describe as a tortuous cliff-hanger and a fitting finale to the Rhodesia saga, see Martin, D. and Johnson, P. (1981) *The Struggle for Zimbabwe*, Zimbabwe Publishing House, Harare, pp.315–8.

[9] Chile's 1978 amnesty law, imposed by decree during military rule, prevented prosecution of individuals implicated in certain criminal acts committed between 11 September 1973 and 10 March 1978, the first period of Pinochet rule when a state of siege was in force and repression was harshest.

[10] See Chap. 1 above.

[11] Ibid.

to do is inapplicable to the issue of such amnesties. Can it ever be a benefit to anyone that public office was applied to torture, murder and maim people instead of upholding their dignity as human beings by protecting them? Settled practice of States stretching from as far back as the fifteenth-century trial at Bresach of a war criminal alleged to have trampled underfoot the laws of God and humanity, to the setting up in 2000 of a United Nations sponsored Special Court for the trial of people alleged to have committed crimes against humanity in Sierra Leone suggests that national amnesty for crimes against humanity may no longer be an option under international law. But even if it were accepted only as an exception to the norm, the conditions that would trigger operation of the exception appear to be insurmountable, judging by current State practice.[12]

Drawing from international human rights law and general international law, Chapter 5 examined the legal criteria, satisfaction of which triggers operation of the exception to the general prohibition against national amnesty laws that purport to expunge criminal and/or civil liability of agents of a prior regime alleged to have violated basic human rights of individuals. This checklist would have to be met in its entirety. Such national amnesty laws ought:

(1) to have been voluntarily adopted by the new regime, and not merely to have been imposed upon it by the offending regime;[13]
(2) to constitute a necessary pillar of the State's constitution or to be a fundamental policy of the new administration;[14]
(3) not to offend contemporary standards and notions of justice in the light of developments since adoption by the UNGA of the UDHR (1948) and subsequent emergence of a universal culture of human rights;
(4) everything considered, to be reasonable and consistent with norms *jus cogens*.

Chapter 5 concluded that State practice of acquiescing with some and rejecting other national amnesty laws is indicative of the process of custom. The strong prohibition under international human rights law and general international law against breach of basic human rights of individuals, coupled with emerging and continuing State practice of reviewing acceptability under international law of national amnesty laws that purport to expunge criminal and/or civil liability of agents of a prior regime alleged to have violated basic human rights of individuals inspires vehemently the view that after custom has run its full course on this issue, a fully fledged binding norm of customary international law will result that adds rather than subtracts from the gains of

---

[12] See Chap. 5 above.
[13] On imposed and elective amnesties see Chap. 1 above.
[14] One from which no exceptions were intended or are permissible.

the positive human rights law tradition, to prohibit for all time such national amnesty laws. The setting up recently of the Special Independent United Nations Court in Sierra Leone and adoption of the Statute of the proposed International Criminal Court[15] (ICC) buttress rather than weaken earlier decisions of the United Nations to set up tribunals that prosecute offences against the whole of humanity in the former Yugoslavia and in Rwanda. Exceptions to that prohibition would have to be construed very narrowly. An exception paradigm with a four-point checklist was suggested. Chile type amnesty laws, which failed on each of the four requirements, are not sustainable under international law. Although South Africa type amnesty laws satisfy the first two requirements, they succumb on the last two, making them unsustainable under international law.

Chapter 6 examined the scope of the positive human rights law tradition in relation to the national amnesty laws tradition that it dominates. The question it addressed was whether it could still be said that there was a residual function in international law of the national amnesty laws tradition. It showed that the positive human rights law tradition has diversified and become both encompassing and specialised to make vain any claims that the national amnesty laws tradition is applicable even as an exception to the dominant positive human rights law tradition. Few are the areas of human life, if any, that are still not protected generally or specifically through supervisory United Nations or regional treaty instruments. In fact, some writers refer to over-regulation in the effort of universal and regional organisations to promote and to encourage human rights observance. Therefore, it appears that the scope if any of national amnesty laws that expunge criminal and/or civil liability of agents of a previous regime alleged to have violated basic human rights of individuals is unsustainable under international law. Therefore, regardless of whether they are Chile/Peru type imposed national amnesty laws, or South Africa type elected national amnesty laws, or Zimbabwe type policy oriented national amnesty promulgations, national amnesty provisions that purport to expunge criminal and/or civil liability of agents of a previous regime alleged to have violated basic human rights of individuals are in the custody of the process of custom. There is strong evidence to support the view that when this process comes to an end, a norm of customary international law will emerge that prohibits such national amnesty provisions. This of course does not affect other types of amnesties, of which there are several.

---

[15] Rome Statute of the International Criminal Court, UN Doc. A/CONF.183/9 (1998).

BIBLIOGRAPHY

Akhavan, P. (1996) 'The Yugoslav Tribunal at Crossroads: The Dayton Peace Agreement and Beyond', *Human Rights Quarterly*, vol. 18 No. 1, p.259.

Alexy, R. (1999) 'A Defence of Radbruch's Formula', in Dyzenhaus, D. (ed.) *Recrafting the Rule of Law: The Limits of Legal Order*, Hart Publishing, Oxford, p.15.

Allot, P. (1977) 'The People as Lawmakers: Custom, Practice, and Public Opinion as Sources of Law in Africa and England', *Journal of African Law*, vol. 21, p.1.

Allot, P. (1999) 'The Concept of International Law', *European Journal of International Law*, vol. 10, p.31.

Alston, P. (1991) 'The Purposes of Reporting', in *Manual on Human Rights Reporting*, United Nations Centre for Human Rights, United Nations Institute for Training and Research, p.14.

Amerasinghe, C. F. (1994) 'Interpretation of Texts in Open International Organisations', *British Yearbook of International Law*, vol. 45, p.175.

Anand, R. P. (1986-II) 'Sovereign Equality of States in International Law', *Recueil des cours*, 197, p.13.

Anonymous, (1996) 'Human Rights in Peace Negotiations', *Human Rights Quarterly*, vol. 18 No. 2, p.249.

Atkinson, R. *et al.* (10th ed. 1990) *Introduction to Psychology*, Harcourt Brace Jovanovich, London.

Bassiouni, M. (1992) *Crimes Against Humanity*, Martinus Nijhoff, Dordrecht/London.

Bell, C. (2000) *Peace Agreements and Human Rights*, Oxford University Press, Oxford.

Bin Chen (1998) 'The Importance of Custom and the Process of its Formation in Modern International Law', *James Cook University Law Review*, vol. 5, p.27.

Birkett, J. (1947) 'International Legal Theories evolved at Nuremberg', *International Affairs*, vol. 23, p.317.

Boister, N. and Burchill, R. (1999) 'The Pinochet Precedent: Don't Leave Home Without it', *Criminal Law Forum*, vol. 10, p.405.

Bos, M. (1980) 'Theory and Practice of Treaty Interpretation', *Netherlands International Law Review*, vol. 27, p.3.

Bradley, A. W. and Ewing, K. D. (12th ed. 1997) *Constitutional and Administrative Law*, Longman, London.

Braude, C. and Spitz, D. (1997) 'Memory and the Spectre of International Justice: A Comment on AZAPO. *AZAPO v President of the Republic of South Africa*', *South African Journal on Human Rights*, vol. 13 No. 2, p.269.

Brierly, J. L. (6th ed. 1963) *The Law of Nations*, Oxford University Press, Oxford.

Brown, C. (2000) 'Cosmopolitanism, World Citizenship and Global Civil Society', in Caney, S. and Jones, P. (eds) *Human Rights and Global Diversity*, Frank Cass, London, p.7.

Brownlie, I. (1982) 'Recognition in Theory and Practice', *British Yearbook of International Law*, vol. 53, p.197.

Brownlie, I. (3rd ed. 1983) *Basic Documents in International Law*, Clarendon Press, Oxford.

Brownlie, I. (5th ed. 1998) *Principles of Public International Law*, Oxford University Press.

Brysk, A. (1994) *The Politics of Human Rights in Argentina: Protest, Change, and Democratization*, Stanford University Press, Stanford CA.

Byers, M. (2000) 'The Law and Politics of the Pinochet Case', *Duke Journal of Comparative and International Law*, vol. 10, p.415.

Captori, F. (1986) 'Human Rights: The Hard Road Towards Universality', in Macdonald, R. St J. and Johnston, D. M. (eds) *The Structure and Process of International Law*, Sweet and Maxwell, New York, p.977.

Cassel, D. (1998) 'Transitional Justice and the Rule of Law', *American Journal of International Law*, vol. 92, p.601.

Cassese, A. (1986) *International Law in a Divided World*, Clarendon Press, Oxford, p.78.

Cassese, A. (1994) *International Law in a Divided World*, Clarendon Press, Oxford.

Cassese, A. (1995) *Self-Determination of Peoples: A Legal Appraisal*, Cambridge University Press, Cambridge.

Cassese, A. (1998) 'Reflections on International Criminal Justice', *Modern Law Review*, vol. 61 No. 1, p.1.

Cassese, A. (1999) 'The Statute of the International Criminal Court: Some Preliminary Reflections', *European Journal of International Law*, vol. 10 No. 1, p.144.

Chaibong, H. (2000) 'The Cultural Challenge to Individualism', *Journal of Democracy*, vol. 11 No. 1, p.127.

Chapman, A. R. (1996) 'A "Violations Approach" for Monitoring the International Covenant on Economic Social and Cultural Rights', *Human Rights Quarterly*, vol. 18 No. 1, p.23.

Chen, B. (Greed (ed.) 1951) *The International Law of Recognition*, Stevens and Sons, London.

Cheng, B. (1965) 'United Nations Resolutions on Outer Space: Instant International Customary Law', *Indian Journal of International Law*, vol. 5, p.23.

Chesterman, S. (2000) 'An Altogether Different Order: Defining Crimes Against Humanity', *Duke Journal of Comparative and International Law*, vol. 10, p.307.

Chigara, B. (2000) 'Pinochet and the Administration of International Criminal Justice', in Woodhouse, D. (ed.) *The Pinochet Case: A Legal and Constitutional Analysis*, Hart Publishing, Oxford, p.115.

Chigara, B. (2000) 'The International Tribunal for the Law of the Sea and Customary International Law', *Loyola of Los Angeles International and Comparative Law Review*, vol. 22 No. 4, p.433.

Chigara, B. (2001) *Legitimacy Deficit in Custom: A Deconstructionist Critique*, Ashgate, Aldershot.

Chigara, B. (2001) 'From Oral to Recorded Governance: Reconstructing Title to Real Property in 21st Century Zimbabwe', *Common Law World Review*, vol. 30 No. 1, p.36.

Chinkin, C. (1993) *Third Parties in International Law*, Clarendon Press, Oxford.

Christenson, G. A. (1987) 'The World Court and Jus Cogens', *American Journal of International Law*, vol. 81, p.93.

Churchill, R. R. and Lowe, A. V. (1991) *Law of the Sea*, Manchester University Press, Manchester.

Cohen, S. (1996) 'Government Responses to Human Rights Reports: Claims, Denials, and Counterclaims', *Human Rights Quarterly*, vol. 18, p.517.

Conlon, P. (1995) 'Lessons From Iraq Sanctions Committee as a Source of Sanctions Implementation Authority and Practice', *Virginia Journal of International Law*, vol. 35 No. 3, p.633.

Corbett, P. E. (1925) 'The Consent of States and the Sources of the Law of Nations', *British Yearbook of International Law*, vol. 6, p.20.

Craig, P. (1990) *Public Law and Democracy in the United Kingdom and the United States of America*, Oxford University Press, Oxford.

Craven, M. (1994) 'Towards an Unofficial Petition Procedure: A Review of the Role of the UN Committee on Economic, Social and Cultural Richts', in Drzewicki, K. *et al.* (eds) *Social Rights as Human Rights: A European Challenge*, Abo Akademi University Institute for Human Rights, Finland, p.91.

Craven, M. C. R. (1995) 'What's in a Name? The Former Yugoslav Republic of Macedonia and Issues of Statehood', *Australian Yearbook of International Law*, vol. 16, p.199.

Crawford, J. (1976–77) 'The Criteria for Statehood in International Law', *British Yearbook of International Law*, vol. 48, p.93.

Crawford, J. (1979) *The Creation of States in International Law*, Clarendon Press, Oxford.

Davies, M. (1996) *Delimiting the Law*, Pluto Press, London.

Derrida, J. (1981) *Positions* (translated by Alan Bass), *The Athlone Press*, London.

Derrida, J. (1981) *Dissemination* (translated by Barbara Johnson), University of Chicago Press, Chicago.

Derrida, J. (1982) *Margins of Philosophy* (translated by Alan Bass) University of Chicago Press, Chicago.

Detter, T. (1962) 'The Organs of International Organisations Exercising their Treaty-Making Power', *British Yearbook of International Law*, vol. 38, p.421.

Dixon, M. (3rd ed. 1998) *Textbook on International Law*, Blackstone Press, London.

Dorjahn, A. P. (1946) *Political Forgiveness in Old Athens*, AMS Press, New York.

Dugard, J. (1997) 'Is the Truth and Reconciliation Process Compatible with International Law? An Unanswered Question', *South African Journal on Human Rights*, vol. 13 No. 2, p.258.

Dugard, J. (1997) 'Retrospective Justice: International Law and the South African Model', in McAdams, A. J. (ed.) *Transitional Justice and the Rule of Law in New Democracies*, University of Notre Dame Press, Paris, p.269.

Dugard, J. (1999) 'Dealing with Crimes of a Past Regime. Is Amnesty Still an Option?', *Leiden Journal of International Law*, vol. 12, p.1000.

Dworkin, R. (3rd ed. 1990) *Law's Empire*, Fontana Press, Glasgow.

Dyzenhaus, D. (1998) *Judging the Judges, Judging Ourselves*, Hart Publishing, Oxford.

Dyzenhaus, D. (1999) 'Recrafting the Rule of Law' in Dyzenhaus, D. (ed.) *Recrafting the Rule of Law: The Limits of Legal Order*, Hart Publishing, Oxford.

EC Foreign Ministers Declaration on the Guidelines on Recognition of new States in Eastern Europe and the Soviet Union of 16 December 1991 (1993) *European Journal of International Law*, vol. 4 No. 1, p.72.

Elliot, C. and Quinn, F. (2nd ed. 1998) *English Legal System*, Longman, London.

An Etymological Dictionary of the English Language (1909) Clarendon Press, Oxford.

Evensen, J. (1952) 'The Anglo Norwegian Fisheries Case and its Legal Consequences', *American Journal of International Law*, vol. 46, p.609.

Feather, N. T. (1998) 'Reactions to Penalties for Offences Committed by the Police and Public Citizens: Testing a Social-cognitive Process Model of Retributive Justice', *Journal of Personality and Social Psychology*, vol. 75 No. 2, p.528.

Feinberg, J. (1973) *Social Philosophy*, Eaglewood Cliffs, Prentice Hall.

Fell, G. S. (1991) 'Street-crime Victim Compensation, Retributive Justice, and Social-contract Theory' in Sank, D. and Caplan, D. I. (eds) *To Be a Victim – Encounters with Crime and Injustice*, Plenum Press, New York/London.

Fenrick, W. J. (1999) 'Should Crimes Against Humanity Replace War Crimes?', *Columbia Journal of Transnational Law*, vol. 37 No. 3, p.767.

Fernandez-Arnesto, F. (1998) *Truth, a History and a Guide for the Perplexed*, Black Swan, London.

Fitzmaurice, G. (1956) 'The Foundations of Authority of International Law and the Problem of Enforcement', *Modern Law Review*, vol. 19, p.1.

Fitzmaurice, G. (1957-II) 'The Principles of International Law Considered from the Standpoint of the Rule of Law', *Recueil des cours*, vol. 92, p.1.

Franck, T. (1990) *The Power of Legitimacy Among Nations*, Oxford University Press, New York/Oxford.

Franck, T. (1992) 'The Emerging Right to Democratic Governance', *Australian Journal of International Law*, vol. 46, p.86.

Freeman, M. (1999) 'Genocide and Gross Human Rights Violations in Comparative Perspective', *Ethnic and Racial Studies*, vol. 22 No. 6, p.1072.

Friedrichs, D. (1983) 'Victimology: A Consideration of the Radical Critique', *Crime and Delinquency*, vol. 29, p.283.

Gaeta, P. (1999) 'The Defence of Superior Orders: The Statute of the International Criminal Court versus Customary International Law', *European Journal of International Law*, vol. 10 No. 1, p.172.

Garaway, C. (1999) 'Superior Orders and the International Criminal Court: Justice Delivered or Justice Denied?' *International Review of the Red Cross*, vol. 81 No. 836, p.785.

Gareton, M. A. (1999) 'Chile 1997–1998: The Revenge of Incomplete Democratisation', *International Affairs*, vol. 75, p.261.

Geis, G. (1990) 'Crime Victims: Practice and Prospects', in Lurigo, A. *et al.* (eds) *Victims of Crime*, Sage, Newbury Park, CA, p.251.

Geras, N. (2000) *Amnesty: Rights and Wrongs*. Paper presented at Conference on Amnesty, Truth and Reconciliation, University of Hull, 10 April 2000.

Gerdes, L. C. *et al.* (2nd ed. 1988) *The Developing Adult*, Butterworths, London.

Gewirth, A. (1982) *Human Rights: Essays on Justification and Applications*, The University of Chicago Press, Chicago/London.

Ghandhi, P. R. (1998) *The Human Rights Committee and the Right of Individual Communication, Law and Practice*, Ashgate, Aldershot.

Glenn, H. P. (2000) *Legal Traditions of the World*, Oxford University Press, Oxford.

Goldston, J. A. (1999) 'Race Discrimination in Europe: Problems and Prospects', *European Human Rights Law Review*, Issue 5, pp.462–483.

Greenwood, C. (1992) 'New World Order or Old? The Invasion of Kuwait and the Rule of Law', *Modern Law Review*, vol. 55 No. 2, p.153.

Greppi, E. (1999) 'The Evolution of Individual Criminal Responsibility under International Law', *International Review of the Red Cross*, vol. 81 No. 835, p.531.

Griset, P. L. (1991) *Determinate Sentencing – The Promise and the Reality of Retributive Justice*, State University of New York Press, Albany.

Gutto, S. B. O. (1995) 'The OAU's New Mechanism for Conflict Prevention, Management and Resolution and the Controversial Concept of Humanitarian Intervention in International Law', *Proceedings of the African Society of International and Comparative Law*, vol. 7, p.348.

Halderman, H. (1962) 'Legal Basis For United Nations Armed Forces', *American Journal of International Law*, vol. 56, p.488.

Hamilton, E. and Huntington, C. (eds) (1964) *Plato: The Collected Dialogues*, Pantheon, New York.

Harries, K. (1997) 'Social Stress and Trauma: Synthesis and Spatial Analysis', *Social Science and Medicine*, vol. 45 No. 8, p.1251.

Harris, D. J. (5th ed. 1998) *Cases and Materials on International Law*, Sweet and Maxwell, London.

Hart, H. L. A. (2nd ed. 1994) *The Concept of Law*, Clarendon Press, Oxford.

Hayner, P. B. (1994) 'Fifteen Truth Commissions – 1974 to 1994: A Comparative Study', *Human Rights Quarterly*, vol. 16, p.597.

Hayner, P. B. (2001) *Confronting State Terror and Atrocity*, Routledge, New York.

Henkin, L. (2nd ed. 1979) *How Nations Behave*, Columbia University Press, New York.

Higgins, R. (1963) *The Development of International Law Through the Political Organs of the United Nations*, Clarendon Press, Oxford.

Higgins, R. (1994) *Problems and Process: International Law and How We Use It*, Clarendon Press, Oxford.

Hovannisian, R. G. (ed.) (1999) *Remembrance and Denial: The Case of the Armenian Genocide*, Wayne State University Press, Detroit MI.

Jennings, R. and Watts, A. (eds) (9th ed. 1992) *Oppenheim's International Law*, Longman, London.

Jones, M. A. (5th ed. 1996) *Textbook on Torts*, Blackstone Press, London.

Kairys, D. (1982) *The Politics of Law: A Progressive Critique*, Pantheon Books, New York.

Kelley, H. H. (1973) 'The Process of Causal Attribution', *American Psychologist*, vol. 28, p.107.

Kelsen, H. (1934) 'The Pure Theory of Law: Its Method and Fundamental Concepts, Part I', *Law Quarterly Review*, p.475.

Kelsen, H. (1935) 'Pure Theory of Law (Part II)', *Law Quarterly Review*, vol. 51, p.518.

Kelsen, H. (1967) *The Pure Theory of Law*, University of California Press, Berkeley.

King, C. S. (1983) *The Words of Martin Luther King*, Fount, London.

King, M. L. Jr (1981) *Strength to Love*, Collins Fount Paperbacks, Philadelphia.

Koskenniemi, M. (1989) *From Apology to Utopia: The Structure of International Legal Argument*, Finnish Lawyers' Publishing Company, Helsinki.

Koskienemi, M. (1995) 'International Law in a Post-Realist Era', *Australian Yearbook of International Law*, vol. 16, p.1.

Kritsiotis, D. (1993) 'The Legality of the 1993 US Missile Strike on Iraq and the Right of Self-defence in International Law', *International and Comparative Law Quarterly*, vol. 45, p.162.

Kritz, N. J. (ed.) (1995) *Transitional Justice: How Emerging Democracies Reckon with Former Regimes*, United States Institute of Peace Press, vol. 1, p.1.

Kwakwa, E. (1995) 'Internal Conflicts in Africa: Is There a Right of Humanitarian Action?' *African Yearbook of International Law*, p.9.

Lapidoth, R. (1992) 'Sovereignty in Transition', *Journal of International Affairs*, vol. 45, p.325.

Lauterpacht, H. (1948) *Recognition in International Law*, Cambridge University Press, Cambridge.

Lauterpacht, H. (1966) *The Function of Law in the International Community*, Archon Books, Hamden/Connecticut.

Lauterpacht, H. (1976-IV) 'The Development of the Law of International Organisations by the Decisions of International Tribunals', *Recueil des cours*, vol. 152, p.377.

Lee, R. (1995) 'Rule Making in the United Nations: *Opinio Communitatis*', *New York University Journal of International Law and Politics*, vol. 27 No. 33, p.57.

Lippmann, M. (1998) 'The Pursuit of Nazi War Criminals in the United States and in other Anglo-American Legal Systems', *California Western International Law Journal*, vol. 29 No. 1, p.1.

Macpherson, C. B. (1997) 'Human Rights as Property Rights', *Dissent*, vol. 24 No. 1, p.72.

Mak, T. D. (1995) 'The Case against an International War Crimes tribunal for the Former Yugoslavia', *International Peacekeeping*, vol. 2 No. 4, p.536.

Malanczuk, P. (ed.) (7th ed. 1997) *Akehurst's Modern Introduction to International Law*, Routledge, London/New York.

Marks, S. (2000) *The Riddle of all Constitutions: International Law, Democracy, and the Critique of Ideology*, Oxford University Press, Oxford.

Martin, D. and Johnson, P. (1981) *The Struggle for Zimbabwe*, Zimbabwe Publishing House, Harare.

Martinez, M. (1996) *National Sovereignty and International Organisations*, Kluwer Law International, The Hague.

Maunu, A. (1995) 'The Implied External Competence of the European Community after the ECJ Opinion 1/94 – Towards Coherence or Diversity', *Legal Issues of European Integration*, vol. 2, p.115.

McAdams, A. J. (1997) *Transitional Justice and the Rule of Law in New Democracies*, University of Notre Dame Press, London.

McCoubrey, H. and White, N. D. (3rd ed. 1999) *Textbook on Jurisprudence*, Blackstone Press, London.

McDougal and Associates (1987) *Studies in World Public Order*, New Haven Press, New Haven.

McGoldrick, D. (1991) *The Human Rights Committee, Its Role in the Development of the International Covenant on Civil and Political Rights*, Clarendon Press, Oxford.

McKenna, A. J. (1992) *Violence and Difference*, University of Illinois Publishing Co., Illinois.

McShane, M. D. and Williams, F. P. (1992) 'Radical Victimology: A Critique of the Concept of Victim in Traditional Victimology', *Crime and Delinquency*, vol. 38 No. 2, p.258.

Mejia, R. M. (1999) 'The Struggle against Impunity in Guatemala', *Social Justice*, vol. 26 No. 4, p.55.

Mendelson, M. H. (1995) 'The Subjective Element in Customary International Law', *British Yearbook of International Law*, vol. 66, p.177.

Mendelson, M. H. (1989) 'The Nicaragua Case and Customary International Law', *Coexistence*, vol. 26, p.85.

Merrills, J. (2nd ed. 1981) *Anatomy of International Law: A Study of the Role of International Law in the Contemporary World*, Sweet and Maxwell, London.

Mill, J. S. (4th ed. 1869) *On Liberty*, Longmans, Green, Reader, and Dyer, London.

Milne, A. J. M. (1984) 'The Idea of Human Rights: A Critical Inquiry', in Dowrick, F. E. (ed.) *Human Rights: Problems, Perspectives and Texts*, Gower, Aldershot.

Motala, Z. (1995) 'The Promotion of National Unity and Reconciliation Act, the Constitution and International Law', *Comparative and International Law Journal of Southern Africa*, vol. 28 No. 3, p.338.

Mugerwa, N. (1968) 'Subjects of International Law', in Sorensen, M. (ed.) *Manual of Public International Law*, p.247.

Muller, A. (1995) *International Organisations and their Host States: Aspects of their Legal Relationships*, Kluwer Law International, The Hague.

Murphy, S. D. (1999) 'Democratic Legitimacy and the Recognition of States and Governments', *International and Comparative Law Quarterly*, vol. 48 No. 3, p.545.

Nelson, J. J. and Green, V. M. (1980) *International Human Rights: Contemporary Issues*, Human Rights Publishing Group, New York.

Neuwahl, N. A. (1991) 'Joint Participation in International Treaties and the Exercise of Power by the EEC and its Member States: Mixed Agreements', *Common Market Law Review*, vol. 28, p.717.

O'Donnell, G. (2000) 'The Judiciary and the Rule of Law', Journal of Democracy, vol. 11 No. 1, p.25.

O'Flaherty, M. (1996) *Human Rights and the UN: Practice before Treaty Bodies*, Sweet and Maxwell, London.

Oda, S. (1968) 'The Individual in International Law', in Sorensen, M. (ed.) *Manual of Public International Law*, Macmillan, London, p.495.

Oppenheim, L. F. L. (1st ed. 1906) *International Law: A Treatise*, vol. 2, p.264.

Orentlicher, D. (1991) 'Settling Accounts: The Duty to Prosecute Human Rights of Violations of a Prior Regime', *Yale Law Journal*, vol. 100, p.2537.

Parry, C. (1949) 'The Treaty Making Power of the United Nations', *British Yearbook of International Law*, vol. 20, p.108.

Ratner, S. R. and Abrams, J. S. (2nd ed. 2000) *Accountability for Human Rights Atrocities in International Law*, Oxford University Press, Oxford.

Rawls, J. (1986) *A Theory of Justice*, Oxford University Press, Oxford.

Rawls, J. (1994) 'The Main Idea of the Theory of Justice', in Singer, P. (ed.) *Ethics*, Oxford University Press, Oxford.

Rawls, J. (1999) *A Theory of Justice*, Oxford University Press, Oxford.

Reisman, W. M. (1990) 'Sovereignty and Human Rights in Contemporary International Law', *American Journal of International Law*, vol. 84, p.866.

Rivers, J. (1999) 'The Interpretation and Invalidity of Unjust Laws', in Dyzenhaus, D. (ed.) *Recrafting the Rule of Law: The Limits of Legal Order*, Hart Publishing, Oxford, p.40.

Robertson, G. (1999) *Crimes Against Humanity: The Struggle for Global Justice*, Allen Lane, London.

Roht-Arriaza, N. (ed.) (1995) *Impunity and Human Rights in International Law and Practice*, Oxford University Press, New York.

Rotberg, R. I. and Thompson, D. (eds) (2000) *Truth v. Justice: The Morality of Truth Commissions*, Princetown University Press, Princeton.

Roth, B. R. (2000) *Governmental Illegitimacy in International Law*, Oxford University Press, Oxford.

Ryan, C. M. (1997) 'Sovereignty, Intervention, and the Law: A Tenuous Relationship of Competing Principles', *Millennium Journal of International Studies*, vol. 26 No. 1, p.77.

Schabas, W. A. (2000) *Genocide in International Law*, Cambridge University Press, Cambridge, p.2.

Scharf, M. P. (1996) 'Swapping Amnesty for Peace: Was There a Duty to Prosecute International Crimes in Haiti?' *Texas International Law Journal*, vol. 31 No. 1, p.1.

Schneider, J. (1963) *Treaty Making Power of International Organisations*, Rue Du Cardinal Lemoine, Paris.

Schwendinger, H. and Schwendinger, J. (1970) 'Defenders of Order or Guardians of Human Rights?', *Issues in Criminology*, vol. 7, p.72.

Seyested, F. (1964) 'Is The International Personality of Intergovernmental Organisations Valid vis-a-vis Non-Members?' *Indian Journal of International Law*, vol. 4, p.233.

Shklar, J. N. (1987) 'Political Theory and the Rule of Law', in Hutchinson, A. C. and Monahan, P. (eds) *The Rule of Law: Ideal or Ideology*, Carswell, Toronto, p.1.

Simmonds, N. E. (1986) *Central Issues in Jurisprudence: Justice, Law and Rights*, Sweet and Maxwell, London.

Skinner, B. F. (1953) *Science and Human Behaviour*, McMillan, New York.

Sornarajah, M. (2000) *The Settlement of Foreign Investment Disputes*, Kluwer, The Hague.

Sornarajah, M. (2001) *Developing Country Perspective of International Economic Law in the Context of Dispute Settlement.* Paper presented at Manchester University School of Law Conference on Perspectives in International Economic Law, 4 May 2001.

Steiner, H. J. and Alston, P. (1996) *International Human Rights in Context*, Clarendon Press, Oxford.

Stotzky, I. P. (ed.) (1993) *Transition to Democracy in Latin America: The Role of the Judiciary*, Westview Press, Boulder CO.

Symposium of the European Journal of International Law (1999) 'The International Criminal Court: The US v. the Rest?' *European Journal of International Law*, vol. 10 No. 1, p.93.

Teitel, R. G. (2000) *Transitional Justice*, Oxford University Press, Oxford.

Tocqueville, A. (Commager, H. S. (ed.) 1946) *Democracy in America*, Oxford University Press, Oxford.

Tutu, D. (1999) *No Future Without Forgiveness*, Rider, London.

United Nations (1991) *The World's Women 1970–1990: Trends and Statistics*, United Nations Publication.

Van Bueren, G. (1995) *The International Law on the Rights of the Child*, Martinus Nijhoff, London.

van Schaack, B. (1999) 'The Definition of Crimes Against Humanity: Resolving the Incoherence', *Columbia Journal of Transnational Law*, vol. 37 No. 3, p.787.

Varouxakis, G. (1997) 'John Stuart Mill on Intervention and Non-Intervention', *Millennium Journal of International Studies*, vol. 26 No. 1, p.57.

Vignes, D. (1983) 'The Impact of International Organisations on the Development and Application of Public International Law', in Macdonald, R. St J. and Johnston, D. M. (eds) *The Structure and Process of International Law*, Sweet and Maxwell, New York, p.809.

Vincent, R. J. (1986) *Human Rights and International Relations*, Cambridge University Press, Cambridge.

Warbrick, C. (1992) 'Recognition of States', *International and Comparative Law Quarterly*, vol. 41 No. 2, p.473.

Warbrick, C. and McGoldrick, D. (1999) 'The Future of Former Head of State Immunity after *Ex parte Pinochet*', *International and Comparative Law Quarterly*, vol. 48 No. 4, p.937.

Watson, J. B. and Raynor, R. (1920) 'Conditioned Emotional Reactions', *Journal of Experimental Psychology*, vol. 3, p.680.

Watts, A. (1994) 'The Legal Position in International Law of Heads of Governments and Foreign Ministers', *Hague Recueil*, 247, p.9.

Weatherill, S. (1995) *Law and Integration in the European Union*, Clarendon Press, Oxford.

Wedgwood, R. (1999) 'The International Criminal Court: An American View', *European Journal of International Law*, vol. 10 No. 1, p.93.

Weissberg, G. (1961) *The International Status of the United Nations*, Oceana, Dobbs Ferry.

Welscher, L. A. (1991) *Miracle, A Universe: Settling Accounts with Torturers*, Penguin Books, London.

Wheeler, N. J. (2001) 'Humanitarian Vigilantes or Legal Entrepreneurs: Enforcing Human Rights in International Society', in Jones, P. and Caney, S. (eds) *Human Rights and Global Diversity*, Frank Cass, London, p.139.

Wheeler, S. and Shaw, J. (1994) *Contract Law: Cases, Materials and Commentary*, Oxford University Press, Oxford.

White, N. (1996) *The Law of International Organisations*, Manchester University Press, New York/Manchester.

Whiteman, M. (1977) 'Jus Cogens in International Law', *Georgia Journal of International and Comparative Law*, p.607.

Yearbook of the International Law Commission (1950) II.

Yearbook of the International Law Commission (1976) II.

Young, J. (1986) 'The Failure of Criminology: The Need for a Radical Realism', in Matthews, R. and Young, J. (eds) *Confronting Crime*, Sage, London.

Zacher, M. W. (1970) *Dag Hammaskjold's United Nations*, Columbia University Press, New York/London.

Zacklin, R. 'Beyond Kosovo: the United Nations and Humanitarian Intervention', The Josephine Onoh Memorial Lecture 2000, Studies in Law Series, University of Hull.

Zwanenburg, M. (1999) 'The Statute of the International Criminal Court and the United States: Peacekeepers under Fire', *European Journal of International Law*, vol. 10 No. 1, p.124.

BBC NEWS, 'Mozambique Picks up the Pieces', http://news6.thdo.bbc.co.uk/hi/english/world/africa/newsid_734000/734865.stm.

'Mugabe Terror Moves From Farm to Factory to Continue Reign of Terror', *Guardian*, Monday 8 May 2000.

'Mugabe's Army Hands Out Guns', *Guardian*, Sunday 7 May 2000.

'National Reconciliation: Is Truth Enough?' *The Economist*, 26 August 2000, p.72.

'Take Me to Court if You Dare, Smith Tells Mugabe', *Guardian*, Friday 27 October 2000.

'US Loses Seat on Human Rights Body', *Financial Times*, Friday 4 May 2001.

'War Crimes Prosecutor in Frosty Talks with President', *Guardian*, 24 January 2001.

'Way Cleared for Milosevic Trial', *Sunday Times*, 24 June 2001.

INDEX

acceptance and rejection of amnesties 58,
        65, 75–90, 167–8
act of state doctrine 89, 146–7
African Charter on Human and Peoples'
        Rights 70–1, 108, 119
American Convention on Human Rights
        33, 70–1, 108, 114–15
Anti-Racism Information Service 132
apartheid *see also* South Africa
    attribution theory 101
    confessions 81–2
    crimes against humanity 7, 11, 74–5, 101
    customary international law 74–5, 148–9
    declarations 149
    denouncement of 149
    forgiveness and 94–5
    imposed national amnesty laws 9, 11
    investigations, difficulties in 80–2
    negligence with regard to 11
    opinio communitatis 149–50
    property rights 63–4
    reasonableness 111
    resolutions 149
    secrecy and 80–1
    Truth and Reconciliation Commission,
        failures of 82–3
    UN Charter 149
    victims' rights 61–4, 82–5
armed forces 158–9
attribution theory
    apartheid 101
    causal 101–2
    human rights 165–6
    international law 101–6, 165
    international organisations 166
    United Nations 166

Belgium 159–61
benefit theory 59–62

children
    Committee on the Rights of the Child
        136, 141–3

convention on 141–3
    monitoring compliance 141–3
    reporting procedure 141–2
    supervision 141
Chile 55, 113–14, 119–20, 123, 127, 170
    see also Pinochet, General
classical conditioning theory 53–5
claw back clauses 65
codification
    national amnesty laws 110, 117–19
    norms 78
    official records, in 117–19
    opinio communitatis 78
    Zimbabwe 117–19
Commission on Human Rights 32–3
Committee against Torture 136,
        137–40
Committee on Economic, Social and
        Cultural Rights 134–7
Committee on Elimination of
        Discrimination against Women 136,
        140–1, 144
Committee on Elimination of Racial
        Discrimination 129–32
Committee on the Rights of the Child 136,
        141–3
community sentences 84
compensatory nature of acceptance of
        amnesties 60
conciliation 130–1
confessions 81–2
Congo 78, 160–1
constitutions
    grundnorm 73
    linking of amnesties, to 109
    legal rights 98
    norms and 35–6
    political instrument, as 97
    role of 96–8
    social order 96–7
    South Africa 73–5, 94–5, 97–8, 104–5,
        113
conventions *see* treaties and conventions

crimes against humanity *see also* genocide
  act of state doctrine 89
  apartheid 7, 11, 74–5, 101
  classification, as 85–6
  customary international law 89–90
  definition 7–8
  examples of 86
  extradition 36, 38
  fear 4
  former Yugoslavia 86
  immunity 89, 146–52
  individual responsibility for 89
  international criminal tribunals 77–8, 89
  International Law Commission 79
  intervention 101
  investigations 18
  jurisdiction 22, 36, 39–40
  jus cogens 37, 148
  mens rea 12
  peacetime, committed in 7
  Pinochet 143
  prosecutions 18–21, 36
  public office 169
  Rwanda 86
  South Africa 74, 80–1
  state practice 77–80
  superior orders defence 89
  time limits 7
  torture 7, 74, 148–9
  treaties and conventions, 85–6
  war crimes, distinguished from 7
customary international law
  acceptance or rejection of 71–2
  ambiguity 151
  apartheid 74–5, 148–9
  crimes against humanity 89–90
  declarations 126
  democracy 52
  environment 67
  extradition 26
  genocide 87, 89, 149, 151–2
  human rights 123, 169–70
  immunity 17, 149
  incorporation doctrine 26–7
  inconsistency 151–2
  individual responsibility 89
  International Court of Justice 56, 76–7, 150
  International Criminal Court 154, 164
  legal practice 77
  making and unmaking 75–6
  motivations for asserting 59–73

  norms 36, 59–73, 123, 151
  Nuremberg Principles 153–4
  Pinochet 17
  prohibition of amnesties, emergence of 170
  prosecutions 26
  reconciliation 20–1
  resolutions 126–7
  restoration 100–1
  South Africa 73–4
  state practice 56, 58, 59, 76–7, 109, 169–70
  superior orders defence 152–3, 162
  torture 74, 89
  transformation doctrine 27
  United Nations 126–7
  values expressed in 89–90

decentralisation 35
declarations
  apartheid 149
  customary international law 126
  enforcement 48
  El Salvador 63
  illegality 167
  national amnesty laws 5–6
  racial discrimination 131
  state practice 80–5
  state sovereignty 28–9
  UN General Assembly 126, 129
definition of amnesia 8–9
democracy 52, 167
developing countries 69–70, 78
diplomatic relations 159–61
diplomatic tool theory 64
disappearances 55
discretion
  acceptance and rejection of amnesties 168
  challenging 101–6
  constraints 92–124
  escape route theory 95
  human rights 168–9
  impact of amnesties 58
  international law, limits under 23–40
  jus cogens 164
  models, choice of 92–124, 168–9
  norms 164
  opinio communitatis 92–106, 126
  reasonableness 110–11
  state practice 57–91
  state sovereignty 56, 58
  victims 47

discrimination 86–9 *see also* racial
　　discrimination, sex discrimination
dualism 27
due process 61, 78, 167
duress 9

early warning procedure 132
Economic and Social Council 31–2
El Salvador 58, 63–4, 114–15, 127, 168
elective national amnesty laws 9, 12–13
emergency procedure 133–4
enforcement *see also* prosecutions
　　communal 39–40
　　declarations 48
　　human rights 39–42
　　International Covenant on Civil and
　　　　Political Rights 31–2, 108
　　International Covenant on Economic,
　　　　Social and Cultural Rights 136
　　judiciary 41–2
　　legal rights 47–8
　　rule of law 42
　　torture 116
　　treaties and conventions 88–9
environment 67, 123
equality before the law 1, 4, 53, 167
escape route theory 95–6
European Convention on Human Rights
　　70–1, 108
European Union 73
executive
　　decisions 12
　　deference of 16
　　fairness 113
　　restraints on 43–5
exhaustion of local remedies 70, 131
extradition 16–17, 26, 36, 38

fairness
　　executive 113
　　international criminal tribunals 114–15
　　justice 3–4, 58–9, 71, 83, 99, 163
　　legal rights 113–14
　　legitimacy 15
fear 4
federalism 44
forgiveness 94–5, 107
former Yugoslavia 10–12 *see also*
　　Milosevic, Slobodan
　　crimes against humanity 86
　　escape route theory 95–6
　　institutional restraints 95–6

International Criminal Tribunal 4, 24,
　　77, 86
　　torture 39

Geneva Conventions 161
genocide
　　convention on 86–7
　　customary international law 87, 89, 149,
　　　　151–2
　　definition 151–2
　　discrimination 86–7
　　homicide 161
　　prohibition of amnesties 86–7
globalisation 107
Graeco-Roman tradition 106–7, 122–3
grave breaches of international law 159–61
group rights 136
grundnorms 28, 73–4

Haiti 84–5, 120
heads of state 60–1, 146–52
homicide 161
hostages 88
human rights
　　attribution theory 165–6
　　communal dimension to 38
　　customary international law 123, 169–70
　　developing countries 69–70
　　discretion 168–9
　　enforcement
　　　　communal 39–40
　　　　judiciary 41–2
　　imposed national amnesty 10–12
　　impunity 129–45
　　legal rights 163
　　national amnesty laws as breaching 5–6,
　　　　165
　　norms 37
　　opinio communitatis 165
　　positive tradition 107–21, 125–62
　　　　competing and parasitic 127–9
　　property rights, as 13, 38–9, 58, 163
　　state sovereignty 10
　　treaties and conventions 99, 129–45
　　victims 21–2, 70–1, 163–4
　　wrongs against the state, breaches of as
　　　　96
Human Rights Commissioner, creation of
　　67
Human Rights Committee 31–2, 69–70
　　acceptance of 70
　　composition 32

Human Rights Committee (*continued*)
  independence of 32
  International Covenant on Civil and
    Political Rights 132–4
  legality of national amnesty laws 120
  natural justice 115–16
  state sovereignty 69, 107–8
  supervisory function of 32
  workload 69–70
humanity *see* crimes against humanity

identification of international law 73–5
immunity 145–61
  act of statute doctrine 146–7
  crimes against humanity 17, 89, 146–52
  customary international law 17, 149
  heads of state 60–1, 146–52
  International Criminal Court 157, 161
  international criminal tribunals 145
  Nuremberg principles 89
  official acts 147–8
  personae materiae 146–7
  Pinochet 17, 60–1, 89, 120, 146–52
  private/public divide 146
  ratione materiae 60, 146–7
  superior orders defence 146, 152–5,
    162
  torture 89, 148–9
  United Nations 30–1
implementation standards 136–7
imposed national amnesty laws 9–12
  apartheid 9, 11
  contractual nature of 9
  duress 9
  human rights 10–12
  international laws, as 10, 74
  legitimacy 10–11
  Milosevic 10
  negotiated amnesties 9–10
  Pinochet 9–10
  prosecutions 11
impunity
  Chile 55
  diplomatic relations 159–61
  disappearances 55
  human rights, violation of 129–45
  International Criminal Court 159,
    161
  Rwanda 159
  state needs doctrine 54–5
incorporation doctrine 26–7, 74
Indemnities 156, 159

individual right of petition
  African Charter on Human and Peoples'
    Rights 70–1, 108
  American Convention on Human Rights
    70–1, 108
  European Convention on Human Rights
    70–1, 108
  international law 71
  nature of 70–1
  procedural rights 71
  torture 139
International Court of Justice
  customary international law 56, 76–7,
    150
  establishment of 24
  United Nations General Assembly 127
International Covenant on Civil and
    Political Rights
  Economic and Social Council 31–2
  emergency procedure 133–4
  enforcement of 31–2, 108
  Human Rights Committee 132–4
  implementation standards 136
  inter-state reports 133
  minimum requirements 128–9
  monitoring compliance with 132–4
  Peru 115–16
  recommendations 32
  remedial mechanism 133
  reports 31, 133
  state sovereignty 69
  United Nations 31
  Universal Declaration of Human Rights
    128–9
  victims 47
    communications of 31
International Covenant on Economic,
    Social and Cultural Rights
  Committee on Economic, Social and
    Cultural Rights 134–7
  enforcement 136
  group rights 136
  implementation standards 136–7
  monitoring compliance with 134–7, 145
  reporting procedure 135, 145
  treaty supervisory bodies 136
International Criminal Court 155–61
  armed forces 158–9
  customary international law 154, 162
  due process 78
  grave breaches of international law
    159–61

International Criminal Court (*continued*)
  immunity 157, 161
  impunity 159, 161
  indemnities 156, 159
  intervention 49, 156–9
  jurisdiction 158–61
  opt-out 158–9
  permanent establishment of 24, 78, 142
  political prosecutions 152
  reconciliation 121–2
  Statute on 155, 162
    ratification of 155
  superior orders defence 152–5, 162
  time limits 121
  truth and reconciliation commissions 121–2
  UK debates on 156–9
  United States 158
  vexatious prosecutions 156
international criminal tribunals *see also* International Court of Justice, International Criminal Court
  crimes against humanity 77–8, 89
  establishment of 24, 142–3
  fairness 114–15
  former Yugoslavia 6, 24, 86
  immunity 145
  natural justice 114
  Rwanda 24, 86
international law *see also* customary international law
  application of 73–5
  attribution law 101–6, 165
  'bystander', as 101–6
  discretion 23–40
  dualism 27
  European Union 73
  grave breaches of 159–61
  grundnorms 28
  identification of 73–5
  imposed national amnesty 10
  incorporation law 74
  individuals and 71
  integration of 26–7
  jus cogens 36–7
  legality of national amnesty laws 119–21
  legitimacy 91
  making and unmaking of law 75–90
  monism 27–8
  national law and 23–40, 164–7, 170
  norms 36–7

  peremptory 36–7
  positive law theory 65
  prosecutions 14, 120–1
  relations between states governing 72–3
  role of 24–5, 64–5
  South Africa 74–5
  state practice 26, 39, 65
  state responsibility 25
  state sovereignty 29–34, 39, 66–7
  truth and reconciliation commissions 121–2
International Law Commission
  conduct, examples of 79–80
  crimes against humanity 79
  Draft Articles 25–6, 78–80
  opinio communitatis 79
  state responsibility 25–6, 78–80
  vicarious liability 78–80
international organisations *see also* United Nations
  attribution theory 166
  creation of 30–4
  role of 34–5
  rules of 33
  state sovereignty 30–4
intervention
  crimes against humanity 101
  International Criminal Court 49, 156–9
  state needs doctrine 49
  state sovereignty 67–9
  treaties and conventions 165
  United Nations 69
investigations
  apartheid 81–2
  crimes against humanity 18
  difficulties in 80–2
  escape route theory 95
  perpetrators, advantages to 18

judiciary
  enforcement 41–2
  human rights 41–2
  moral and political morality, of 43
  rule of law 41–4
  United States 44
  victims 41–2
jurisdiction
  crimes against humanity 22, 36, 39–40
  hostages 88
  International Criminal Court 158–61
  torture 37–8
  universal 39–40, 159–61

jus cogens
  crimes against humanity 37, 148
  discretion 164
  international law 36–7
  norms 36–7, 164
  Norway 151
  Pinochet 17
  state sovereignty 35–6
  torture 38
justice
  constructivist 98–9
  deference of 2
  equality before the law 4
  evidence, of 3
  fairness, as 3–4, 58–9, 71, 83, 99, 163
  legal rights, pre-determined 4
  legitimacy 98–9
  political measures, deference to 2
  principles, practice of 3
  rehabilitation 22
  retribution 3
  social contract, as 3
  transformative 1, 5
  transitional 1, 5
  Universal Declaration of Human Rights
      98–9
  utilitarianism 2–4
  victims 83

Kosovo 68
Kurds 68
Kyoto Protocol 94

laissez-faire 62
legal rights
  consistency 15–16
  constitutions 98
  enforcement 47–8
  executive decisions 12
  fairness 113–14
  human rights, as 163
  justice 4
  moral grounds for existence of 43
  natural justice 113–14
  obliteration of 64
  ownership of 14
  positive 80, 98
  pre-determined 4
  sacrifice of 64–5
  state sovereignty 63–4
  threshold 18
  transfer of 13–18, 163

Universal Declaration of Human Rights
      108
  victims 4, 14–18, 62–3, 91, 163–4
legality of national amnesty laws 119–21,
      163–4
  Chile 119–20, 123
  Haiti 120
  Human Rights Committee 120
  international law 119–21
  Peru 119
  South Africa 120, 123–4
  state practice 57
legitimacy 2
  fairness 15
  imposed national amnesty 10–11
  international law 91
  justice 98–9
  power and 60
  weakening of 15

Maslow's hierarchy of needs 48–53
migrant workers 136
Milosevic, Slobodan 10, 68, 95–6
minority groups 119
monism 27–8
monitoring
  children, 141–3
  Human Rights Committee 32
  International Covenant on Civil and
      Political Rights 132–4
  International Covenant on Economic,
      Social and Cultural Rights 134–7,
      145
  non-governmental organisations 144,
      164
  recommendations 129
  reporting requirements 143–5
  sex discrimination 140–1
  torture 137–40
  treaties bodies, by 129–45, 162, 164,
      170
    efficacy, of 144–5
  violations approach 143
multinationals 107

natural justice 112–16
  administrative law 112–13
  El Salvador 114–15
  Human Rights Committee 115–16
  international criminal tribunals 114
  legal rights 113–14
  Peru 115–16

natural justice (*continued*)
  Pinochet 114
  South African Constitution 113
  victims 113
non-governmental organisations
  monitoring 144, 164
  opinio communitatis 93
  racial discrimination 131–2
  role of 93, 164
norms
  benefit theory 59–62
  codification 78
  constitutions and 35–6
  customary international law 36, 59–73,
    123, 151
  discretion 164
  emerging 59–73
  human rights 37
  international law 36–7
  jus cogens 36–7, 164
  motivations for asserting 59–73
  opinio communitatis 92–3
  self-determination 99–100
  state
    assertions of 59–73
    practice 39
    society and, differences between 35
    sovereignty 35–6
  treaties and conventions 36, 151
Norway 150–1
Nuremberg trials 89, 153–4

official acts 147–8
official records, codification in 117–19
opinio communitatis
  apartheid 149–51
  challenging 101–6, 123, 149–51
  codification 78
  customary international law 150
  discretion 92–106, 123
  fisheries 150–1
  human rights 165
  International Law Commission 79
  non-governmental organisations 93
  norms 92–3
  Norway 150–1
  resolutions 93
  United Nations General Assembly 93
  United States 123
  Universal Declaration of Human Rights
    128
  victims 165

peace, crimes committed during times of
  7
peacekeeping forces 152
Peru 115–16, 119
Pinochet, General
  allegations against 16–17
  benefit theory 60
  crimes against humanity 143
  customary international law 17
  escape route theory 95
  extradition 16–17
  heads of state 60–1, 146–52
  immunity 17, 60–1, 89, 120, 146–52
  imposed national amnesty 9–10
  institutional restraints 95
  jus cogens 17
  natural justice 114
  rejection of national amnesty laws
    168
  torture 17, 89, 148
politics and law 96
positive law theory 65
procedural rights 71
property rights
  apartheid 63–4
  human rights 13, 38–9, 58, 163
  state sovereignty 29–30
  transfer of 13–22, 29–30, 38, 163–4
  victims 13–22, 38, 163–4
prosecutions
  counter-productivity of 18–19
  crimes against humanity 18–21, 36
  customary international law 26
  escape route theory 95
  fear 4
  imposed national amnesty 11
  international law 120–1
  military attitude to 19
  perpetrators, advantages to 18
  political 152
  purpose of 55
  state needs doctrine 55
  vexatious 156
  victims' response to 46–7, 55
  violence, resulting from 22
  war crimes 24

racial discrimination *see also* apartheid
  Anti-Racism Information Service 132
  Committee on Elimination of Racial
    Discrimination 129–32
  communications procedure 131

racial discrimination (*continued*)
  conciliation 130–1
  Convention, monitoring compliance
    with 130–2
  declarations 131
  early warning procedure 132
  exhaustion of local remedies 131
  non-governmental organisations 131–2
  reporting procedures 131–2
  resolutions 126–7
  state practice 132
  United Nations 126–7, 130–1
  urgent procedure 132
reasonableness
  apartheid 111
  Chile 114
  discretion 110–11
  El Salvador 14–15
  national amnesty laws 110–12
  victims 112
recognition of states 52
recommendations
  African Charter on Human and Peoples'
    Rights 71
  American Convention on Human Rights
    70–1
  commissions, of 71
  European Convention on Human Rights
    71
  implementation of 71
  International Covenant on Civil and
    Political Rights 32
  monitoring 129
  sex discrimination 140
  United Nations 129
reconciliation *see also* truth and
    reconciliation commissions
  beneficiaries, stigmatisation of 118
  customary international law 20–1
  International Criminal Court 121–2
  methods of 18–19
  South Africa 104–5
  state needs doctrine 49–50
  victims, injustice to 121
  Zimbabwe 117–19
rehabilitation of governments 1, 22
relativism 1
reporting
  children, 141–2
  disaggregation 145
  International Covenant on Civil and
    Political Rights 31, 133

International Covenant on Economic,
    Social and Cultural Rights 135, 145
  monitoring 143–5
  racial discrimination 131–2
  sex discrimination 140–1, 144
  standardisation of 145
  torture 138–9
  training 145
  treaties and conventions 164
resolutions
  apartheid 149
  customary international law 126–7
  opinio communitatis 93
  racial discrimination 126–7
  United Nations 93, 126–7
retribution 3
rule of law 42–5
  democracy 167
  enforcement 42
  inconsistent application of 15
  judiciary 41–4
  rule of reason, as 42–3, 95
  security needs 53, 56
  state needs doctrine 53–4
  United States 44–5
  victims 47
  Zimbabwe 168
Rwanda 11
  grave breaches of international law
    159–61
  impunity 159
  International Criminal Tribunal 24, 77,
    86

sacrifice, idea of 19–20, 22
security
  physiological needs of state 52–3
  rule of law 53, 56
  state needs doctrine 52–3, 56
self-constituting law 4, 24, 127
self-determination 99–100
sex discrimination
  Committee on the Elimination of
    Discrimination against Women 136,
    140–1, 144
  convention on 140–1
  monitoring compliance 140–1
  reporting procedure 140–1, 144
  recommendations 140
Sierra Leone 78, 90, 123, 142, 169–70
social good, amnesties as 2
social contract, justice as 3

South Africa *see also* apartheid
  acceptance of national amnesty laws 58,
    168
  community orders 84
  Constitution 73–5, 94–5, 97
    natural justice 113
    reconciliation and 104–5
    role of 97–8
  crimes against humanity 74, 80–1
  criminals, maintaining power of 84
  customary international law 73–4
  ecclesiastical tradition 94–5
  forgiveness 94
  globalisation 107
  Graeco-Roman tradition 106–7
  grundnorm 73–4
  international law 74–5
  legality of national amnesty laws 120,
    123–4
  natural justice 113
  politics and law 97
  reconciliation 104–5
  unity, need for 107
  victimisation 61
  victims 61–4, 113
sovereignty *see* state sovereignty
state needs doctrine 167
  classical conditioning theory 53–5
  democracy 52
  equality 53, 167
  impunity, problem of 54–5
  international obligations 52
  intervention 49
  Maslow's hierarchy of needs 48–53
  physiological needs of states 51–2
  prosecutions 55
  recognition of states 52
  reconciliation 49–50
  rule of law 53–4
  security needs 52–3, 56
  treaties and conventions 50–1
state practice 1–22
  citizens, treatment of 6
  crimes against humanity 77–80
  customary international law 56, 58, 59,
    76–7, 109, 169–70
  declarations of deference to state
    amnesty laws 80–5
  development of 23
  discretion 57–91
  divergence in 76–7
  international law 26, 39, 65

national amnesty laws
  acceptance and rejection 58, 65,
    75–90
  deference to declarations of 80–5
  legality of 57–8
  prohibition or authorisation of
    57–91
  norms 39
  racial discrimination 132
state responsibility 25–6, 78–80
state sovereignty
  decentralisation 35
  declaration of national amnesty as
    exercise of 28–9
  discretion 56, 58
  external 29
  human rights 10
  Human Rights Committee 69, 107–9
  individual liberty and 48
  internal 29
  International Covenant on Civil and
    Political Rights 69
  international law 29–34, 39, 66–7
  international organisations, effect of
    creation of 30–4
  intervention 67–9
  jus cogens 35–6
  legal rights 63–4
  norms 35–6
  physiological needs of states 51
  power and 59–60
  property rights of victims, transfer of
    29–30
  regulation of 64–5
  society and, distinction between 35
  territorial 29
  treaties and conventions 36–7
  UN Charter 68–9
sub-communities 41–2
superior orders defence
  crimes against humanity 89–90
  customary international law 152–3, 162
  illegality 153–4
  immunity 146, 152–5, 162
  International Criminal Court 152–5,
    162
  Nuremberg principles 153–4
  peacekeeping forces 152
  United States 152

terrorism 116
time limits 7, 121

torture
  Committee against Torture 136, 137–40
  convention on 74, 87–8, 137–40
  crimes against humanity 7, 74, 148–9
  customary international law 74, 89
  definition of 87
  derogations, prohibition from 87–8
  enforcement 116
  former Yugoslavia 39
  immunity 89, 148–9
  individual right of petition 139
  information, receiving 139
  inquiries, conducting 139
  inter-state complaints 139
  jurisdiction 37–8
  jus cogens 38
  monitoring compliance 137–40
  Peru 116
  Pinochet 17, 89, 148
  prevention of 14
  prohibition of amnesties 87
  reporting procedure 138–9
  reservations 139
  supervision 140
transfer
  legal rights 13–18, 163
  property rights 13–22, 29–30, 163
  state, to 21–2, 29–30
transformation doctrine 27
treaties and conventions *see also* particular
      treaties and conventions
  claw back clauses 65
  crimes against humanity 85–6
  denials 145
  derogations 65
  discrimination 88–9
  enforcement 88–9
  human rights 99, 129–45
  intervention 165
  monitoring compliance 129–45, 162,
      164, 170
  national laws, breach of 103–4
  negotiations of 62
  norms 36, 151
  reporting requirements 131–2, 135,
      138–45, 164
  state needs doctrine 50–1
  state sovereignty 36–7
  supervisory organs, with 33–4,
      129–45, 162, 164, 170
  values, in 85–9
  Vienna Convention 36, 103–5

tribunals *see* international criminal
      tribunals
truth and reconciliation commissions
  attribution theory 101
  apartheid 82–3
  goodwill, need for 122
  International Criminal Court 121–2
  international law, in 121–2
  parasitic nature of 127
  role of 121
  victims 82–3, 121

United Nations *see also* Human Rights
      Committee
  acceptance and rejection of amnesties
      167–8
  apartheid 149
  attribution theory 102, 166
  bystander, as 102–3
  Charter 30–1, 68–9, 125–8, 149
  Commission on Human Rights 32–3
  customary international law 126–7
  declarations 126, 129
  equality 28
  force of, persistent and increasing
      universal 125–7, 167–8
  General Assembly 93, 126–7, 129
  Human Rights Commissioner, creation
      of 67
  International Court of Justice 127
  International Covenant on Civil and
      Political Rights, enforcement of 31
  intervention 69
  juridical personality of 31
  national amnesty laws, inconsistent and
      intermittent force of 125–7
  negligence 11
  opinio communitatis 93
  privileges and immunities 30–1
  racial discrimination 126–7, 130–1
  recommendations 129
  resolutions 126–7
  state sovereignty 68–9
  treaty supervisory bodies 167
United States
  environment 94, 123
  federalism, restraints on 44
  International Criminal Court 158
  judiciary 44
  Kyoto Protocol 94
  opinio communitatis 123
  peacekeeping forces 152

United States (*continued*)
  rule of law 44–5
  superior orders 152
Universal Declaration of Human Rights
  International Covenant on Civil and
      Political Rights 128–9
  justice 98–9
  legal rights 108
  opinio communitatis 128
  positive human rights 127–8
  weaknesses of 127–8
  Zimbabwe 118
utilitarianism   2–4
utility of national amnesty laws, claimed
    166

vexatious prosecutions 156
vicarious liability 78–80
victims
  apartheid 61–4, 82–5
  benefit theory 62
  discretion 47
  due process 61
  exhaustion of local remedies 70
  forgiveness, expectations of 82
  human rights 21–2, 70–1, 163–4
  individual petition, right of 70–1,
      108
  individualism 96
  information needed by 82
  International Covenant on Civil and
      Political Rights 31, 47
  judiciary 41–2
  justice, need for 83
  legal rights of 4, 14–18, 62–3, 91,
      163–4
    enforcement 47–8
    exchange of 14–18
    pre-determined 4
    recognition of 46

neglect of 46
  opinio communitatis 165
  perpetrators, cleansing the 61–3
  post-violation era, as 45–8
  property rights of, transfer of 13–22, 38,
      163–4
  prosecutions
    exoneration, from 46–7
    response, to 55
  reasonableness 112
  reconciliation 121
  rule of law 47
  South Africa 61–4, 113
  sub-communities 41–2, 45
  system 46
  test of victimhood 45–6
  truth commissions, failures of 82–3, 121
  victimisation 61
Vienna Convention on the Law of Treaties
    36, 103–5
violence 20–2, 91

war crimes 7, 24
women *see* sex discrimination
World Trade Organisation 24–5

Yugoslavia *see* former Yugoslavia

Zimbabwe
  acceptance of national amnesty laws 56,
      168
  African Charter on Human and Peoples'
      Rights 119
  codification 117–19
  government policy, change of 117–19
  minority groups 119
  reconciliation 117–19
  rule of law 168
  Universal Declaration of Human Rights
      118–19